FOUR DECADES OF
INDIA-BANGLADESH RELATIONS
Historical Imperatives and Future Direction

FOUR DECADES OF INDIA-BANGLADESH RELATIONS

Historical Imperatives and Future Direction

Editor

Smruti S Pattanaik

Institute for Defence Studies and Analyses, New Delhi

GYAN

Four Decades of India-Bangladesh Relations :
Historical Imperatives and Future Direction

ISBN : 978-81-212-1166-6

Published in 2012 in India by
Gyan Publishing House
23, Main Ansari Road, Daryaganj,
New Delhi - 110002
Phones : 23282060, 23261060
Fax : (011) 23285914
E-mail: books@gyanbooks.com
website: gyanbooks.com

Laser Type Setting : Rajender Vashist, Delhi

Printed at: Salasar Imaging Systems, New Delhi-110035

Content

Preface

The current volume is the result of a dialogue between the Institute for Defence Studies and Analyses (IDSA), New Delhi and the Bangladesh Institute for International and Strategic Studies (BIISS). For the first time, the scholars of the two premier think tanks–IDSA and BIISS have come together to discuss important aspects of India-Bangladesh relations. The volume provides both Indian and Bangladeshi perspectives and is a valuable addition to the existing literature on the subject which would be relevant to the policy makers of the two countries. The contributors have examined the issues keeping the future of bilateral relations in mind. Thus, the focus is on the future of India-Bangladesh relations. In the recent past, the two countries have worked closely to improve their relations and forged close inter-connectivity, keeping the regional perspectives in mind. The dialogue took place at IDSA in May 2011.

The book comprises thirteen chapters discussing the entire gamut of bilateral relations and the way forward. The first chapter titled "Consonance and Dissonance: Issues and Trends in Indo-Bangladesh Relations" provides a historical background to the relations between the two countries and the issues that have bedeviled the bilateral relations. This chapter discusses the synergy between the two countries during the liberation war, relations between them during different regimes in power and a detailed survey on a host of issues that have emerged as a challenge.

The chapter by Arvind Gupta titled "Trends in Indian Foreign Policy" discusses global and regional developments and factors affecting India's foreign policy. It examines the contours of India's neighbourhood policy and the challenges it confronts, and examines the trends in India's foreign policy. It briefly contextualizes India-Bangladesh relations of the wider neighbourhood and explores areas where the two countries can cooperate.

"South Asia and the International Order" by Segufta Hossain, examines in detail major power interests in the region during the cold war period and the developments in the post- cold war era. Post-9/11 developments again attracted the attention of the international community as the global war on terror gained momentum. This chapter places Bangladesh in the regional context and discusses the potential that the country has and the challenges it is facing. The chapter provides recommendations to overcome these challenges.

Ashok Behuria's chapter on "South Asia: Regional Security Challenges", deals with the challenges that the countries of the region are facing in terms of social, economic and security challenges and the continuation of political instability in some of the infant democracies in the neighbourhood, that have posed serious a problem to stability. The author argues that security dilemmas and differences in the perception of the regimes have prevented the building of a regional security architecture, and suggests that a multi-track dialogue at various levels is essential to move away from the current impasse which breeds distrust.

Sreeradha Datta's chapter on "India-Bangladesh Cross-Border Connectivity" discusses India's efforts to develop a rail and road network that would facilitate trade and transit that Bangladesh is trying to establish with the countries of the region. It provides details of cross-border connectivity and new road and rail links that are being established as part of improving trans-boundary connections. The chapter details prospects of border trade and future connectivity in terms of connecting the energy grid to deal with the shortage of power.

The chapter "Bangladesh-India Connectivity: A Focus on Transit" by Ishtiaque Selim, deals in detail with the longstanding issue of transit, various routes that exist which can be used for the proposed transit route, and examines various schools of thought that exist in Bangladesh regarding provision of transit to India. It also deals with studies that have been undertaken to look at the transit issue and various infrastructure challenges that would emerge as a hindrance to the process. This chapter argues that transit would generate revenue for Bangladesh and create opportunities for employment.

Anand Kumar in his chapter "Indo-Bangladesh Trade: Problems

and prospects", provides an Indian perspective on the issue of trade. The author delineates various hurdles to India-Bangladesh trade which includes various tariff regimes, illegal trade, smuggling, trade in service and problems of the Non-Tariff Barrier (NTB). The chapter examines whether the Free Trade Agreement can be a way out. The chapter examines the recent developments in bilateral trading relations and suggests measures on how to improve trade. The author argues that private players need to be encouraged to play a larger role in terms of investment.

Mahfuz Kabir's chapter on "Bangladesh-India Trade and Investment: Bangladeshi Perspectives", analyses in detail the volume and composition of bilateral trade, issues like trade deficit, establishing bilateral and regional free trade area, tariff and non tariff barriers, and suggests trade facilitation measures. The author suggests some measures on improving trade between Bangladesh and India from Bangladesh's perspective.

In her second chapter titled "Cooperation on Water Issue: Bangladesh Perspective", Segufta Hossain examines water as a security concern for Bangladesh in terms of water scarcity. She examines the low riparian anxieties by looking at the issue of Farakka and the proposed river linking project in India and also the controversy surrounding the Tipaimukh Dam. The chapter analyses in detail the challenges to cooperation vis-à-vis water and the constraints in the way of optimizing any such cooperation. The chapter has a section on recommendations on how to overcome the challenges to cooperation between the two countries.

Medha Bisht in the chapter on "Water problems in Bangladesh: External and Internal Dimensions", deals with three aspects of water security – water reliability, water quality and water quantity. These three issues are discussed taking into account the internal and external dimensions of the water problem that Bangladesh is facing. It also deals with broader problems like river pollution which affect the quality and wastage of the water which could be mitigated by water harvesting and using it judiciously. The chapter also deals in detail with the India-Bangladesh water engagement and related bilateral problems.

The chapter on "Bangladesh-India Cooperation on Energy Issues: Bangladesh Perspectives" by Mahfuz Kabir analyses the energy requirement of the growing economies of the two countries and the energy security problems they face in terms of the rising price of crude oil, developing alternative sources to meet their energy need and diversification of their energy market. The author argues that the two countries can jointly explore energy sources and cooperate by institutionalizing joint monitoring of pilferage, harmonize oil prices to curb cross-border informal trade, and share information and experience in renewable energy, nuclear energy and energy conservation.

The chapter on "Transcending India-Bangladesh Relations: Framing Mutual Security Parameters" deals with the factors that make cooperation on security issues imperative rather than it being a choice, given a host of non-traditional challenges that would require a cooperative effort. The problems of border management, issues of smuggling, illegal migration and the need to chart out a cooperative security framework are dealt with in detail. The chapter also analyses bilateral and multilateral cooperative frameworks that exist for such cooperation on security. The author argues that cooperation on security assumes greater importance as it is security issues that generate mistrust and suspicions that percolate to other areas of bilateral ties.

Shaheen Afroze's chapter on "Security Dynamics and Bangladesh-India Relations: Bangladeshi Perspectives", deals with various challenges the countries are facing. The chapter details how the security concerns of India are impacting on Bangladesh-India relations. It analyses the border-related security challenges which includes killings on the border, illegal migration, problems of enclaves and the delay in implementing the 1974 boundary agreement, and suggests measures on how to meet some of these challenges. The author argues that given the sensitive nature of the issues that confront the two countries, both the governments should be responsive to the mood and sentiment of the people while resolving the problems.

The book also comprises some important documents including latest MoUs and agreements related to India-Bangladesh relations as annexures which would be useful to those researching on India-Bangladesh relations.

Last but not the least, I would like to thank all the contributors of this volume for adhering to the deadlines and submitting their chapters, bearing with various editorial queries, being open to various editorial suggestions and comments and resubmitting their drafts on time. I would like to sincerely thank Director General IDSA Dr Arvind Gupta, for his unstinted support now and earlier as the head of the South Asia Centre. Without his emphasis to publish the book in time, this effort would have got delayed.

I take this opportunity also to remember the late AKM Abdus Sabur, for his selfless support when both of us were making efforts from 2007 to start the bilateral dialogue between IDSA and BIISS which could not happen for one reason or the other. It was only in 2009 when he visited IDSA to attend a conference, that we both finalized the draft of the MoU which was signed in 2010. A special mention needs to be made for Ambassador Virendra Gupta, former deputy director who wanted me to explore the possibility of restarting the bilateral when I was a visiting fellow at Dhaka University in 2007. I also would like to especially thank Dr Shaheen Afroze, Research Director BIISS, for coordinating this programme with me and the Director-General BIISS, Imrul Quayes and former DG IDSA, Shri N.S.Sisodia, for taking keen interest to see that the bilateral is held after a break of almost ten years. My sincere thanks to my colleagues at the South Asia Centre for all their help in successful conduction of this bilateral at IDSA in May 2011. I would like to especially mention Gulbin and Pramod who took special care of the delegates from the BIISS,and Dr Uttam Kumar Sinha an expert on water issues, for presenting a paper on water security at this bilateral.

I would like to express my personal thanks to Dr Ashok K. Behuria, Coordinator, South Asia Centre, for his support and encouragement and bearing with my insistence to submit his chapter in spite of his busy work schedule. I will fail in my duty if I do not thank Mr Vivek Kaushik, Assistant Editor at IDSA, for providing all help with the publication of the volume. The two copyeditors of this volume, Dr Kiran Sahni and Seema Nambiar need to be complimented for a meticulous job and putting up with last minute editing. My sincere thanks to Shri Amit Garg and his team at Gyan Publishing House, for working round the clock to see that the book is published in time.

Smruti S. Pattanaik
Editor

List of Contributors

Dr Smruti S Pattanaik is a Research Fellow at the Institute for Defence Studies and Analyses (IDSA). She is a PhD from the South Asian Studies Division of School of International studies, JNU. She joined IDSA in 1998. Her main areas of interest are politics of identity in South Asia, army in politics and foreign policy issues. She was a Kodikara Fellow at the Regional Centre for Strategic Studies, Colombo. She was a visiting Asia fellow at the department of international relations, Dhaka University in 2004 and 2007. She was a post doctoral fellow at the Centre for International Relations and Research (CERI) in Paris in 2008, visiting fellow at Peace Research Institute Oslo (PRIO) in 2009. She is the author of "*Elite perceptions in foreign policy: Role of print media in influencing Indo-Pak relations, 1989-99*" (2004) and has edited a book titled *South Asia: Envisioning a Regional Future* (2011). Her current project focuses on "India Neighbourhood Policy". She is the book review Editor of Strategic Analysis, IDSA journal published by francis and Taylor. Dr Pattanaik coordinates the Pakistan Project of IDSA. She is member of various taskforce of IDSA focusing on India's neighbours. She has written around 50 articles and 20 book chapters in various national and international publications.

Dr Arvind Gupta is the Director General of IDSA, New Delhi. He is an officer of the Indian Foreign Service and earlier held the Lal Bahadur Shastri Chair at the Institute. Prior to joining the IDSA, Dr Arvind Gupta was Joint Secretary at the National Security Council Secretariat from 1999 to 2008. During his tenure at the NSCS, he dealt with a wide spectrum of national security issues. He has served in the Ministry of External Affairs and Indian Missions abroad on various diplomatic assignments. His current interests include: the impact of globalization on India's security; security in South Asia, foreign policy and diplomatic challenges before India, energy security, climate change, institutional reform, India's neighbours, internal security, technology and security issues. He has a number of publications to his credit.

Ms. Segufta Hossain is Research Fellow at Bangladesh Institute of International and Strategic Studies (BIISS). Her areas of interest are Strategic Issues, Environment and Environmental Security. Some of her important publications are: "North Korea's Nuclear Test: Implications for East Asian Security", BIISS Journal, Vol. 27, No. 4, October 2006; "Bangladesh's Foreign Minister's Visit to China: Issues, Outcomes, and Future Exploration", Bangladesh Foreign Policy Survey (BFPS), Quarterly, Vol. 7, No. 1, June-August 2006; "Maoist People's War in Nepal: Issues and Concerns", BIISS Journal, Vol. 27, No. 1, January 2006. She has also co-authored articles in various journals and edited books, such as: "Migrant Labours, Remittance Inflow and Economic Development" in Golam Mohammad (ed.), National Security Bangladesh 2009, BIISS and The University Press Limited, 2010; "Urban Environmental Change: A Case Study on Eastern Dhaka City Wetlands Transformation from 1963-2009", *BIISS Journal*, Vol. 31, No. 2, April 2010; "Bangladesh (Part II)" in Caroline Ziemke-Dickens and Julian Droogan (eds.), Asian Transnational Security Challenges: Emerging Trends, Regional Visions, The Council for Asian Transnational Threat Research (CATR) and Centre for Policing, Intelligence and Counter Terrorism (PICT), Macquarie University, 2010; "Non-Traditional Security of Bangladesh 2008: Food Security" in Sheikh Md Monirul Islam (ed.), National Security Bangladesh 2008, BIISS and The University Press Limited, 2009; "Non-Traditional Security of Bangladesh" in M. R. Osmany (ed.), Whither National Security Bangladesh 2007, BIISS and UPL, 2008.

Dr Ashok Behuria obtained his Ph.D. from School of International Studies, Jawaharlal Nehru University in 1995. For his Ph.D. he worked on Ethno-communal violence as a factor in India-Pakistan relations during the 1980susing the linkage theory framework. He joined International Centre for Peace Studies (ICPS) in 1996 and worked as Assistant Director, Associate Editor of *Weekly Kashmir Trends*, Assistant Editor of *Journal of Peace Studies*. He joined IDSA in 2003 and has been working as Research Fellow on issues relating to South Asia in general and Pakistan, Sri Lanka and Nepal in particular. He has written a number of research articles, monographs and commentaries on various regional and international issues. He is the coordinator of South Asia Centre at IDSA.

Dr. Sreeradha Datta is the Director of Maulana Abul Kalam Azad Institute for Asian Studies (MAKAIAS), Kolkata. Earlier, she was a Research Fellow at Institute for Defence Studies and Analyses (IDSA), New Delhi. Prior to joining IDSA, she was Coordinator (Research) with South Asian Centre for Strategic Studies, New Delhi (1996-99) also the Editor, *South Asia Watch* (1997-1999). She has been recipient of the Kodikara Fellowship (1997). She was selected for International Visitors Leadership Programme, USA (2006); She is a regular participant in Indo-Bangladesh Track II dialogues and also has been working on climate change and water security issues in South Asia. Some of her selected publications are : *Caretaking Democracy: Political Process in Bangladesh 2006-08* (New Delhi: IDSA, 2009); *Changing Security Dynamics in Southeast Asia* (Co-edited) (New Delhi: Magnum, 2008); *Bangladesh: A Fragile Democracy* (New Delhi: Shipra, 2004).; *The Northeast Complexities and its Determinants* (New Delhi: IDSA/Shipra, 2003) and *Islamic Militancy in Bangladesh : The Treat from Within, in South Asia : Spectre of Terrorism* (Ed.) P R Kumaraswamy, Ian Copland (New Delhi) Routledge, 2008.

Mr. Ishtiaque Selim is Research Fellow at Bangladesh Institute of International and Strategic Studies (BIISS). He joined BIISS in 2006. His areas of interest are regional integration and security issues

Dr. Anand Kumar is an Associate Fellow at IDSA, New Delhi. After completing his PhD from School of International Studies, Jawaharlal Nehru Univesity (JNU), he joined the IDSA in 2007. His area of specialization is Bangladesh, Maldives, Counter-terrorism, South Asian politics and low intensity conflicts. His latest article "Shaikh Hasina's Visit to India and the future of Indo-Bangladesh Relations" has been published by the Royal Society for Asia Affairs, London, in their official journal, *Asian Affairs*.

Dr Mohammad Mahfuz Kabir is currently a Research Fellow at Bangladesh Institute of International and Strategic Studies (BIISS). He holds PhD in International Economics from School of Economics and Finance, Curtin University of Technology, Australia. He worked on the issues of regional cooperation, SAARC, BIMSTEC and

BIMSTEC-Japan cooperation, which have been published in journals and books from Bangladesh and abroad. Recently he worked as an expert in the background studies on "external sector performance" and "comprehensive national security" components of the Sixth Five Year Plan (2011-2015) of Bangladesh. His areas of research interest include regionalism, international trade, panel data econometrics, and partial and computable general equilibrium models.

Dr. Medha Bisht is an Associate Fellow at the Institute for Defence Studies and Analyses (IDSA), New Delhi. Ms. Bisht has a doctorate from Diplomatic and Disarmament Studies Division, Jawaharlal Nehru University. She wrote a PhD on Multi-Satekeholder Negotiations on Security and Development. Dr Bisht has been a contributory author to various reports commissioned by the United Nations, IDRC Canada and the Government of India including the Progress of Women in South Asia (2005) & (2007) published and supported by UNIFEM. Since 2007 she has been one of the contributors (India section) to the Landmine Report published by the International Campaign to Ban Landmines, Canada. International Negotiations and Civil Society Participation, Multi Stakeholder Processes, Bhutan, Transnational Water Issues and Dams in South Asia, Anti-Personnel Landmines. Some of her important publications are: "Advocacy Groups and Multi-Stakeholder Negotiations: Redefining Frameworks of Diplomatic Practice," *International Studies*, 45.2, 2008; "India's Development Diplomacy: Re-Engaging Afghanistan," *Peace and Conflict Monitor*, University of Peace, May 5, 2009; "Poverty and Governance in South Asia: Issues and Concerns" in Ashok Behuria (ed.), *India and its Neighbours: Towards a New Partnership*, 2008; "Red Star Rising," *Asian Affairs*, May 2008, Brunel Academic Publishers Ltd, United Kingdom and "Sanitation And Waste Management: A Perspective of Gender and Diplomacy" in Sudarshan and Pande (ed.), *Ensuring Public Accountability through Community Action*, ISST, 2007.

Dr. Shaheen Afroze is Research Director at Bangladesh Institute of International and Strategic Studies (BIISS). She has done her Ph.D. in International Relations from University of Glasgow, UK in 1994. Her areas of interests are: South Asian Studies, Inter-state Relations in South Asia, Foreign Policy and Security of Small States, Gender Studies. Some of her **significant publications are:** 'India-Pakistan Rivalry and the Role of Small States: A Bangladesh Perspective',

Regional Studies, Summer 2003, (Islamabad, Pakistan); 'Bangladesh-China Relations: An Assessment', in *Asian Security and China in the Period 2000-2010,* (Asian Security Review, IDSA, New Delhi, India, 2003); 'Gendering Economic Development: Change or Continuity?' in P. R. Chari and Sonika Gupta edited *Evolving a Theoretical Perspective on Human Security*, (New Delhi, Institute of Peace and Conflict Studies), 2002; "India-Pakistan Nuclear Arms Race: Response of the Non-Nuclear Weapon States of South Asia", *BIISS Papers*, No. 17, December 1998 and "Non-Compliance of the Small States of South Asia: A Theoretical Perspective", *Theoretical Perspectives*, Vol. 3., No. 1, 1996; "Nuclear Rivalry and Non-Nuclear Weapon States in South Asia: Policy Contingency Framework", *BIISS Journal*, Vol. 16, No.4, 1995 and "Do Small States Behave Differently from Big States? A Critique of Maurice East's Alternative Model", *BIISS Journal*, Vol. 14, No.1, 1993.

1

Consonance and Dissonance: Issues and Trends in India-Bangladesh Relations

Smruti S Pattanaik

"India seeks to build a new future with Bangladesh. The time has come to chart a new path. We are ready to pursue a bold vision for our relations, based on mutual respect and mutual benefit"

Prime Minister Manmohan Singh, January 2010

India has been extremely important factor in Bangladesh's political discourse, first in the context of state formation based on the two-nation theory in 1947 and later in the emergence of a secular Bangladesh in 1971. The factor of geography has further added to their complex relations making India an important component of Bangladesh's foreign policy. From being an important partner in the country's liberation, India has been portrayed as an 'unfriendly' country and many anti-India elements due to their various vested interests have often attributed 'motives' to India's role in the liberation war thereby questioning the basis of a close relationship. In spite of such views India and Bangladesh have shared historic synergy and India's role in the liberation war only augmented these ties. Though one witnessed an erosion of the close relationship; the two countries remained important for each other in terms of security and economic dependence. Throughout the eighties India was also too embroiled in its own problems to devote much time to Bangladesh though it jealously guarded any attempt to breach what it considered to be its 'strategic periphery'. Its focus on the neighbourhood remained confined to preventing any outside power from interfering, but at the same time, given the difficult relations between the two, it could not play the role of regional power. It got involved in bilateral nitty-gritty and in many cases it could not exhibit magnanimity, as bilateral issues were debated within the narrow framework of regime interests, domestic politics and narrowly defined national interests that remained security centric. The end of the Cold War and the politics of power blocs brought about a major change in international political dynamics that significantly influenced the politics in the region. The two countries attempted to address some of the bilateral issues that had bedevilled their relations but with limited success. However India's attitude changed after I.K. Gujral became prime minister and emphasised that India would not expect reciprocity in its relations with its smaller neighbours - with the exception of Pakistan. This set a positive tone in the bilateral relations. The relations between the two have been determined by regime interests more so in the case of Bangladesh apart from factors of ideology.

Different Regimes and India Bangladesh Relations

The historical socio-cultural ties that transcend national boundaries unfortunately have not helped the two countries to overcome bilateral political difficulties. The relations in the initial phase were shaped by historical episode of the liberation war when India shared excellent relations with the Bangladesh government in exile. This extraordinary coordination set the tone for bilateral relations after liberation. The relationship that started with shared memories of sacrifices made for the birth of the new nation also shaped the outlook of the two countries. An example of this was the signing of Treaty of Peace and Friendship that encompassed the shared vision of peace and security. The Treaty got embroiled in the domestic politics of Bangladesh till it lapsed in 1996 after 25 years of ignominious existence. Even when it was in existence the Awami League (AL) which was the chief architect of the Treaty refused to acknowledge it and allowed the treaty to die its natural death. India also did not want any extension of this treaty. The Treaty had its existence and relevance during the Cold War period when many countries were hostile to the creation of Bangladesh and some including Pakistan even refused to recognise it. Bangladesh was an infant democracy – a new nation with few strong institutions or a strong military. The Treaty did play a limited role in providing a security umbrella in the formative stage of the state. The two countries also shared similar values based on democracy and secularism and followed a similar trajectory in their nation building effort.

Both the countries also took many initiatives to resolve some of the pending issues soon after liberation to help them to outgrow the antagonism that prevailed during the Pakistan period. Demarcation of borders and exchange of enclaves were very important issues for changing the tone and texture of relationship. Unfortunately the matter got embroiled in a legal battle in India and the transfer of Tinbigha could not take place in time, leading to mistrust and suspicion between the two countries. Similarly the land boundary agreement was not ratified by India - given the differences in the perception of the two countries regarding its ratification. While Bangladesh ratified the Treaty even though it did not publish it in the official gazette, that denied it legal sanctity; India argued that the Treaty could not be ratified unless the boundary demarcation is complete[1]. Though the position did not alter the ground situation as the border remained undemarcated until 2010, nevertheless this added to the trust deficit. The advantage of a well defined and demarcated boundary was not lost on the leadership in India. The then minister for external affairs Sardar Swaran Singh said in the Lok Sabha:

> *It is in our interest that we should ensure smooth demarcation of boundary in accordance with the Agreement as the advantage that will accrue to both countries as a result of a friendly atmosphere will far outweigh any seeming dissatisfaction in any locality. The continuance of unsettled borders creates problems. As a result of the Agreement, there should be no reasons for such problems to arise.*

The rise of rightist political parties after the assassination of Sheikh Mujib led to the projection of India as the main 'enemy' and these parties often questioned Bangladesh relationship with India terming it as a 'surrender of sovereignty'. Moreover in the post 1975 period Bangladesh's placed greater emphasis on its relations with Muslim countries, both for political and economic reasons. As the secularists were politically marginalised, due to General Zia's political programme of promoting 'Bangladeshi nationalism' rehabilitating the religious political parties, the entrenched bureaucracy and political class were inherently anti-India. The personal relationship between the leaders of the two countries was not good. As an analyst pointed out: "Just as Zia could not afford to be seen as following Mujib's footsteps or adopting a conciliatory stance towards India, neither could Indira Gandhi be seen to be conciliatory towards a military regime which is opposed to Mujib's goals"[2]. However the two countries signed a trade agreement in 1976 to improve their economic relations with India agreeing to offer coal at a cheaper price.

Similarly India after 1975 did not pay much attention to its relations with Bangladesh. It was critical of the military takeover in Dhaka. Some of the pro-Mujib groups took shelter in India and carried out cross border raids. This also strengthened the belief that India would not support any government other than that of the AL. These alleged cross border attacks by the *Kader bahini* also created anger in Dhaka especially when military government was trying to consolidate after a series of coups and counter coups. Zia's frequent requests for the handing over 'miscreants' were disregarded by Delhi. The two countries resorted to rhetoric, followed by skirmishes on the border over contested claims and were even prepared for military action which indicated the rising tensions between the two countries. However the two countries agreed to form joint enquiry commission to look into the matter of cross-border raids that were allegedly being conducted from India with the help of the Indian border force. As was pointed out by a scholar, "Zia made an effective scapegoat of the Indian government by combining accusations of territorial aggression with the cry of 'Islam in danger"[3]. Zia's own perception of India and his initiative to diversify Bangladesh's foreign policy also distanced both countries. Zia also had realised that the circumstances under which he took over, especially after failed coup of Khalid Musharraf, any pro India stance or any emphasis on forging close ties would be politically suicidal for him. India's internal tryst with democracy after the imposition of emergency was another factor that kept it busy. With the change of government in New Delhi; the Janata Party for the first time came to power. Prime Minister Morarji Desai was keen on developing good relations with India's neighbours to effect a change in the policy followed by his predecessors. President General Zia ur Rahman and Morarji Desai met on the sidelines of the non-alignment summit and agreed to have an interim agreement on Farakka in 1977.

This agreement was possible as the decision was taken at the highest level to concede to Bangladesh's demand for 63 per cent of water from Ganges. The inland water treaty was renewed and new routes were added to the existing routes. Prime Minister Morarji Desai accommodated Bangladesh's demand for market access for some products and the economic relations continued even after Mrs Gandhi returned to power. However, road and rail transit remained closed even though the agreement has provision for such facilities to be extended to India. Article 5 of the 1972 trade agreement provided for "mutually beneficial arrangements for the use of their waterways, railways and roadways for commerce between the two countries and for passage of goods between two places in one country through the territory of the other." However this got embroiled in politics and rail and road routes to transport goods from one part of India to its other part in the Northeast remained suspended. Over a period of time vested interests did not wanted these routes to be reopened for political reasons. The flow of Chakma refuges to India and unfolding insurgency in Chittagong only added to the enduring problems between the two.

General Ershad's tenure did not see any significant change in Bangladesh's approach. Given the domestic compulsions and the lack of legitimacy due to his military takeover the atmosphere was not conducive for any breakthrough in bilateral relation even though the two countries signed a MoU on water sharing at Farakka in 1982 and 1985. The assassination of Indira Gandhi and assumption of power by Rajiv Gandhi brought some change in India's neighbourhood policy. He agreed with long standing Dhaka's proposal to involve Nepal for augmenting the lean season flow by constructing storage in Nepal; this could not fructify as Kathmandu did not agree to it because it would have submerged large tracts of land in Nepal. In 1982 the relations between the two countries improved after the signing of a MoU on Farakka. Bangladesh wanted to sign a long term treaty on water sharing at Farakka and then rely on a link canal within Bangladesh that was to be built to augment water to address its water problems during lean season without depending on India. However, it could not marry its public posture with the contemplated link canal plan of the government[4]. The likely adverse reaction to any proposal which resembled an earlier Indian proposal prevented the water resources minister in the Ershad government from going public[5]. Writing in the context of water sharing, which holds true for India-Bangladesh relations, an Indian analyst said that it is the "over simplified 'nationalistic' view that tended to carry greater weight in the bureaucratic and political processes in both countries"[6]. India also got involved in regional politics for defending its sphere of influence. The Assam agitation against illegal immigrants had its impact on bilateral relations. Thus domestic politics on either side left its imprint. The construction of a fence, mobilisation of border forces on both the sides and firing on the border became a regular feature between the two countries. Bangladesh also demanded transfer of Tinbigha on lease for vehicular traffic and laid claims over the New Moore Island and Mahuri *char*.

With the dawn of democracy the relationship began to appear more hopeful; however India got dragged into the electoral politics of Bangladesh and emerged as a factor in the ideological contest between the two countries. The unresolved Farakka issue coupled with Tinbigha became a major problem. The BNP propagated that India wanted desertification of Bangladesh given the dam it has built in Farakka. During the first BNP government, Bangladesh's relations with India, were often marked by a confrontational attitude. Begum Zia went to the extent of describing insurgents from the Northeast as being the sun of freedom (*mukti surya*) thus vitiating the bilateral atmosphere. Even though she visited India in 1992, bilateral tension continued. However, the Tin Bigha Corridor was finally leased to Bangladesh and opened for use by Bangladeshi passengers and vehicular traffic on 26 June 1992[7]. Her announcement that Bangladesh would not allow its territory to be used against India did not resonate with what was happening on the ground. Bangladesh raised the Ganges water issue in 1993 at the Commonwealth Summit in Cyprus and later in 1995 at the UN General Assembly. Coupled with this, Babri Masjid demolition in India, Indian diplomatic premises in Dhaka were attacked, there were also attacks on minorities and their places of worship in Bangladesh. Prime Minister Narasimha Rao's decision not to attend the Dhaka SAARC summit citing security reasons only aggravated tensions.

The relations between the two countries were dominated by differences on water sharing and repatriation of Chakma refugees from India. The Awami League assumed power in 1996 and the two countries signed the much needed treaty on water sharing at Farakka. It was felt that the thorny issue of water sharing had contributed substantially towards embittering the relations between the two. With the signing of the Treaty it was believed that India and Bangladesh would be able to concentrate on larger issues.

The enunciation of a policy based on non-reciprocity also known as 'Gujral doctrine'[8] was greatly appreciated and sparked a hope that the two countries would emerge as partners in forging mutually beneficial ties. The fragile coalition politics prevented any breakthrough in India's relations with Bangladesh[9]. In 2001, 16 BSF personnel were killed by Bangladesh in Pyrduwah giving rise to tension in the border. However, India acted with utmost restraint. The BJP led National Democratic Alliance (NDA) government assumed power in 2001 and was keen on developing good relations with its neighbours. Brajesh Mishra was sent to Bangladesh as a personal envoy of Prime Minister Vajpayee to felicitate Begum Zia for her party's victory in the election. To achieve a breakthrough the NDA government downplayed the post election violence in Bangladesh in which minorities were targeted resulting in their temporary migration to India. It was felt that the BNP government was not keen on improving relations with India[10]. The Kolkota-Dhaka bus service and Dhaka-Agartala bus service were also introduced during the NDA period. Keeping the 2007 elections in mind Begum Zia visited New Delhi and praised India's contribution to the liberation war. The visit towards the end of her tenure was to win the confidence of Hindu minorities in Bangladesh rather than to improve relations.

The relations between the two countries improved substantially during the caretaker government regime. The army chief, Moen U Ahmad's visit to India was significant. During this period for the first time Indian soldiers who had participated in the liberation war were invited to jointly celebrate victory day in Bangladesh in December. This was the first time any such effort was made by the Bangladesh military. Commerce Minister Jairam Ramesh visited Dhaka to launch the India Bangladesh Chamber of Commerce and Industries in 2007. The two countries have revived the Dhaka-Kolkota train service – the 'Moitree Express' that runs between the two cities.

The Awami League's landslide victory in the December 2008 elections endorsed popular support for the party. The battle cry of "Save the country and Islam by voting for Bangladesh Nationalist Party and its alliance" did not succeed. The party in its election manifesto had pledged that it would establish regional connectivity. The commerce Minister of Bangladesh Col (retd) Faruk Khan speaking at a business conference in July 2009 said, "We said in the manifesto that if elected, we would give a boost to regional trade by building Chittagong and Mongla ports as regional gateways. We have the mandate of the people for going ahead for regional integration." Prime Minister Hasina visited India in January 2010 and the two countries signed a 51 point joint communiqué that clearly provided future direction to India Bangladesh relations and delineated priority areas for the two governments to collaborate. The two countries exchanged strip map[11]. The Land Boundary Agreement is pending for ratification before the Indian parliament during the current budget session.

Involving the provinces of India bordering Bangladesh in New Delhi's relationship with Dhaka signals a new dimension in India's foreign policy. This can partly be attributed to the nature of coalition politics and partly due to the fact that the border provinces of India have much stake in the national policy towards India's neighbours. Often accusations have been made that the geographically peripheral states of India are not consulted while New Delhi frames its bilateral ties even though these states have close economic and socio-cultural connection with Bangladesh. India's relationship with Bangladesh impinges on the life of the people living in these states bordering Bangladesh. The four chief ministers of Assam, Tripura, Mizoram and Meghalaya were part of the prime minister's entourage and the chief minister of Paschimabanga refused to accompany the prime minister because of disagreement over Teesta water sharing.

Trends in Bilateral Relations

(i) Issues of Trade: Compulsions of Asymmetry

The India-Bangladesh bilateral trade agreement was signed in 1980 and has been periodically extended since then. During Commerce and Industry Minister Anand Sharma's visit to Dhaka the ready-made garment export quota was increased from previous 8 million to 10 million pieces[12]. It is likely that this effort would help the hosiery industry in Bangladesh and provide investment opportunities for contract manufacturing by Indian firms. In addition to this during Prime Minister Manmohan Singh's visit in September 2011 India allowed duty free access to 46 Bangladeshi textiles items. This has evoked sharp criticism from garment manufacturing industries in India[13]. India is the biggest export destination of Bangladesh outside the Western world[14].

The laboratory testing for *hilsa* is now conducted at the Benapole border and BSTI has been involved in certifying products. In the JWG meeting held in May 2010, India agreed to assist in strengthening BSTI. Fourteen land customs posts/ integrated check posts have been upgraded for bilateral trade between the two countries. There is progressive reduction of items on the negative list. Earlier the two countries had signed Business Protection and Promotion Agreement (BIPA) to facilitate investment. This agreement provides for repatriation of capital investment, non-operating profits, loan repayments, royalty payments and service fees without delay and on a non-discriminatory basis[15]. Apart from extending credit lines; India has undertaken several infrastructure projects to improve connectivity in the bordering states. The provision of border *haats* in the 1974 trade treaty is being implemented now. Out of the total one billion dollar credit line which India had extended projects worth US$750 million has already been signed between Exim Bank of India and Economic Relations Department of Bangladesh[16].

Connectivity and Transit

India has long been asking for transit to its Northeast through Bangladesh. However in late nineties trans-shipment was proposed as a way out. This would have dealt with the concerns raised by Bangladesh security analysts and have been profitable for Bangladesh truckers who would have carried Indian goods from one side of the border to the other. A dry run was conducted to test the viability and profitability of such exercise in July 1999. However, the proposal could not take off as it was feared that it may impact Awami League's political fortunes as the elections were round the corner. Given these domestic sensitivities I.K.Gujral the then Prime Minister of India wrote: "In keeping with the policy of asymmetry, we have not insisted that

India's trade with Peoples Republic of Bangladesh

Values in US $ Millions

S.No.	*Year*	*2006-2007*	*2007-2008*	*2008-2009*	*2009-2010*	*2010-2011*
1.	**EXPORT**	1,629.57	2,923.72	2,497.87	2,433.77	3,606.39
2.	%Growth		79.42	-14.57	-2.57	48.18
3.	India's Total Export	126,414.05	163,132.18	185,295.36	178,751.43	251,135.89
4.	%Growth		29.05	13.59	-3.53	40.49
5.	%Share	1.29	1.79	1.35	1.36	1.44
6.	**IMPORT**	228.00	257.02	313.11	254.66	446.75
7.	%Growth		12.73	21.82	-18.67	75.43
8.	India's Total Import	185,735.24	251,654.01	303,696.31	288,372.88	369,769.13
9.	%Growth		35.49	20.68	-5.05	28.23
10.	%Share	0.12	0.10	0.10	0.09	0.12
11.	**TOTAL TRADE**	1,857.57	3,180.74	2,810.98	2,688.44	4,053.15
12.	%Growth		71.23	-11.62	-4.36	50.76
13.	India's Total Trade	312,149.29	414,786.19	488,991.67	467,124.31	620,905.02
14.	%Growth		32.88	17.89	-4.47	32.92
15.	%Share	0.60	0.77	0.57	0.58	0.65
16.	**TRADE BALANCE**	1,401.57	2,666.70	2,184.76	2,179.11	3,159.64
17.	India's Trade Balance	-59,321.19	-88,521.83	-118,400.95	-109,621.45	-118,633.24

Note: Since 2006-07, Petroleum figures are being computed from Import Daily trade Returns (DTRs) to genetate country-wise/port-wise tables. Up to 2005-06 consolidated petroleum import figures were being received from the Petroleum Ministry.

Source: Department of Commerce, Government of India http://commerce.nic.in/eidb/iecnt.asp

Bangladesh grant us transit rights. By conceding transit to be the sovereign right of Bangladesh, it was possible for us to fertilise the mind of that country about how to make the best use of transit facilities for its own economic and social developments"[17]. The two countries have not been able to sign a transit treaty during Prime Minister Manmohan Singh's visit as agreement on Teesta could not be reached. In the context of transit Bangladesh is now discussing whether it needs to levy transit fee or whether there is any international precedence for this. A Bangladesh minister termed imposition of transit fee as 'uncivilised' creating more controversy. There are also doubts whether Bangladesh infrastructure would be able to handle such a transit. India's one billion dollar loan is aimed at improving and developing infrastructure in Bangladesh. Though some security analysts have cited security reasons while arguing against transit to India the situation is slowly changing. Bangladesh's own desire to grow economically and emerge as an economic hub and a land bridge between South and South East Asia has made it to look at connectivity as an opportunity. It has exhibited a regional outlook by granting such facilities to Nepal and Bhutan thereby connecting the north-eastern part of the region. The two countries have signed an inland waterway transit agreement that facilitates transport of goods between one part of India to the other. The road and rail transit between the two had stopped during the 1965 war. The genuine desire for enhancing economic engagement often takes political colour in Bangladesh.

Connectivity between the two countries is equally important for the economic development and investment opportunities it would provide. The two countries signed a Framework Agreement on Cooperation for Development and pledged:

> *To promote trade, investment and economic cooperation, which is balanced, sustainable and builds prosperity in both countries. Both Parties shall take steps to narrow trade imbalances, remove progressively tariff and non-¬tariff barriers and facilitate trade, by road, rail, inland waterways, air and shipping. Both Parties will encourage the development of appropriate infrastructure, use of sea ports, multi-modal transportation and standardization of means of transport for bilateral as well as sub-regional use.*[18]

Illegal Immigration, Smuggling and Management of Border

India and Bangladesh share a 4096 km-long border. Of this, 180 kms lie along the river line. Radcliffe was asked to draw the boundary keeping the Muslim and Hindu majority areas in mind while taking into account 'other factors'. The award said: "The province offers few, if any, satisfactory natural boundaries, and its development has been on the lines that do not well accord with a division by contiguous majority areas of Muslims and non-Muslims majorities". This has made the management of the India Bangladesh border difficult in cases where the boundary cuts across villages, and homes, dividing families and rendering the boundary irrelevant to the people staying near the border making it prone to violation. Smuggling of cattle, illegal immigration and killings due to firing on the border have emerged as new challenges to the two countries. India has built fence on the India-Bangladesh boundary but this has not been enough for dealing with the challenge of porous border. At one level the building of fence reflects a sense of distrust between the two countries; at other level it is a sign of the lack of cooperation over the management of the border and the differences in approach to security and other related issues. This also reflects absence of an empathetic attitude towards each other's concerns. While India imposes night curfew near the border such strict a restriction is not imposed on the other side of the border in Bangladesh. Moreover, "The existing border cum-fencing...Was constructed at varying distance of about 900 mts, 700 mts, 500 mts and 300 mts from the zero line of the international border and at some place fencing was constructed at about 400 mts to 1000 mts away"[19].

The two countries now have joint and coordinated patrols in place since last July. Referring to coordinated border patrol while making a suo motto statement in the parliament on the prime minister's visit S.M. Krishna said: "We hope this will greatly reduce the scope for incidents on the border and strengthen mutual trust and goodwill among the border guarding forces and people living in the border areas. We hope that problems arising from illegal border crossings and related difficulties will be better addressed by both sides"[20]. In both cases of cattle smuggling- that has led to a majority of firing incidents at the border - and illegal immigration, the reluctance of political class to address the issue is palpable. While illegal immigrants have emerged as a major vote bank for political parties in India the cattle smuggling has a criminal-political nexus. In both the cases there is a clear reluctance to take steps to address the issue as these two issues are highly politicised and sensitive and involve high political stakes.

The government has given directions to the border security forces to use non-lethal weapons and not to fire until threat is posed to their security. The border force feels such a policy has emboldened the smugglers who are taking advantage of this. The government instructs the border force not to shoot but it also wants them put an end to smuggling. Thus there is a dichotomy in India's approach. At the same time government's reluctance to legalise cattle trade which would substantially reduce border firing reflects further confusion. The smuggling of cattle which runs into crores induces the carrier to risk his life and as a result they often enter into confrontation with the Border Security Force (BSF) of India to see the trade continues without hindrances[21]. This has given rise to bribe and other mode of inducement[22]. The government needs to tackle cattle smuggling seriously. To stop the smuggling of cattle the state police of other states should prevent the transport of cattle from other parts of the country to reach the border. But this might be difficult as there is no legal barrier on transport of cattle from one state to another within India. Legalising this trade would be a politically explosive issue in India. Therefore the only way forward is to have more dialogue and adopt a practical approach to deal with the issue. According to the Indian home minister more Indians are killed in the firing than Bangladeshis. Unfortunately due to the lack of interest of India's national media the killing of Indians also largely remains unreported, and it appears as a one sided story. Any border incidents between India and Pakistan finds immediate mention in the national daily but news on India-Bangladesh border is conspicuous by its absence.

The issue of illegal immigration is also another explosive topic between India and Bangladesh. Bangladesh in the past has denied the existence of any such illegal immigration. According to the *Economist* every one of Bangladesh's poorest 32 districts (out of 64) shares a border with India[23]. The border states of India also do not share similar views on immigrants from Bangladesh. While Tripura does not have any such problem and is rather happy with the cheap work force provided by migrant labourers from across the border, Assam has a huge problem which has fed into the identity politics in the state and has made Assamese a linguistic minority in their state. The demographic profiles of the Northeast states have changed over a period of time. This, perhaps, to a large extent explains the rather high rate of growth of the Muslim population in Assam, estimated at 77.42 per cent between 1971 and 1991[24] which is much higher compared to the all India level. West Bengal politics is dominated by the sharing of water with Bangladesh. India earlier had proposed introduction of work permit to allow Bangladeshi workers to work on legally valid work permits. However there is no response from Bangladesh on this proposal. Such illegal immigration and unauthorised crossing is likely to pose challenge to Bangladesh also. Bangladesh has frequently accused that many of its wanted criminals are hiding in India.

Indian insurgent groups have found shelter in Bangladesh and the issue of illegal immigration that includes human trafficking are two important issues that have challenged Indian policy makers. This has remained a major sore point leading to political contestation that has often become part of domestic politics.

Adding to the discomfiture Prime Minister Manmohan Singh's remark made to editors at a closed door meeting regarding radicalism and anti-Indianism in Bangladesh was leaked to the media thus creating a huge furore. The fear of the emergence of radical groups in Bangladesh that can be used against India is real and is shared by many. India has been a victim of terrorism sponsored from across the borders. Some of these elements have used India's open and porous border to infiltrate into India. Without cooperation from Bangladesh India's security remains vulnerable to cross border infiltration by non-state actors.

Water Sharing

The two countries established Joint River Commission (JRC) in 1972 to look into the matter of river water sharing. The agenda of the joint river commission is:

(a) to maintain liaison between the participating countries in order to ensure the most effective joint efforts for maximising the benefits from common river systems to both the countries,

(b) to formulate flood control works and to recommend implementation of joint projects,

(c) to formulate detailed proposals on advance flood warnings, flood forecasting and cyclone warnings,

(d) to study flood control and irrigation projects so that the water resources of the region can be utilised on an equitable basis for the mutual benefit of the peoples of the two countries, and

(e) to formulate proposals for carrying out coordinated research on problem of flood control affecting both the countries.

(f) The commission shall also perform such other functions as the two governments may, by mutual agreement, direct it to do.

The joint river commission did not meet between 2005-2010.

Water sharing has emerged as a major problem area between the two countries. In 1996 India and Bangladesh signed the Ganges water treaty after prolonged negotiation that factored in 40 years of data (1949-88) on the flow of the river. States like Bihar are complaining that their interests were not taken into consideration while signing the treaty with Bangladesh and have demanded a review of the treaty. Morarji Desai also visited Bangladesh in April 1979 and the two countries agreed to establish Joint river commission. Even after signing the Farakka Treaty in 1996 the issues of water sharing remain contentious. Though the treaty is up for review every five years; Bangladesh has not asked for abrogation of the treaty. Controversy has surrounded the quantum of water and the suspicion that India is withdrawing water and depriving Bangladesh of its legitimate share. The matter is rendered complex "by the absence of official information about the operation of the treaty. The greater enemy of the treaty was the classification of information, i.e. the treatment of all information regarding flows and releases as secret"[25]. Moreover Bangladesh insistence on 'historic' flow does not take into account climate change and increase in population thereby nurse grievances on imaginary ground.

The following is details of the Ganges water sharing during the lean period.

Period	*Average of total flow 1949-88 (cusecs)*	*India's share (cusecs)*	*Bangladesh's share (cusecs)*
Jan			
1-10	107, 516	40, 000	67, 516
11-20	97, 673	40, 000	57, 673
21-31	90, 154	40, 000	50, 154
Feb			
1-10	86, 323	40, 000	46, 323
11-20	82, 859	40, 000	42, 859
21-28	79, 106	40, 000	39, 106
March			
1-10	74, 419	39, 419	35, 000
11-20	68, 931	33, 931	35, 000*
21-31	64, 688	35, 000*	29, 688
April			
1-10	63, 180	28, 180	35, 000
11-20	62, 633	35, 000*	35, 000*
21-30	60, 992	25, 992	29, 688
May			
1-10	**67, 351**	**35, 000***	**32, 351**
11-20	**73, 590**	**38, 590**	**35, 000**
21-31	**81, 854**	**40, 000**	**41, 854**

*Three ten day periods during which 35, 000 cusecs shall be provided.
Source: http://www.hcidhaka.org/shar_ganga.php.

Conclusion: Future Direction

The two countries have signed a number of agreements on cultural exchanges during the prime minister's visit. Earlier the two countries had celebrated the 150th birth anniversary of Rabindranath Tagore who has written the national anthem of both the countries[26]. There are also plans to celebrate the Nazrul centenary together. There have often been complaints in Bangladesh that Indian channels do not carry TV programmes of Bangladesh whereas Bangladesh cable operators beam the Indian channel network in Dhaka. While it is difficult to force the private players who are driven by market economy; an MoU was signed between Doordarshan and Bangladesh Television. The two countries are exploring the possibilities of jointly co-producing programmes. India also announced 300 additional scholarships for

Bangladesh students annually for five years to study in India. Two hundred scholarships are provided under *Muktijoddha* scholarship scheme by the government of India to higher secondary-level students and 478 scholarships for graduate-level students. Such educational and cultural exchanges are likely to help in furthering people to people relations between the two countries. India has a separate category to facilitate visas for medical treatment and medical attendant. Multiple entry visa is provided for this. The two countries have approached the international tribunal for the Law of Sea to settle their maritime disputes. Bangladesh decided to approach the international tribunal during the BNP period.

Porous borders have made security of the two countries intertwined. Without mutual cooperation dealing with pan South Asian terrorist groups is impossible. Bangladesh has been victim of countrywide bomb attacks, suicide attacks and attacks on its pluralist culture. These common challenges should provide synergy for greater cooperation. Thus cooperation should go beyond regimes that are in power by making people a stakeholder in the process. Often it is questioned whether this cooperation and good relations would be sustained in case there is a change of regime in Dhaka. New Delhi's desire for a sustainable long term ties with Bangladesh is evident from its investment in long term projects. Uncertainty regarding India-Bangladesh relations remains a factor as the main opposition party in Bangladesh has been opposed to closer ties with India. The past does not generate much hope as far as the BNP government is concerned. Bangladesh's help in the arrest of ULFA main functionaries hiding in that country reassures that cooperation on the issues of security is possible. Similarly in the past India played a major role in facilitating the signing of CHT peace accord in 1997 that facilitated the return of Chakma refuges to Bangladesh who had taken refuge in India.

The last visit of Prime Minister Manmohan Singh and signing of historical agreement that paved the way for exchange of enclaves and demarcation of boundary got marred by India's inability to sign the Teesta accord. This also demonstrated how the resolution of the longstanding border dispute became peripheral to a mainstream issue like water. The fact that the people in the enclaves are leading a sub-human life did not receive much attention from the civil society, media and policy makers as Dhaka remained stuck on the single issue of the Teesta. The success of the visit was evaluated only through this narrow prism. The longstanding demand of providing 24 hour access through Tin Bigha was also granted[27]. The trade concessions made for textile products were not given the attention they deserved. Understandably, there was hardly any reaction in India to Dhaka's refusal to sign the transit treaty with India as it was clear that allowing transit without a deal on Teesta may mean political hara-kiri for the AL. Even the newspapers in India were critical of last minute fiasco criticising both the central and the state government in India for failing to take the consent of the state and not signing Teesta.

The provinces of India increasingly will play larger role in influencing foreign policy of India. Coalition politics has made it imperative that the regional demands and the views of the provinces affected by any international treaty need to be taken on board. As the states in India are increasing becoming assertive of their rights it would be more difficult for the centre to monopolise the foreign policy domain. Bangladesh has been part of centre-state relations and politics between different parties in India. Both in the context of the Assam agitation and the Farraka issue Bangladesh became a part of India's domestic politics.

The relations between the two countries would be dependent on how New Delhi's manages its ties with provincial capitals in India and the Awami League's ability to manage its domestic political imperatives. The management of internal dynamics would decide the temperature of bilateral relations. Nevertheless, the two countries would be influenced by globalisation and market forces which would blunt the sharp political division to some extent. As former Indian foreign secretary Shyam Saran said: "The stand of interdependence is to provide certain stability to the relationship despite political changes, because the logic of the interdependence will not permit the political relationship to swing from one side to another."[28] India is striving to achieve this in Bangladesh.

Notes

1. For detailed analyses see Smruti S Pattanaik, "India-Bangladesh Land Border: A Flawed Inheritance and Problematic Future", *Strategic Analysis*, Vol. 35(5), August-September 2011, pp. 745-51.
2. Kathryn Jacques, *Bangladesh, India and Pakistan: International Relations and Regional Tensions in South Asia*, Macmillan, London, 2000, p. 103.
3. Kathryn Jacques, Ibid, p. 110.
4. Ben Crow, *Sharing the Ganges: The Politics and Technology of River Development* University Press Limited, Dhaka, 1995, pp.188-190.
5. Ibid, p. 189.
6. Ramaswamy Iyer, "Conflict resolution: Three River Treaties", *Economic and Political Weekly*, Vol. 34 (24), June 12-18, 1999, p. 1513.
7. Ministry of External Affairs, *Annual Report*, 1992-93, http://mealib.nic.in/?2020#India's Neighbours.
8. For the five principles of Gujral doctrine see, I.K.Gujral, *A Foreign Policy for India*, External Publicity, Delhi, 1998, pp. 94-95.
9. For details pertaining this period see, Dennis Wright, "Bangladesh and the BJP, *South Asia Journal,* Vol. 25(3), 2002, pp. 381-93.
10. In an interview with Brajesh Mishra, National Security adviser of the NDA government. July 12, 2010 at New Delhi. For various views on India-Bangladesh relations see Smruti S. Pattanaik, "India's Neighbourhood Policy: Perception from Bangladesh", *Strategic Analysis*, Vol. 35(1), January-February Issue, 2011, p. 81.
11. There are total 162 enclaves (51 in India and 111 in Bangladesh) The Indian enclaves in Bangladesh are located in four districts - Panchagarh, Lalmonirhat, Kurigram and Nilphamari. All of Bangladesh's enclaves lie in West Bengal's Cooch Behar district. The agreement enables Bangladesh to retain the Dahagram and Angarpota enclaves. The headcount revealed that 34,000 people resided in the Indian enclaves in Bangladesh and there were 17,000 inhabitants in the latter's enclaves. 56 enclaves are not inhabited, of which 37 are Indian. "India, Bangladesh settle Boundary Dispute", http://indiatoday.intoday.in/story/india-bangladesh-settle-boundary-dispute/1/150380.html"
12. Out of this three million pieces would be produced by using fabric from India, another three million pieces from fabric either sourced

from India or Bangladesh and remaining two million without any preconditions.

13. "Domestic Textile Firms hit by duty free imports from India." *Business Standard*, September 3, 2011. http://www.business-standard.com/india/news/domestic-textile-firms-hit-by-duty-free-importsbdesh/447912/
14. Ministry of External Affairs, "*Fact sheet on other MoU and Agreements signed with Bangladesh*", http://meaindia.nic.in/mystart.php?id=510118194&flg=1
15. Syed Tashfin Chowdhury, "Delhi Emphasizes Mutual Interest after Dhaka Warning", *Asia Times Online,* July 12, 2011, http://www.atimes.com/atimes/South_Asia/MG12Df03.html
16. The credit line is extended on 1.75 per cent interest rate with a repayment period of 20 years, including a grace period of five years.
17. I.K. Gujral, *A Foreign Policy for India*, n. 8, p. 8.
18. Framework Agreement on Cooperation for Development", http://meaindia.nic.in/mystart.php?id=501018197&flg=1
19. Deputy Commissioner Karimganj M Angamuthu said in a note (dated: 18-05-2009)on the 'Status of Indo-Bangladesh Border Road Cum Fencing in Karimganj District" as cited in *Hindustan Times*, January 31, 2010.
20. Suo Moto Statement by EAM in Lok Sabha on PM's Visit to Bangladesh, September 8, 2011, http://meaindia.nic.in/mystart.php?id=501018214&flg=1
21. Interaction with BSF officers on 3rd May 2012.
22. In the recent case of torture of a Bangladeshi national which was publicized in the media the BSF has sent those involved in the crime to jail, see "8 BSF men Sent to Jail", *Daily Star*, March 15, 2012.
23. "Go East, Old Man" *Economist,* August 30, 2011, http://www.economist.com/blogs/banyan/2011/08/india-and-bangladesh
24. Wasbir Hussain, "Demographic Jitters", *Outlook,* September 20, 2004.
25. Ramaswamy Iyer, n. 6, p. 1515
26. For details of India-Bangladesh Relations see IDSA Task Force Report on "India-Bangladesh Relations: Towards Convergence", especially chapter 3 and 4, IDSA, September 2011.
27. According to the May 16, 1974 boundary agreement India will retain the southern half of South Berubari Union no 12 and adjacent

enclaves, measuring an area of 2.64 square miles approximately, and in exchange Bangladesh will retain the Dahagram and Angarpota enclaves. India will lease in perpetuity to Bangladesh an area of 178 meters by 85 meter 'Tin Bigha" to connect Dahagram with Panbari Mouza (PS patgram) of Bangladesh.

28. "Does India have a Neighbourhood Policy" Lecture at ICWA, September 9, 2009.

2

Trends in Indian Foreign Policy

Arvind Gupta

Indian foreign policy has to adjust to the fast changing world. Since the end of the Cold War, global and regional environment have undergone major change. India has sought to align its foreign policy to new realties. It opened up its economy in 1991 and went nuclear in 1998. In 2005, it sought to normalise its relations with the US. It weathered the global 2008-09 financial and economic crisis with relative ease. It has now begun to focus on the maritime dimension of its foreign policy. Indian foreign policy is driven by national interests and has become more pragmatic. However, given its size and historical legacy, India continues to strive for strategic autonomy in foreign policy.

Bipolarity has ended. US hegemony is under challenge. New powers have risen. A transition to multi-polar world is being made but the contours of the multi-polar world are still not clear.

With the rise of China, India and other Asian countries, the balance of power is shifting from the West to Asia Pacific. Russia is trying to recover its lost position. Newly emerging countries are in different stages of development and are yet to consolidate their power. Nevertheless, they occupy an important place in the global power structure. India, for instance, is playing an important role in several new institutions of global governance like the G-20, BRICS and in the Asia Pacific.

Factors Affecting India's Foreign Policy

The US is in relative decline. Following 9/11, the US got bogged down in Iraq, Afghanistan and uncertainty continues over Iran. The Iraq war has proved to be costly for the US. The current crisis in the

Middle East has exposed the limits of the US influence in the region. The US has shied away from taking a lead in NATO'S operations in the Middle East. In Afghanistan, the US exit strategy is mired in uncertainty over the post withdrawal security situation and whether Taliban would be part of a future political dispensation and if they are, what would be the nature of such a government. Developments in Afghanistan would have implications for the entire region.

The US debt burden ($14 trillion, 100 per cent of GDP) is too huge and will take several years to redress. The global economic and financial crisis of 2008-09 exposed US weaknesses while China came out relatively unscathed. US commitments to its allies are increasingly being questioned. Most experts however agree that it is too early to write off the US. The US is looking for new partners to shape the emerging global order. It wants India as a partner in the future.

China's rise, particularly its military modernisation and assertive foreign policy, is causing a great deal of concern. Will China's rise be peaceful? Will it play by the existing rules or will it set its own norms? How will the US-China relationship pan out? These are some of the imponderables about China's rise. China is also in a state of transition. It is also not clear how the internal situation in China will develop and whether or not it will affect China's ability to play a larger role or its stability. India is naturally interested in the implications of developments in China as both have unsettled border disputes. China has launched a diplomatic offensive to enhance its influence in far flung areas. Its naval modernisation programme is designed to enhance its power projection as well as sea denial capabilities. China is also emerging as a major space power having tested ASAT weapons.

The nature of conflict is also changing. Inter-state wars are becoming less frequent while intra-state conflicts are becoming more frequent. Wars against non-state actors are becoming more common. Terrorism has emerged as a form of warfare between state and non state actors. Both India and Bangladesh face the similar challenge of terrorism. Failed states or failing states pose a major challenge to state sovereignty as well as international security. Such states or regions breed terrorism and organised crime. Unfortunately, these problems do not remain confined within the state boundaries and have a spill over effect on the region as a whole.

Non traditional security issues are becoming dominant. Several developmental issues are being securitised. Climate change, energy security, global health, food security, water security and cyber security are emerging as major issues of international concern.

Human rights have emerged as a key international security issue. International law is evolving towards the legalisation of responsibility to protect (R2P). R2P is a new norm in international law. The recent NATO intervention in Libya was justified under a UNSC resolution which authorised military action under Chapter VII of the UN charter to protect Libyan security forces' strikes against the civilians. The guidelines for outside intervention in the affairs of a state on humanitarian grounds are still unsettled. It is not clear under what circumstances the international community could invoke the R2P to intervene in the internal affairs of a state.

Globalisation has accelerated bringing in its wake opportunities and challenges. Globalisation – the convergence of several technologies – has led to the shrinking of time and space as well as greater interdependence. Interdependence has ensured that the impact of local incidents is felt everywhere and the impact of global developments are felt locally. Thus, no one is immune from negative developments in any part of the world. Advances in technologies have had profound impact on social conditions - how we live, how we think and how we behave. The impact of social networking sites has been palpable in the recent developments in the Middle East.

The structure of the world economy is changing. The share of services in the global economy has increased significantly. Knowledge plays an increasingly greater role in the shaping of the economies. Knowledge economies require a greater emphasis on education, training and skills. The global financial crisis highlighted the fragility of the world economy. High oil prices are a threat to stability of the global economy.

Risks to global stability have increased. Nations and societies are exposed to a variety of risks which appear suddenly and unexpectedly and also spread rapidly. Over the last few years, the world has seen how quickly the financial crisis spread and engulfed the whole region. Pandemics like bird flu and SARS spread across the globe in quick time. Natural disasters like the 2004 tsunami affected scores of countries claiming hundreds of thousands of lives. The eruption of a volcano in Iceland in 2010 disrupted flights to and from Europe for several weeks causing huge economic losses and passenger inconvenience.

Demographic changes in the world are making some countries vulnerable. The Western world is ageing fast while developing countries have youth bulges which can lead to unemployment and social unrest. One fifth of the population of South Asia is between 15-24 years. India alone accounts for 200 million youth. Young adults account for half of the unemployed in this region. The share of youth population in the region is: Sri Lanka 27 per cent, Nepal 38 per cent, Pakistan 37 per cent, Bangladesh 39 per cent and India 32 per cent.[1] Generating employment opportunities for them is a formidable challenge.

Democracy is becoming the norm but democratic institutions are still weak in many countries. In South Asia Pakistan and Bangladesh face challenges to democratic stability and Nepal is in the process of transiting to a stable political order after years of instability. Sri Lanka is engaged in rehabilitation of Tamils displaced during the civil war and is also in the process of finding a political solution to its longstanding ethnic conflict. It is a major concern for India that Western countries are pursuing polices of regime change in the name of democracy and human rights protection. This creates further instability.

Global prosperity depends upon the judicious use of global commons – air, water, cyber space, and earth. Climate change poses an existential threat to global security. The rising level of sea would affect countries like Maldives and Bangladesh badly. Issue of global warming needs to be addressed urgently. Maritime security – piracy, freedom of navigation, protection of Sea Lines of communication (SLOCS) – are becoming important. This would need joint efforts and cooperation among the countries.

Global defence expenditure is increasing - $1.5 trillion. This is a reflection of increased insecurity. Newly rich counties are acquiring weapons on an unprecedented scale. This is despite the fact that the nature of conflict is changing.

India and the World

India is being called upon to adjust to the rapidly changing world. The key tasks before India are to safeguard its national security, to remove poverty and to achieve decent standards of living for its 1.2 billion strong population.

During the Cold War years, India had maximised its autonomy by following a policy of non-alignment. This policy served it well in the bipolar world.

In the post Cold War era, India had to craft a new policy as Soviet Union collapsed and disappeared altogether. India's adjustment to the new realties came in the form of three key developments. First, India opened up its economy in 1991 and slowly started integrating with the world economy. This process is still going on and has brought rich dividends. India is projected to emerge as the second or third largest economy in the world by 2050. This was unthinkable few years ago and is the result of India's policy of economic liberalisation.

Second, India exercised its long delayed nuclear option in 1998 due to the rapidly changing security environment which included WMD proliferation in its neighbourhood. Initially, India was sanctioned but the impact of sanctions has been weathered successfully. India became a de-facto nuclear power with a minimum nuclear deterrence. It follows a policy of no-first use. It has also declared a moratorium on further tests.

Thirdly, India signed a civil nuclear cooperation deal with the US. The agreement was controversial but its positive impact was that international sanctions against India were removed and India became part of the global mainstream. This deal became possible given India's impeccable non-proliferation record and the confidence of the world community that it has been a responsible nuclear state. The nuclear deal is likely to help in boosting economic growth and creating jobs in the country. It will also help fulfil India's growing energy needs. The negative fall out was the impression within the country that India had sacrificed its decision making autonomy. The jury is still out on this.

India's foreign policy challenges are two: an unstable neighbourhood and an assertive China. Both are linked with each other. India's key challenge in the neighbourhood is to improve trust and cooperation, enhance connectivity for greater trade within the region, enhance regional cooperation and safeguard its security through multilateral and bilateral framework of cooperation. India has to factor in the sensitivities of the neighbours for a more durable relationship.

It also needs to take initiative for economic development of the region. India in the past has urged its neighbours to be partners in development and benefit from the vast India market.

In India' neighbourhood, Pakistan and Afghanistan are unstable. Foreign powers are present in the region. The region is the hotbed of terrorism having transnational linkages. The future of Afghanistan remains uncertain after 2014 pull out of western troops from combat operation. Pakistan uses its influence with Taliban to gain strategic depth in Afghanistan that has not allowed peace to return to Afghanistan. Indian workers and its Embassy has been target of Pakistan sponsored Haqqani group in Afghanistan. The Pakistani army's mindset is anti-Indian and they continue to consider India as a threat. As a result, terrorism is used to destabilise India in an asymmetric war. The army continues to play a dominant role in Pakistan and has sabotaged the civilian government's peace initiatives with India. The China-Pakistan nexus is a major security challenge for India. The defence cooperation between them and its presence in Gilgit and Baltistan in Pakistan Occupied Kashmir has been a major concern for India.

A rising China presents its own challenges. The Sino-Indian border is still unsettled and China continues to stake its claim to the state of Arunachal Pradesh. Its decision to issue staple visa to people of Jammu and Kashmir is seen as an attempt to keep pressure on India. China is expanding its presence in the Indian Ocean and also in India's neighbourhood. Given the border dispute and China's aggressive posture vis-à-vis India it will have to manage its relations with China.

Other countries in the region are also unstable in varying degrees. Nepal, after the overthrow of monarchy, continues to be unstable. Peace process is yet to reach logical conclusion as the parties don't have consensus among themselves on reaching agreement on the issue of federalism and the form of future government in the country. Bangladesh successfully held elections in 2008 and transited to democracy. However challenges from the radical elements and terrorists remain a major factor there. The situation is little better elsewhere but these countries face the challenge of poverty and social unrest. India's borders with its neighbours are porous which creates its own set of challenges including infiltration of terrorists and criminals. Relations with Bangladesh have improved considerably in the recent past. The relationship must be made sustainable.

After the demise of the LTTE, Indo-Sri Lankan relations are on the upswing. The trade between the two countries has grown and reached $5 billion in 2011. India is engaged in building infrastructure in Sri Lanka and building houses for the people living in the north who suffered during the long drawn out war. Democracy in Maldives has resulted in the deepening of Indo-Maldives relations. However, recent development in which the government was overthrown by police coup has raised concerns of stability. Moreover, the rise of radical elements in Maldives is also a challenge. The India-Myanmar relationship is being diversified. The two countries have recently signed a Framework Agreement.

Besides the neighbours, India has other major interests - energy, diasporas, trade, investment – in its extended neighbourhood in West Asia and East Asia. India's Look East policy has borne fruit. It is now shaping its Look West policy. India is also trying to rejuvenate its relationship with Central Asia. Africa and Latin America have emerged as new priorities in Indian foreign policy.

India' growth will be affected by its ability to source its energy needs from different parts of the world. Energy security has emerged as key priority in India's foreign policy.

India needs to have sufficient defence preparedness to meet its diverse security challenges. India's defence budget, as a percentage of GDP, is amongst the lowest in the world, and India has to contend with high defence spenders like China and Pakistan with whom it had fought wars in the past.

In order to meet its security and developmental goals, India will have to maintain high economic growth over a long period of time. The growth will have to be inclusive and even. This requires India to improve governance and undertake much delayed reforms. The challenge of improving governance will remain critical for India in the coming decades. The corruption scandals of recent times have undermined India's image in the world. There are also evidence that a vast amount of resources have been siphoned off at the expense of growth and development. In the end, the robustness of India's foreign policy will depend upon the quality of governance at home and management of internal security challenges.

Contours of India's foreign policy

India has unprecedented opportunities to play an important role in global and regional affairs and to safeguard its national interests. It has the political, economic and military tools to play this role in accordance with international law. India is already playing important role in developing connectivity and infrastructure in Afghanistan and has pledged $2 billion for Afghanistan's economic development. It has provided a soft loan of $1 billion to Bangladesh that will finance 14 development projects in Bangladesh with fixed annual interest of 1.75 payable with twenty five years including five years grace period. It is involved in developmental activities in Nepal and Sri Lanka. Nepal and India have recently signed Double tax avoidance agreement. In the above backdrop, it is obvious that India's foreign policy has evolved over the years. India's investment in Sri Lanka has increased. India is involved in nine projects worth US$ 168 million[2].

The following trends have become pronounced.

India' engagement with the world has increased manifold. India now has nearly 30 strategic partnerships with key countries in the world. Relations with these countries are being developed across a wide spectrum. India maintains good relations with major powers and also with newly emerging powers. India is a member of several regional organisations like BRICS, IBSA, and EAS etc. These groupings have become increasingly important in global affairs.

As a non-permanent member of the UNSC for the next two yeas, it is participating in the management of top international security issues. This experience will be useful when India joins the UNSC as permanent member.

India has an important voice in key global negotiations like those on climate change, WTO and elsewhere. Many countries the world are watching India's rise and are positive about India taking a more high profile visible role in international affairs.

The economic dimension of India's foreign policy has become stronger. India's has leveraged its growing economic clout to play an important role in the global governance institutions. India's place in the G20 deserves a mention. India is also participating in the reform of global financial institutions. Foreign investment in India has grown and have crossed $200 billion since 1991. India's share in global trade is growing. Similarly Indian investments in other countries are also growing. India has signed several Free Trade Agreements in the recent years. This has given it a higher profile in world affairs.

Energy security is being given high importance in India's foreign policy. Indian investments in energy sector have grown. India also attracts foreign investment in this sector.

The military dimension of India's diplomacy has become more pronounced. India is playing an effective role in tackling the menace of piracy in the oceans and providing stability in the Indian Ocean region. India's defence cooperation with several countries, particularly with US, Israel, Japan apart from Russia has increased.

India is also part of several counter terrorism working groups along with other countries. India has played a key role in promoting international cooperation on terrorism.

India has followed proactive policy in the neighbourhood. With the exception of Pakistan, India's relations with other neighbours have improved. The prospects for regional cooperation have become brighter and India is now taking greater interest in further regional cooperation.

The Neighbourhood

With Pakistan, India has followed a balanced policy of engagement and persuasion. India's effort is to persuade Pakistan not to let its territory be used for terrorist activities against India. This has been a constant effort. At the same time India has cautiously resumed dialogue with Pakistan which was suspended after the Mumbai attack. It must be admitted that India's policy towards Pakistan has not shown the desired results as yet given the power dynamics. Pakistan Army continues to play important role in shaping its India policy.

India has civilisational and historic links with Afghanistan. It has contributed nearly $2 billion towards the reconstruction of Afghanistan. However, the security situation is a matter of concern and is constraining the growth of India's relations with Afghanistan. The two countries signed a Strategic Partnership Agreement in 2011 October. India has agreed to train the security forces of Afghanistan to prepare the country to face the post withdrawal security situation. It has been supportive of international initiatives that are being undertaken to promote political stability in Afghanistan which includes the talks with Taliban. It firmly believes that a regional approach would help the political stability in

Afghanistan as competing interest impedes long term peace.

India's unique relationship with Bhutan continues to be strengthened. India's assistance to Bhutan has led to significant socio-economic improvements in the country. In 2007 the two countries revised their bilateral treaty and have signed a new treaty taking into account the new geo-political realities and aspirations of both the countries. In the past the two countries have successfully cooperated in flushing out Indian insurgent groups that had taken shelter there. The two countries also share an open border.

India has an open border with Nepal and share age-old socio-cultural and familial links. India has supported Nepal's peace process and multi-party democracy. It is due to Indian efforts that political parties and the Maoists came together on a common platform to establish republic and transit the country to an era of political stability.

The India-Bangladesh relationship has improved significantly in recent years. The economic relationship between the two countries is growing steadily to their mutual benefit. Prime Minister Manmohan Singh visited Dhaka last year and the two countries signed a Framework Agreement for cooperation and development. The two countries share similar concerns relating to terrorism, climate change and realise the importance of developing connectivitiy to foster closer economic collaboration.

Following the defeat of the LTTE, India-Sri Lanka relations have entered a new phase. India has conveyed to Sri Lanka the need for genuine national reconciliation, a meaningful devolution package and a dialogue between the government and the minority parties. India is also contributing towards socio-economic reconstruction in Sri Lanka.

India shares close relations with Maldives. It has been supportive of democratic transition there. Both the countries have recently signed Framework agreement to further their bilateral cooperation. India has also signed defence cooperation agreement with Maldives in 2009 which aims at protecting and securing Maldives vast Exclusive Economic Zone (EEZ)

China occupies high priority in India's foreign policy. The two countries have a congruence of interests on several regional and international issues. Difficult bilateral issues are being handled in the spirit of partnership and mutual understanding.

India and Iran despite some recent difficulties are engaged in promoting bilateral exchanges in a number of areas including energy, trade, commerce and industry, culture etc.

India regards European Union as a strategic partner with shared values of democracy, rule of law, respect for human rights and fundamental freedoms.

India's relationship with the US has shown all round progress. The Indo-US nuclear deal is a landmark development helping India to integrate with the international order.

India continues to maintain a special and privileged partnership with Russia. Russia fulfils India's critical needs in the areas of defence, energy, science and technology and commerce.

Japan remains an important partner for India. The bilateral relationship has been enriched by the intensification of the security dialogue and cooperation.

Africa has assumed a high priority in Indian foreign policy. India's relationship with the African countries is broad-based and growing rapidly.

India is also reaching out to the Latin American continent by its substantial relationships with Brazil, Mexico, Argentina and Colombia.

Central Asia remains an important region for India. India is developing bilateral ties with these countries and is also inclined to play a role in the Shanghai Cooperation Organisation (SCO).

India's Look-East policy is bearing fruit. India's relationship with the ASEAN countries is growing rapidly.

The Gulf region plays an extremely important role in India's energy security. The region also provides employment to nearly five million Indians. The importance of the Gulf for India cannot be overstated.

Domestic factors are playing an increasingly important role in shaping India's foreign policy. This is due to several reasons: many of India's states have borders with India's neighbours with whom they have cultural, social and economic affinities; a large number of Indians live abroad – their well being is important. They also send large remittances to India. More and more Indians are beginning to travel abroad for work, leisure, tourism and pilgrimages. Many Indians live in unstable regions of the world. Indian foreign policy has to cater to the needs of Indian nationals living abroad as was visible in the recent evacuations from Libya.

Challenges Facing Indian Foreign Policy

The following five challenges are key to India's foreign policy.

India needs a clear articulation of its foreign policy goals, The Indian establishment does not articulate foreign policy through white papers or other such authoritative documents. India does not even have a national security document as yet.

India needs to further buildup its political, diplomatic, economic, military and soft power capabilities to deal with new challenges. Indian diplomacy is overstretched. There have hardly been any high level visits to our neighbouring countries. This must change and India needs to engage its neighbour at the highest level.

India will need to maintain its strategic autonomy in a world where it is called upon to engage with all kinds of countries and groupings. The relationship with big powers should not be at the expense of other countries. This will require delicate diplomacy. Food, water, health and energy security must be given high priority in India's foreign policy. It is important that India achieve its national goals which will enable it to play larger global role. Political stability and economic prosperity would play vital role in shaping its foreign policy goals.

India will need to learn to manage its neighbourhood better. Our current engagement is not sufficient. We need to manage risks and opportunities in the neighbourhood better. India needs to take into account the sensitivities of the neighbours while at the same time sensitising them about India's concerns. Regional cooperation needs to be strengthened. People-to-people contacts, particularly in the areas of health, education, tourism, culture, trade need to be bolstered. It is important to develop regional synergy to have a mutually beneficial approach to global issues.

India and Bangladesh

The global geo-political context and the developmental needs of the two countries provide an opportunity to forge closer ties. As mentioned above, India's economic needs and security challenges are enormous. India and Bangladesh are not just neighbours they share similar concern regarding climate change and economic issues. The two countries have embarked on a Look East policy. While India's Look East policy dates back to the early nineties Bangladesh started its Look East policy in 2001. There is a need for the two countries to connect to South East Asian economies. At the same time there is a need for both to integrate with each others economies. The trade between the two countries has grown and recently India agreed to provide duty free access to 47 items thus fulfilling a longstanding Bangladesh demand.

India and Bangladesh have similar concerns on terrorism. Without mutual cooperation it would be difficult for both to meet the challenge of terrorism given the geographical proximity and porous nature of their border. The two can cooperate to develop a synergy in their approach to global terrorism. Both the countries are part of South Asia Association for Regional Cooperation (SAARC) and Bay of Bengal Initiative for Multi Sectoral Technical and Economic Cooperation (BIMSTEC).

Similarly, India and Bangladesh share similar concerns on climate change and related environmental issues. According to a study, the two countries are the most vulnerable to risks related to climate change[3]. The rise in sea levels would also create environmental refugees that would require close collaboration not just between the two countries but such concerns need to be globally articulated to mitigate the problem.

Both the countries face the challenges of economic development. India's major challenge has been to develop its Northeastern region. Though India is building road infrastructure and port to connect the northeast region to outside world through Myanmar, road connectivity for trade through Bangladesh would significantly change the economic landscape of the Northeast. Economic cooperation between the India's Northeast and Bangladesh would boost the Look East policy of the two countries.

India economic growth and its ability to play a larger global role is likely to help the entire region. The two countries can synergise their economic aspirations and adopt a common approach to various trade related challenges they face globally. The two countries also have scope to cooperate on security aspects such as terrorism, drug trafficking and managing and patrolling the vast and porous border to deal with the threats of smuggling, drug trafficking and illicit trade in weapon that can fuel violence and affect stability. The two countries have the potential and political will to develop mutually beneficial parameters for cooperation which will accrue greater economic and political benefits to them. This would be a major challenge for the foreign policies of both the countries.

Notes

1. http://web.worldbank.org/WBSITE/EXTERNAL/COUNTRIES/SOUTHASIAEXT0,,contentMDK:20827027~pagePK:146736~piPK:146830~the SitePK:223547,00.html
2. "India's Investment into Sri Lanka Zooms", Business Standard, November 18, 2011, http://www.business-standard.com/india/news/indian-investment-into-sri-lanka-zooms/455827/
3. "Bangladesh and India most risk from Climate Change", http://www.reuters.com/article/2010/10/19/us-climate-bangladesh-idUSTRE69I6LE20101019

3

South Asia and the International Order: A Bangladesh Perspective

Segufta Hossain

Introduction

South Asia is gaining global importance and increasing its influence in international affairs. Intra-regional relations in South Asia are shaped by both the socio-economic and socio-cultural factors. For more than 50 years the political dynamics of South Asian countries have revolved around the region's socio-cultural and historical inheritance, geo-political construction and economic space.[1] Bangladesh could not remain outside the ambit of the changes in the regional and global system. Bangladesh is a nation of strategic importance not only to the South Asian sub-region but also for the larger geopolitical dynamics of Asia as a whole. The geographic location of Bangladesh has made the country geo-strategically important. But this geopolitical location of Bangladesh gives it both strength and weakness from different perspectives. Against this backdrop, this chapter tries to discuss the potentialities and challenges faced by Bangladesh in the context of present world order. This study is divided into five sections. The first section provides a brief introduction. The second section deals with the present world order; the third section focuses on South Asia in the context of present global situation; the fourth section deals with the potentialities that Bangladesh offers and the challenges that the country faces in the present world order and the last section consists of the conclusion and recommendations.

Present International Order: Post Cold War Phase

In the immediate aftermath of World War II, Europe was drawn into a Cold War between the US and Soviet Union who were competing to bring the countries of Europe under their influence. After 1975 the world witnessed a second Cold War. Fundamental changes took place in the international system, transforming it into a multi-polar system as economic forces increasingly interlocked with political factors in shaping history even though the world was divided into two major power blocs while some countries formed the non-aligned movement.[2] With the end of the Cold War and the fact that there remained only one superpower on the global scene, i.e. the United States, it is widely perceived that the world order established after the World War II, is yielding place to a new one.[3] The end of the Cold War in the early 1990s has changed the political scenario of the world by furthering the process of democratisation. The reduction in East-West tensions also reduced inter-state conflicts, some of which had occurred due to the ideological rivalry between the superpowers during the Cold War.

The end of the Cold War also brought about fundamental changes in the international order which has since altered the nature of international conflict. Since the late 1980s, the main threat to regional and global peace has come, not from major inter-state confrontations, but from other sources: internal conflicts, i.e., conflicts occurring within the borders of states.[4] Besides these conflicts, newer threats, that were even beyond the control of the major powers of the world were also coming to the forefront. The most notable of these are, religious militancy, terrorism, North-South conflict, climate change and competition for the scarce resources. It can be said that the end of the Cold War has brought both stability and instability into the international politics. With the collapse of communist regimes in Eastern Europe and the disintegration of the Soviet Union, the bipolar international system of the Cold War period disappeared, yielding place to a predominantly unipolar system under the leadership of the United States, especially from a military/political point of view.[5]

Economic forces, as much as politics determined the outcome of the Cold War. Although the United States is a great power, from an economic point of view, the international order can be defined as multipolar rather than unipolar as there are other economic powers as well. There are other economic cooperation organisations like the

European Union, the Organisation of Asia-Pacific Economic Cooperation which are playing important role in shaping the geo-economics of the world. There are however many other nation-states that remain outside of these regional economic integration groupings or organisations.[6] Thus, the international order of the post-Cold War era is actually a mixture of the unipolar and multipolar system in which at least five major powers, the United States, Europe, China, Japan and Russia, dominate the international affairs.[7] According to another point of view, the era of world poles is over and there has now emerged a coalition of powerful states, including the United States, Japan, Germany and other powerful states of Europe, whose aim is to dominate the rest of the world in the strategic and economic sphcres.[8] Although the coalition partners have clashes of interests among themselves, they also have a convergence of interests rooted in their desire to gain control over natural resources, industrial raw materials and markets of the developing countries. The politico-military strategy adopted for the purpose is meant to influence political systems in the developing world.[9] They also seek to control economic and technological potential by creating and imposing international controls and monitoring regimes affecting nuclear and space technology, environment management, trade and investment policies.

For developing countries the present situation has become more difficult and complex to handle and it has forced them to re-appraise their domestic, economic, defence and foreign policies. South Asia, which has always been a region where great power competition has been played and managed. It also has been a region of great importance for the industrialised democracies.[10] The primary significance of the states of South Asia lies in the fact that there is competition between the superpowers for influence over the states. Following the end of the British rule, India and Pakistan emerged as two new independent states. Bangladesh won its freedom from Pakistan in 1971 after fighting a nine month long war of liberation. The security scenario of the South Asian region has been dominated by the developments between India and Pakistan. Territorial claims over Jammu and Kashmir have remained the main issue between the two countries. Pakistan became an American ally by joining the South-East Asia Treaty Organisation (SEATO) and the Central Treaty Organisation (CENTO). Shortly afterwards India became one of the co-founders of the Non-Aligned Movement and came closer to the Soviet Union.

Post 9/11

The fall of the Berlin Wall in 1989 and the disintegration of Soviet Union in 1991 inaugurated a period of extreme optimism, with the dominance of the market economy and globalisation which was considered to be the universal solution to economic disparities and restrictive trade regimes that existed in the past. Since the end of the Cold War, the nature of security challenges has changed radically. The 9/11 attacks and its consequences have again marked a significant change in the global security scenario. Terrorism and non state actors now dominate the security discourse. The September 11, 2001 attack brought the transitional phase that followed the end of the Cold War to an unexpected close.[11] Following these attacks, international terrorism received the attention of the global community. US retaliatory measures against the perpetrators of terrorist attacks coupled with a purposefully defined and concerted counter-terrorism strategy brought international terrorism and counter-terrorism to the centre-stage of international politics.[12] The 9/11 incident revealed the vulnerability of even the strongest power of the world to the acts of terrorism. Since then the international community has become increasingly concerned with the quest for security. A global war on terror began in the aftermath of 9/11.

The US decision to bring the perpetrators of 9/11 to justice brought the war close to South Asia. Pakistan emerged as its major ally in this war on terror being fought in Afghanistan. This also brought the international coalition force to Afghanistan and it along with NATO participated in what is termed as 'Operation Enduring Freedom'. The consequences of this war are being felt across the region. In the aftermath of 9/11, Bangladesh as a developing Muslim country was under the scrutiny of the US. As Bangladesh is against all forms of terrorism and violence, the country strongly condemned the 9/11 terrorist attacks. According to the US State Department's *Background Note on Bangladesh.*

> Bangladesh has become a valuable United States ally in our global efforts to defeat terrorism. As part of these efforts, the Government of Bangladesh has begun to address problems of money laundering and weak border controls to ensure that Bangladesh does not become a terrorist safe-haven. Bangladesh's strong national identity and moderate Islamic

tradition help it serve as a key player in combating extremism.[13]

South Asia in the Present International Context

South Asia plays an important role in the international system of today. It had hardly any role in global geo-politics prior to World War II. In 1947 the British withdrew from the region and India and Pakistan emerged as independent countries. The region played an important role in bringing together Afro-Asian nations on to a common platform against colonialism, imperialism and made serious attempts for decolonising the states that remained under foreign rule in Asia and Africa. South Asia was seen as the leader in the development of what was termed the Third World.[14] A major offshoot of British imperialism in South Asia was the growing bitterness and distrust between the core-nation India and peripheral states, especially Pakistan, Bangladesh and Nepal.[15]

With the demise of British imperialism in the South Asian region, competition began among the global powers to increase their influence in this region. The factors responsible for the involvement of major global powers in South Asia are as follows: narrow and intense nationalism; urgent need for economic development; domestic instability in the South Asian periphery; and common suspicion of the peripheral nations against the 'hegemony' of the core nation – India.[16] South Asia's security dynamics till 9/11 stemmed primarily from indigenous roots, with external factors impacting and, on occasion, aggravating or distorting them.[17]

The relevance of South Asian security for the international polity, during the Cold War period, essentially revolved around Indo-Pakistan relations, Sino-Indian conflictual relations and the issues relating to nuclear proliferation. The Cold War and bipolarity failed to change the security dynamics of this region although Pakistan was allied to the United States and India was close to the Soviet Union. This situation changed after the Sino-India conflict following which the US started supplying weapons to India which they stopped doing after the 1965 war between India and Pakistan. Pakistan's relations with China grew stronger as a result of 1963 border agreement. Later, China emerged as a major source of defence equipment for Pakistan after the US sanctions following the 1965 war. Pakistan also played a major role in the Sino-US rapprochement by facilitating Henry Kissinger's secret visit to Beijing in 1969. In the 1971 conflict US sent its nuclear capable

USS Enterprise to the Bay of Bengal. However the Treaty of Peace and Friendship that India signed with the then Soviet Union in August 1971 prevented the US from playing any significant role in the 1971 war. Though peace returned temporarily to South Asia, the Soviet intervention in Afghanistan in 1979 led to the re-emergence of South Asia as a major theatre of super power rivalry. The nuclearisation of South Asia and the subsequent Kargil war again focussed international attention on South Asia. The anti-Soviet jihad in Afghanistan emerged as a major source of instability in the region.

The emergence of Taliban and their brand of religious obscurantism again drew international attention to the region. The events of 9/11 have changed the geo-politics of the South Asian region with the involvement of extra regional powers like the USA due to the global war on terror. The internal security dynamics of some countries in South Asia have also changed. The greatest shift in the security dynamics is that the USA has become more concerned about the South Asian security scenario. The recent developments in the South Asia region draw the attention of the international community due to the fact that not only the international system affects these countries but also the developments within these countries impinge on the interaction of the states at global level.

The Bangladesh Perspective

Bangladesh is one of the most densely populated and least developed countries which is trying to evolve into a developing country. Geopolitically, Bangladesh is situated in the South Asian region with less than two per cent of the world land mass but is home to 20 per cent of the total population of the world.[18] The country is has a strategically important location in South Asia. Its unique position serves to makes it a bridge between East and South Asia. In the changed South Asian geo-strategic scenario, Bangladesh's geopolitical importance has increased due to at least to three factors. First, Bangladesh began to be referred to as the third largest Muslim country in the world and the second in the region. The second factor is Bangladesh's location within the 'geo-strategic frontier' of India, South Asia's most powerful country. And third is Bangladesh's close proximity to China, Asia's largest power, considered as the strategic rival of both the US and India.[19] Bangladesh has made enormous progress in the security and human development sectors. The country is trying to strengthen democracy, accelerate economic growth and strengthen social development. For this, the government has taken several measures to eradicate corruption, effect institutional reforms, promote human rights, the rule of law and the socio-economic condition of the country through alleviation of poverty, elimination of illiteracy, empowerment of women, etc.

Potential of Bangladesh

Social

Bangladesh has achieved much success in the social sector. Since poverty alleviation is a major goal of the government, much emphasis has been laid on the socio-economic development of the underprivileged groups. Bangladesh has achieved remarkable progress in the field of primary schooling, gender parity in primary and secondary education, reducing the under-five mortality rate and the incidence of communicable diseases as well as improving indicators relating to the environmental changes.[20] According to the *Bangladesh Literacy Survey,* 2010 of Bangladesh Bureau of Statistics the national literacy rate (7 years and over) is 57.53 per cent consisting of 60.15 per cent males and 54.84 per cent females.[21] The country has achieved immense success in reducing the infant mortality rate. According to the *Statistical Year Book of Bangladesh 2009* the infant mortality per 1000 live births which was 57 in 1998 went down to 41 in 2008.[22] Life expectancy at birth has also gone up from 56.1 in 1990 to 66.8 in 2008.[23]

The social sector improvement in Bangladesh can be seen by the increased enrolment in primary schools, girls' education, immunisation, micro-credit, birth control, physical mobility and social safety nets, population with access to improved sanitation, women's empowerment and female economic participation, etc. Bangladesh is among the 16 countries to have received UN recognition for being on track to achieve Millennium Development Goal (MDG)4 i.e. reduced child mortality.[24] Of the 52 MDG targets, Bangladesh is on track on 19 of them, and 14 of them need attention. Bangladesh continues to mainstream MDGs in its national development goals as embodied in successive poverty reduction strategy papers. Over time Bangladesh has sought to achieve MDGs along with other development goals through a series of policies and strategies.

Regarding women's status and gender equality, Bangladesh outperforms other South Asian countries on many counts. Sixty-two per cent of women are economically active in Bangladesh, which is not only the highest in Bangladesh but ranks above the average 50 per cent among the developing countries.[25] The micro-credit innovation and the readymade garments (RMG) sector in Bangladesh have and continue to revolutionise the earning potential of women. About the half of the country's population lives below the poverty line with 80 per cent living in the rural areas.[26] The burden of poverty also falls on women who constitute half of the total population of the country.

The microcredit programme in Bangladesh, which was actually conceived in the aftermath of the country's liberation in 1971, has rapidly grown during the 1990s and has gained increasing acceptance. The expansion of the micro credit programme has created more opportunities for self employment and earning for women in Bangladesh than many of her South Asian neighbours. In 2008, of the 21.6 million active microcredit borrowers, 92 per cent were women.[27] The Ready Made Garment (RMG) sector is often regarded as a case of the successful empowerment of women in Bangladesh as about 85 per cent of those employed in the RMG sector are women.[28] Progress with regard to gender equality in education is also positive. A World Bank report on *Changing Norms about Gender Equality in Education* found that gender gaps in education have changed in Bangladesh.[29]

The constitution of Bangladesh has given equal rights to women and it has several provisions that provide scope for the advancement of women.[30] The constitution of Bangladesh has also forbidden any kind of discrimination against women in every aspect of life. The government of Bangladesh adopted the National Policy for the Advancement of Women, 1997 with the aim to improve the condition of the distressed and discriminated women of this country and eliminate discrimination against women in every aspect of life and promote gender equality.[31] The National Policy for Women's Advancement, 2008 aims to empower women to become equal partners in development. The Bangladesh government has approved the National Women Development Policy (NWDP) 2011 which has the provision of giving women an equal share in property and equal opportunity in employment and business. The NWDP also secures women's rights in the formulation and implementation of economic policies in sectors like trade, currency and tax. Women are increasingly assuming leadership roles in the executive, legislative, and judicial organs of the state. Women are also actively serving in the law enforcement and national security agencies.

Economic

The economy of Bangladesh is based on agriculture with some three-fifths of the population engaged in farming. The economy of Bangladesh is rapidly growing and changing into market-based economy. Its per capita income in 2010 was estimated at $1,700 (adjusted by purchasing power parity). According to the International Monetary Fund, Bangladesh was ranked as the 47th largest economy in the world in 2010, among the Next Eleven or N-11 index of Goldman Sachs and D-8 economies, with a gross domestic product of $269.3 billion.[32] The RMG sector flourished in Bangladesh in the early 90s and presently has emerged as the major employer. Bangladeshi RMG products are mainly destined for the US and EU markets. The RMG sector is the leading sector of Bangladesh in terms of employment, production and foreign exchange earnings. It alone earns about 78 per cent of the annual foreign exchange earning of the country. The growth rate of RMG exports was over 20 per cent in the last two decades. About 3.5 million people are employed in this sector.[33] The country's RMG sector provides the highest employment after the agriculture, transport, trade and industry sectors. This sector has provided economic opportunities to the largely neglected and economically marginalised sections of the population, thus radically transforming the socio-economic condition of the country. Presently, Bangladesh is the third largest knitwear exporter in the world just after China and Turkey.[34] Bangladesh's textile industry, which includes knitwear and ready-made garments along with specialised textile products, is the nation's number one export earner, accounting for 80 per cent of Bangladesh's exports of $15.56 billion in 2009.[35] The Bangladesh Garments Manufacturers and Exporters Association (BGMEA) has estimated that textile exports will rise from $7.90 billion earned in 2005-06 to $ 15 billion by 2011.[36]

Remittances from Bangladeshis working overseas are a major source of foreign exchange earnings. Officially Bangladesh began exporting manpower in 1976 and by now has become a notable exporter of manpower. Bangladesh's major destinations for exporting manpower are the countries of the Middle East and South East Asia. According to Bangladesh Association of International Recruiting Agencies (BAIRA), 60896 persons were employed in the overseas countries and the total amount of remittance was $950.92 million in 2010.[37] The government of Bangladesh is committed to a market economy and has been formulating policies for supporting and encouraging private investment and eliminating unproductive expenditure in the public sector.

The geographical location of Bangladesh makes it a bridge between South Asia and South East Asia. The country has already taken the decision to join the Asian highway and the Asian railway network. It is building roads to connect itself to Myanmar and to Thailand. It can also connect itself to the Yunan province in China. Transit with India is also under consideration. All these connectivities would increase the potential of Bangladesh becoming a major economic and business hub in Asia.

Security

Almost all the countries in South Asia are affected by terrorist attacks or face the threat of terrorist attacks. Bangladesh is very seriously concerned about terrorism in the region. Bangladesh which is a moderate Muslim country is increasingly under threat from radical elements while its political and economic development continues to be hampered by the forces of corruption, radicalism, and partisan issues.[38] The frustration created by a combination of poverty, corruption, and the lack of good governance due to a stalemated political process is believed by some to have contributed to the increasing radicalisation of society.[39] Almost all South Asian countries are part of certain regional and international mechanisms to fight against the menace of terrorism. Bangladesh is also a signatory to conventions and protocols against terrorism. Bangladesh has achieved immense success in countering terrorism and radicalisation. The law enforcing agencies have arrested, and the judiciary has prosecuted, the masterminds of the terrorist networks which reinforces the country's stated position of condemning terrorism in all its forms and manifestations whether in the name of religion or any other ideology. Law enforcing authorities have continuously targeted terrorist networks and have foiled many such modules from time to time.

Since its participation in UN Peacekeeping Operations, Bangladesh has successfully proved its credentials as an effective peacekeeper. Bangladeshi peacekeepers earned the confidence of international community by their professional ability and sincerity. Bangladesh has participated in operations ranging from simple monitoring and reporting missions to peace building, peace enforcement, humanitarian assistance and have taken part in peace keeping operations aimed at nation building. As of September 2010, Bangladesh is ranked first in terms its contribution to the United Nations peacekeeping operations. Bangladesh Armed Forces started their deployment in the UN peacekeeping mission in 1988 with 15 observers in UNIMOG (Iraq-Iran). Since then it has maintained its position as a leading troop contributor country. Bangladesh armed forces have so far participated in 45 peacekeeping missions in 32 countries and a total of 92,252 members from Bangladesh armed forces have participated in the noble task of peacekeeping.[40] Presently 8,524 UN peacekeepers from the Bangladesh army, navy and air force are deployed in 11 ongoing UN peacekeeping operations in 10 countries.[41] The Bangladesh police also participate in UN peacekeeping operations. Till date 7415 police personnel have taken part in 18 UN peacekeeping missions.[42] At present Bangladesh has the highest number of police personnel deployed in UN peacekeeping operations.[43]

Challenges to Bangladesh

Although Bangladesh has made immense progress in the economic, security and human development spheres, the country still faces some challenges that are yet to be overcome.

Social

Poverty is a big stumbling block to progress in Bangladesh. Bangladesh has been unable to eliminate extreme poverty and hunger. There is a huge disparity between the standards of living in urban and rural areas of the country. The recent economic growth in Bangladesh has not led to a major decline in poverty levels, least of all in rural areas. Around 40 per cent of people live in poverty, with 25 per cent of these classified by the government as 'extreme poor' and unable to take advantage of the productive opportunities emerging from economic growth.[44]

Unemployment has emerged as major concern for the developing countries of the world. Bangladesh also shares these concerns. According to a study of the International Labour Organisation (ILO), the rate of unemployment in Bangladesh in the decade of nineties was 1.9 per cent while the unemployment currently stands at 3.7 per cent.

The ILO figures also show Bangladesh in twelfth position among the top twenty countries in the world where unemployment is rising.[45] The numbers of unemployed in Bangladesh are now an estimated 30 million. The rate at which unemployment is rising gives credence to fears that unemployment would soar to some 60 million by 2015.[46] More than one-third of the employed persons both at the national and rural levels are under-employed.[47] The country also has large-scale disguised unemployment in agriculture, large industries, offices and organisations particularly in the public sector.

The execution of terrorist leaders in 2007 is a clear demonstration of the government's resolve of dealing with such extremists and can be seen as a significant development for containing extremism in Bangladesh.[48] Terrorism is not a new experience for the sub-continent and the rest of the South Asian region. As the menace of terrorism is transnational in nature, Bangladesh is not yet free totally from it. Terrorist activities impacts the security scenario in the country. The recent arrests of some of Pakistani terriorists and Indian insurgent groups operating in Bangladesh have given rise to apprehensions that these extremists could have links with international terrorist organisations.[49]

Economic

The large and medium manufacturing sectors in Bangladesh have been adversely affected by the current global recession as they are mainly export oriented. The export dependence of the economy has also led to a decline in the service sector, particularly in trade and transport, while the financial service sector remains untouched.[50] The crisis did have its impact on Bangladesh's human security scenario in terms of employment, income and working conditions.[51]

Manpower export is an important source of foreign exchange for the country. But this sector is also facing a slowdown. According to the Bureau of Manpower Export and Training (BMET), after a record growth of two years, Bangladesh's manpower export has fallen drastically in 2009.[52] In 2009, about 70,000 Bangladeshi workers were compelled to return home from different countries of the world especially from the Middle East, Malaysia and Singapore. Compared to 2008 there was a 47 per cent decline in overseas employment in 2009.[53] The recent crisis in several countries of the Middle East is likely to reduce overseas employment opportunities for Bangladeshis which will affect remittances to the country.

Bangladesh's need for energy is growing. Energy is vital for running industries and manufacturing plants, and also mechanised agricultural equipment. The country is gradually integrating with the global economy and the demand for energy will increase day by day. The country has one of the lowest rates of per capita energy consumption in the world.[54] About 88 per cent of power is generated by natural gas and around 55 per cent of the country's energy supply is derived from traditional fuels (crop residues, animal dung and fuel wood), 24 per cent from natural gas, 19 per cent from imported oil and coal and the remaining 2 per cent is from hydro-electricity.[55] With the increase of population the demand for energy will naturally grow. The demand for energy in Bangladesh is said to be rising at the rate of 10 per cent or more per year.[56]

Environment

Water is most essential to life, it is also an integral part of economy, society and ecology. The major sources of available water are trans-boundary rivers (76.5 per cent), with rain water and ground water accounting for 23 per cent and 1.5 per cent respectively.[57] Diversion of water from major rivers by the upstream countries causes immense sufferings to society. The consequential negative impacts of water withdrawal can be seen on the socio-economic life, ecology, environment, and river morphology in Bangladesh.

A major obstacle to the economic development of Bangladesh is the lack of resources. An ever increasing population has severely strained the country's limited natural resources. Seventy per cent of Bangladeshis depend on natural resources (wetlands and forests) for their livelihoods.[58] The environmental degradation and depletion of natural resources visible in Bangladesh can be attributed to poverty, over-population and lack of awareness. Degradation of natural capital and biodiversity has a serious and direct impact on the food security, nutrition and income of the poor.

Bangladesh is regarded as one of the countries most vulnerable to climate change and climatic variabilities. Climate change will change the physiography and demography of Bangladesh., By 2050, 70 million people could be affected annually by floods, 8 million by drought and upto 8 per cent of the low-lying lands may become permanently inundated.[59] As a riverine country, Bangladesh faces seasonal floods almost every year. During the monsoon, rivers swell up, and inundate Bangladesh's vast flood plain and submerge a quarter to a third of the land in a typical year and up to two-thirds in the bad years. Cyclones have become more frequent and although droughts are not frequent, they are being experienced in some parts of the country leading to desertification of those areas. The rise in sea level will certainly increase the frequency and severity of flooding along the major estuarine rivers., Salt water intrusion problems will also be exacerbated in coastal aquifers. Climate change will intensify these disasters. According to Dr. Ainun Nishat, former country representative of International Union for Conservation of Nature (IUCN), "We are nature's laboratory on disasters. We don't have volcanoes, but any other natural disaster…."[60] The former secretary general of the United Nations, Kofi Annan, warned that a rise in sea levels could lead to the disappearance of much of the world's largest delta, i.e. Bangladesh.[61] Bangladesh is being threatened by climate change mainly in the form of frequent floods and cyclone storms for its location in the delta of three large rivers – the Ganges, the Brahmaputra and the Meghna – and for its closeness to the Bay of Bengal. The low lying topography, riverine and coastal flooding, tropical cyclones, storm surges, tornadoes, are the main reasons for the natural disasters and their severe effects in Bangladesh. Climate change will lead to increased flooding, drainage congestion, decrease of fresh water availability, disturbance of morphological processes, salinity intrusion, frequent cyclone and storm surge flooding in Bangladesh. The climate change scenario of Bangladesh is given in the following table:

Table 1: Climate Change Scenario for Bangladesh

Year	*Temperature Change (°C) Mean*			*Precipitation Change (%) Mean*			*Sea Level Rise (cm)*
	Annual	*Dec-Feb*	*June-Aug*	*Annual*	*Dec-Feb*	*June-Aug*	*Prediction*
2030	1.0	1.1	0.8	5	-2	6	14
2050	1.4	1.6	1.1	6	-5	8	32
2100	2.4	2.7	1.9	10	-10	12	88

Source: M. Aminul Islam, Climate Change and Development Risk: Local Perspective, *The Daily Star*, March 15, 2008.

Conclusion and Recommendations

South Asia has become a centre of attraction for the major powers of the world. All the major powers of the world are expanding their engagement with this region. Bangladesh, on account of its location, has become important in the regional as well as global geo-politics.

Although Bangladesh has made great progress in the social, economic and security sectors, the country is still facing problems in some areas. Poverty is a major stumbling block in the development of the country. The government has prepared a Poverty Reduction Strategy Paper to promote growth and reduce poverty in the country. NGOs in Bangladesh have been playing a prominent role in poverty alleviation. By and large NGOs work with poor and disadvantaged people independently and also along side government organisations. To eliminate the curse of unemployment, the government has taken several initiatives to enhance employment opportunities in some selected areas of the country. Opportunities for self employment should be created by providing technical and vocational training to the urban poor, the educated unemployed persons and destitute women.

Bangladesh has limited number of export items and export destinations. To overcome the global financial crisis, the country should diversify its export basket and scout for new markets for her export items. The country's manpower export sector is facing a crunch situation. In this case too the country should focus on different destinations for migrant workers. The government should focus on searching out new job destinations such as African countries, Eastern European countries, Central Asian countries, etc to provide overseas employment for its growing population. Energy security is one of the most important policy concerns for Bangladesh. The government is taking various measures to reform the energy sector. It is necessary to promote alternative sources of energy like bio fuel, wind power, hydro power and most importantly solar power. There is also great potential for cooperation on energy issues with SAARC, BIMSTEC and OPEC countries to make the country energy sufficient.

Bangladesh is vulnerable to global warming and climate change. The government is aware of the impact of climate change as well as the country's historical sensitivity to climate variability. The policy options that the government is taking to reduce the impact of climate change include: indirectly addressing the impact of climate change through programmes that reduce vulnerability through poverty alleviation, employment generation, crop diversification; directly addressing the issue of vulnerability to climate variability and extreme events through disaster risk reduction and management schemes; and specifically targeting climate change by mainstreaming climate change into sectoral plans and national policies.

Bangladesh is a land with a unique culture and rich history. The potential of the country has so far remained untapped due to several factors of which geo-political reasons and strategic economic planning stand out as most significant. Bangladesh needs to reassess its own geo-strategic dynamics and focus on its opportunities and challenges within the changing and emerging global security scenario. Bangladesh has overcome some impediments and now looks forward to a bright future. The country has made impressive improvements in key social and human indicators including improved life expectancy, better access to education and health facilities, gender parity in both primary and secondary schools and advancement and empowerment of women. The country is on course to meet the key MDG targets by 2015. It is necessary to overcome the challenges that the country is facing so that the country can achieve its full economic potential.

Notes

1. S.D. Muni, "South Asia as a Region", *South Asian Journal*, August-September 2003.
2. Andreas Wenger and Doron Zimmerman, *International Relations: From the Cold War to the Globalized World, Lynne* Rienner Publishers, USA, 2003.
3. Ramakant and P. L. Bhola (eds), *Post Cold War Developments in South Asia,* RBSA Publishers, Jaipur, 1995, p. ii.
4. Muzaffer Ercan Yilmaz, Resolving Internal Conflicts in the Post-Cold War Era: Is Peacekeeping Enough?, *Journal of Economic and Social Research*, Vol. 8(2), pp. 27-42.
5. Muzaffer Ercan Yilmaz, "The New World Order : An Outline of the Post-Cold War Era", *Alternatives*, Vol. 7(4), Winter 2008, p. 45.
6. Harrison, 2004, cited in Ibid.
7. Muzaffer Ercan Yilmaz, n. 5.
8. Ramakant and P.L. Bhola (eds), n. 3.

9. Ibid.
10. A.Z. Hilali, Cold War Politics of Super powers in South Asia, *The Dialogue*, Vol. 1(2), April-June 2006, p. 69, available at: http://www.qurtuba.edu.pk/thedialogue/The%20Dialogue/1_2/4_Mr.%20Hilali.pdf
11. Andreas Wenger and Doron Zimmerman, n. 2.
12. A.K.M. Abdus Sabur, A.B.M. Ziaur Rahman and Abu Saleh Md. Yousuf, "International System: The Role of Diplomacy in the Context of Bangladesh", in Mufleh R. Osmany (ed.), *Whither National Security Bangladesh 2007*, Bangladesh Institute of International and Strategic Studies and The University Press Limited, 2008, p. 129.
13. U.S. Department of State, "Background Note: Bangladesh", http://www.state.gov/r/pa/ei/bgn/3452.htm
14. Devin T. Hagerty (ed.), *South Asia in World Politics,* Rowman and Littlefield, 2005.
15. Pramod K. Mishra, *South Asia in International Politics,* UDH Publishers, Delhi, 1984, p. 2.
16. Ibid.
17. Shireen M. Mazari and Mr. Fazlur Rahman, "South Asian Security: International Context", *Policy Perspectives,* 3(1), January 2006.
18. Shaheen Afroze and Abul Kalam Azad, "Structural and Systemic Aspects of National Security", in Mufleh R. Osmany (ed), *Wither National Security Bangladesh 2007*, n. 12, p. 23.
19. Brig Gen Sakhawat Hussein, ndc, psc (Retd), "Geo-strategic importance of Bangladesh", *The Daily Star*, February 19, 2006.
20. "Millennium Development Goals: Bangladesh Progress Report 2009, General Economics Division, Planning Commission, Government of the People's Republic of Bangladesh.
21. Bangladesh Bureau of Statistics, *Report on the Bangladesh Literacy Survey*, 2010, Ministry of Planning, June 2011.
22. Bangladesh Bureau of Statistics, *Statistical Yearbook of Bangladesh 2009*, Ministry of Planning, July 2010.
23. Ibid.
24. "Bangladesh", United Nations Development Programme, at: http://www.undp.org.bd/mdgs.php
25. Mahbub-ul-Haq, Human Development Report (1997), cited in Lailufar Yasmin, "Law and Order Situation and Gender-based Violence: Bangladesh Perspective", *RCSS Policy Studies* 16, 2000, p. 23.

26. "Microcredit Programs in Bangladesh: Giving a Chance to the Poor", Palli Karma Sahayak Foundation (PKSF), at: http://www.pksf-bd.org/index.php?option= com_ content&view= article &id=91
27. M. Shahidul Islam and Suvi Dogra, Women Empowerment in Bangladesh: The Rise of the Other Half, *ISAS Working Paper*, No. 119, 6 January 2011, at: http://www.isas.nus.edu.sg/Attachments/PublisherAttachment/ISAS_Working_Paper_119_-_Email_-_Women_Empowerment_in_Bangladesh_ 07012011124244.pdf
28. Amena Mohsin, "Gendering the Nation and Endangering Gender: Bangladesh National Regimes", *BIISS Journal*, 30(3), July 2009, pp. 239-270.
29. Niels Hugo Blunch and Maitrevi B. Das, "Changing Norms about Gender Equality in Education: Evidence from Bangladesh", *Working Paper* S4404, World Bank, 2007.
30. Article 9 of the Constitution of Bangladesh states that special representation in the local government institutions shall be given, as far as possible, to peasants, workers and women. Article 10 emphasizes on the participation of women in all spheres of national life. Article 15 asserts the provision of basic necessities. According to Article 19 the state shall endeavour to ensure equality of opportunity to all citizens. Article 20 states that work is a right, a duty and a matter of honour for every citizen who is capable of working. Article 28 gives details of not to discriminate against any citizen on grounds only of religion, race, caste, sex or place of birth and clearly states that women shall have equal rights with men in all spheres of the state and of public life. Article 29 states the equality of opportunity for all citizens in respect of employment. See for details, the Constitution of the People's Republic of Bangladesh, Ministry of Law, Justice and Parliamentary Affairs, available at: http://www.bdlaws.gov.bd/chapter.php?id=367
31. "National Policy for the Advancement of Women", 1997, Ministry of Women and Children Affairs, Government of the People's Republic of Bangladesh, available at: http://www.nfpcsp.org/agridrupal/sites/default/files/National_Policy_for_the_Advancement_of_Women_1997.pdf
32. "Economy of Bangladesh", available at: http://en.wikipedia.org/wiki/Economy_of_Bangladesh
33. Bangladesh Garment Manufacturers and Exporters Association (BGMEA), at: http://www.bgmea.com.bd/home/pages/aboutus

34. Bangladesh Knitwear Manufacturers and Exporters Association (BKMEA), at: http://www.bkmea.com/at_a_glance.php
35. *The Financial Express*, 22 June 2010.
36. "Economy of Bangladesh", n. 32.
37. Bangladesh Association of International Recruiting Agencies (BAIRA), available at: http://www.hrexport-baira.org/flow_of_migration/flow_migration_dec.pdf
38. Bruce Vaughn, "Islamist Extremism in Bangladesh", *CRS Report for Congress*, 31 January 2007, available at: http://www.italy.usembassy.gov/pdf/other/RS22591.pdf
39. Ibid.
40. "Bangladesh for Global Peace, Democracy and Development" United Nations Wing, Ministry of Foreign Affairs, Government of the People's Republic of Bangladesh, May 2011.
41. Ibid.
42. Ibid.
43. Ibid.
44. Rebecca Holmes, John Farrington, Taifur Rahman and Rachel Slater, "Extreme Poverty in Bangladesh: Protecting and Promoting Rural livelihoods, at: http://www.odi.org.uk/resources/download/1586.pdf
45. Enayet Rasul, "Unemployment is turning into a very serious issue", *The Financial Express*, January 26, 2008.
46. Ibid.
47. "Unemployment", *Banglapedia*, 10, p. 247.
48. Golam Mohammad, A K M Nazrul Islam and Segufta Hossain, Bangladesh (Part II), in Caroline Ziemke-Dickens and Julian Droogan (eds.), *Asian Transnational Security Challenges: Emerging Trends, Regional Visions,* Council for Asian Transnational Threat Research and Centre for Policing, Intelligence and Counter Terrorism, Macquarie University, 2010, p. 69.
49. *The Daily Star*, November 24, 2009.
50. Abul Kalam Azad, Mohd. Mahfuz Kabir and Benuka Ferdousi, "Global Economic Crisis and Its Impact on Bangladesh", in Golam Mohammad (ed), *National Security Bangladesh 2009*, Bangladesh Institute of International and Strategic Studies (BIISS) and The University Press Limited, 2010.

51. Ibid.
52. Bureau of Manpower, Employment and Training, Government of the People's Republic of Bangladesh, at: http://www.bmet.org.bd/BMET/viewStatReport.action?reportnumber=11
53. Abu Taher Salahuddin Ahmed, Segufta Hossain and Mohammad Jasim Uddin, n. 48.
54. Nawrin Samrina, "Energy Security of Bangladesh: Issues, Perspectives and Strategic Implications of Natural Gas", *ACDIS Occasional Paper*, available at: https://www.ideals.uiuc.edu/bitstream/2142/36/1/SamrinaOP.pdf
55. See for details, http://www.discoverybangladesh.com/meetbangladesh/energy.html
56. K.B. Sajjadur Rashid, "Energy Security Beyond 2020", *The Daily Star,* April 24, 2007.
57. NWMP, "National Water Resources Management Plan", Bangladesh, *Main Report*, 2, July 2001.
58. "Current Conditions: Environment", USAID, available at: http://www.usaid.gov/bd/programs/environ.html
59. Ibid.
60. Mason Inman, "Where warming hits hard", *Nature Reports Climate Change*, January 15, 2009, at: http://www.nature.com/climate/2009/0902/full/climate.2009.3.html, accessed on: June 28, 2009.
61. "Bangladesh exposed to global warming, Annan", *BBC News*, 14 March, 2001, at: http://news.bbc.co.uk/2/hi/americas/1220036.stm

4

Regional Security Environment in South Asia: Overcoming the Constraints

Ashok K. Behuria

South Asian countries lack an integrated view of regional security. In the absence of an overarching view of common security, each of them tends to develop an isolated view of its own security and takes measures to address its concerns in an individual way. Regional organisations like the South Asian Association for Regional Cooperation (SAARC) have not been able to come up with a common view on regional security. On the critical issue of terrorism, which has posed a common challenge to state security and stability, the countries have not reached a consensus even on the definition of terrorism. As a result, the SAARC convention on terrorism (1988) and the Additional protocol (2004) have remained mere documents.

Interstate relationships are mired in mutual suspicions and the temptation to take advantage of the faults in each other's society is very high. This has led the countries in the region to work at cross purposes with one another and perpetuate an environment of distrust and insecurity. There is a precipitate lack of political will to set aside differences and evolve common grounds for cooperation. This is despite the fact that there is a natural sense of togetherness, reinforced by historical, cultural and social factors, which ought to have compelled these countries to synchronise their foreign, security and economic policies. This would have also automatically unlocked the hidden potential for growth and prosperity in the region. In this context, there is a need for looking at common concerns to enable a regional security perspective. This chapter makes an attempt to outline the regional security environment against the backdrop of changing geo-political situation and emphasises the point that there is an urgent need for developing a regional outlook in the field of security.

Situating South Asia

South Asia is home to 23 per cent of the world's population and half of the world's poor. As per World Bank estimates, about 500 million people live on less than US $ 1.25 per day.[1] It is a fact that the countries in the region registered remarkable growth during the last decade (about six per cent in all) despite the socio-economic and political challenges they encountered, and managed to draw a significant number of their population out of poverty. However, grave challenges remain for all countries to sustain the path of progress. About 260 million people still do not have access to basic health facilities and 387 million lack access to safe drinking water. The countries in the region rank lower in the Human Development Index table. The region remains one of the least integrated regions of the world and there are strong barriers to the flow of trade and commerce, investment and movement of people. The main reason for the integration-lag in the region is the reluctance of the states to adopt policies, which could connect them with the rest of the countries in the region.

Moreover, most of the countries have internal security threats and are afflicted with common threats of insurgency, militancy and terrorism. These distract the attention of the leadership away from the immediate issues of governance, corruption and inclusive development and pose a critical challenge to their economic growth. In many cases, these threats in one country are sponsored by another. Hence there is an interlocking of threats which makes the security situation in the region quite complex. The root causes of insurgencies in South Asian states lie in poor governance, an unjust system of resource distribution, imbalanced growth and ethnic disharmony. All the countries are afflicted by common problems of crisis of governance, corruption, lopsided economic growth, demands for representative politics, as well as ethnic and communal conflicts. The adverse security situation in most of these countries has inevitable impact on the economic situation, which in turn constrains the capacity of the states to address the issues outlined above. The resultant economic disparity, poverty, illiteracy and unemployment have provided the ideal condition for growth of radicalism and extremism, which has in turn affected the national regional security situation in a major way and further retarded the economic growth. A vicious cycle of underdevelopment-conflict-underdevelopment has sapped the energies of most of these states in the region and retarded the process of regional cooperation initiated through SAARC since the mid 1980s.

Global and Regional Situation

The post cold war and especially post-9/11 global security situation has turned its focus on intra-state issues with global ramifications. The phenomenon of international terrorism drawing upon perverted interpretation of religious ideals and principles has threatened global peace. There is an international consensus now to fight this menace at all levels. The international efforts to attack the Taliban regime in Afghanistan was premised on the belief that the fall of the Taliban would usher in a new era in not just Afghanistan but the entire region by putting an end to the terrorism it was generating. However, despite a decade of international intervention Afghanistan remains embroiled in conflict and violence. The Taliban are ascendant and Afghanistan does not have the resources to equip and maintain its national security forces. The revenue generating capacity of the Afghan state is low enough (US$ 1.7 billion for 2011)[2] to sustain the present strength of 323,000 soldiers of the Afghan National Security Forces (ANSF), on which alone more than US$1 billion is being spent annually. Moreover, the ANSF is poorly trained, equipped and motivated to take on the Taliban elements. Some analysts say that in the post-withdrawal scenario, the Afghan National Army (ANA) or Police (ANP) may not be able to stand up to the Taliban. The growing attacks by Afghan forces on their trainers have led people to think that even in the post withdrawal phase, many of the former soldiers may melt into Taliban ranks. Without long-term international commitment to provide continued assistance over at least another decade coupled with a targeted effort to increase the capacity of the Afghan state, it is impossible to imagine any substantive change in the Afghan security situation in any near future.

In the case of Pakistan, the Islamist militancy has spread to the interior, apart from the Tehrik-e-Taliban[3] Pakistan (TTP) in the tribal areas. Security analysts in Pakistan are now talking about a new group called "Punjabi Taliban"[4], which, they say, is working with both, the TTP and the Al Qaeda. Moreover, the attacks on the defence and security facilities (on GHQ on October 10, 2009, on PNS Mehran naval base on May 22, 2011) and the arrest of a serving brigadier, Ali Khan in May 2011 on charges of organising a coup, reveal that a section within the armed forces are sympathising with the extremists and that they would like the army to emerge as a radical Islamist force in the days to come. The radicalisation of society is creating an inevitable impact on the army. The terms of societal discourse in the Pakistani society today are being determined by the militant sympathisers. The military today feels compelled to conform to this discourse.[5] The murders of Salman Taseer (the Governor of Punjab) and Shahbaz Bhatti (the Federal Minister) for speaking out against the blasphemy laws of Pakistan and the muted reaction from the Pakistani elite to such heinous acts signify the growing trend of intolerance in Pakistani society at large. The Pakistani strategy of nurturing radical elements as assets for asymmetric use against India and in Afghanistan has had a deleterious impact on Pakistani society and this is likely to affect the regional security situation for a long time.

The protracted process of constitution-making in Nepal and the accompanying political instability has weakened the state capacity for resisting any fresh militancy, in case the state relapses into anarchy due to the ongoing political deadlock on several issues (reintegration, federalism, form of government, etc.) being debated now. The youth wing of the Maoist party— the Young Communist League— is yet to reconcile to the top leadership's decision to adapt to democracy in Nepal. Non-Maoist political parties do not trust the Maoists and suspect that they may capture power through ballot and enforce their revolutionary agenda. The Maoists on the other hand are weary of the treatment meted out to them by the mainstream parties. The fragmentation of the political parties is worsening the political scenario further. The Nepalese society is passing through a prolonged political churning process. Even if the direction of political change has so far been in the right direction, its pace has been too slow and sluggish to inspire confidence amongst external observers about the sustainability of the process. The Nepalese political parties have been too suspicious of India's role and each party has blamed India for supporting the other to its disadvantage. While India does have concern over Maoist efforts to use China as a balancer, its ability to influence and change the Nepalese internal political dynamic is grossly exaggerated— as is its sway over the Madhesh political entities. The India bogey is unlikely to resolve the internal issues of Nepal. The Nepalese political parties will have to shun their mutual suspicions and come together to evolve a constitution, which can address the problems unique to Nepal. They should also refrain from knocking at New Delhi's door to resolve internal political problems and intra party political rivalry in Nepal.

In Bangladesh, despite the huge political capital reaped by Sheikh Hasina's Awami League (AL) in the last 2008 elections, her government is fast losing its popularity because of lack of focus on substantive issues. The AL government's decision to dispense with the caretaker government system through a constitutional amendment (preceded by the Supreme Court's verdict in May 2011 that this provision was unconstitutional) and its recent overreaction to the Bangladesh National Party's (BNP) protest rally in Dhaka on March 12, 2012, demonstrated the all-too familiar pattern of extreme bipolarity in Bangladeshi politics. The AL government's intolerance of political opposition reflects poorly on the ongoing democratic process in Bangladesh. As can be seen from the impressive turn-outs in the political rallies organised by the opposition forces led by the BNP, the tug of war between the two main political parties is likely to lead to political instability and the gains made on the security front may be lost if the attention of the government stays excessively focused on how to defend itself against the political onslaught unleashed by the opposition on the streets.

In Sri Lanka, the government seems to have won the war but lost the momentum for peace making. There is a sense of triumph amongst the majority Sinhalese population, which seems averse to any concession to the Tamils. The Rajapaksa government is not according enough attention to the need for evolving a political solution to the ethnic issue. The victory of the Tamil National Alliance, which is being considered by the government as a remnant of the militant Liberation Tigers of Tamil Eelam (LTTE), in the Tamil areas in the north, indicates that the deep sense of alienation amongst the Tamils continues. This is so despite the elimination of the LTTE from the scene, which could flare up again if the government continues to disregard their genuine demands. The Rajapaksa government's policy of laying emphasis on economic development as a means to resolve the ethnic issue is being rejected by the Tamils as can be seen by their backing of the TNA. The international opprobrium of the gross human rights violations by the security forces in Sri Lanka during the war against the LTTE has created the context for building international pressure on the Rajapaksa government to attempt a political solution. However, given the prevalence of ultra-nationalist Sinhalese-Buddhist sentiments in Sri Lanka, Rajapaksa is not expected to concede anything politically to resolve the Tamil issue. This is clear from his apathy towards Indian persuasion to start a reconciliation dialogue amongst several stakeholders and his ambivalence on the 13th amendment—that was effected under the India-Sri Lanka agreement in 1987.

In Maldives, the nascent experiment with democracy is being put to test as the first elected President, Nasheed was forced to resign in early 2012 after clashes between his supporters and sections of the police reached a point of crisis. The forces opposed to Nasheed are supporters of ex-President Gayoom who have pledged their commitment to the democratic process. However, there are disturbing signs of political groups using Islamic extremism as a tool to mobilize popular support. It remains to be seen how it pans out in the next elections. The role of the police and the Army in the recent change also reflects the state of the democratic process in Maldives which had recently transited to democracy.

Bhutan transisted to democracy in 2008 and held their first ever elections based on adult franchise. Interestingly, it conducted a mock election in 2007 to apprise people of the democratic system that the Monarch was trying to introduce. Bhutan now has a constitutional monarchy and a biparty system. However the King continues to remain a dominant factor in the Bhutanese polity. The election excluded Lhotshampas (Southern Bhutanese of Nepalese origin) who were expelled from the kingdom in 1990[6]. This remains a contentious issue in Bhutan. Most of the refugees are in the process of being settled in different parts of the world with the effort of the UNHCR. These refugees are demanding their right to return. In the future this may emerge as a major challenge to Bhutan.

Apart from these developments which have their bearing on the regional security environment, India's overwhelming presence— in terms of its size, population, resources, and defence capability— has also induced a sense of insecurity among South Asian states. The shift in the Indian approach towards its neighbours since the end of the cold war has not so far assured them of India's benign intentions[7]. As a growing economy, and a stable democracy aiming at the high chair in global politics, India does not anymore want to be constrained at the regional level. In the absence of a regional consensus to get SAARC rolling, primarily because of Pakistan's recalcitrance, India has struck bilateral agreements with some of its neighbours to demonstrate the benefits of economic cooperation at the regional level. Its bilateral economic relationship with Bhutan, Sri Lanka, Bangladesh and Nepal offers some hope of a regional structure of cooperation slowly emerging, riding on the back of such bilateral agreements. It has also involved its neighbours in other regional organisations like Bay of Bengal Initiative for Multisectoral Technical Economic Cooperation (BIMSTEC) and Indian Ocean Rim Countries Economic Cooperation (IOR-EC). Pakistan's decision to embark on a process of granting Most favoured Nation (MFN) status to India since October 2011 also indicates that the winds of change for the better may have started blowing in the region. This may enable meaningful economic cooperation to begin with, and gradually lead to a constructive dialogue on difficult issues relating to security and foreign policies of the states in the region.

Existing Security Dilemmas

Some nagging cases that epitomise the regional security dilemmas are the Islamist militancy in Pakistan and the Indian state of Jammu and Kashmir, the ethnic Tamil issue in Sri Lanka, the left-wing extremism in India, and the secessionist demands in some states. In most of these cases, the root causes may have been internal. However, in most of the cases the ability of the states to address these issues has been seriously constrained by the involvement of external actors. Use of terror and subversion as an instrument of foreign policy[8] has worsened the security situation in the entire region. Often, the instruments of terror have come home to roost and complicated the internal security situation in sponsoring countries. The rising Islamist insurgencies in Pakistan and Afghanistan exemplify this condition of 'militantisation' of societies in many of the South Asian states.

Interestingly, the states have realised quite early that terrorism has to be handled collectively, which can be observed in the SAARC resolutions in November 1987, which acknowledged "the danger posed by the spread of terrorism and its harmful effect on peace, cooperation, friendship and good neighbourly relations and which could also jeopardize the sovereignty and territorial integrity of states". It reflected the resolve of the states "to take effective measures to ensure that perpetrators of terrorist acts do not escape prosecution and punishment by providing for their extradition or prosecution, and to this end"[9] an additional protocol on terrorism was signed in January 2004 in Islamabad, calling upon the states "to prevent and suppress the financing of terrorist acts by criminalising the provision, acquisition and collection of funds" for terrorist acts. However, despite such commitments, there has not been any appreciable movement in favour of containing the common threat of terror in a collective manner.

The situation in Afghanistan and Pakistan remains as problematic as ever. International efforts to stabilise Afghanistan over the last one decade have not been able to contend with the Islamist extremism fuelled by the Taliban and its allies in the Af-Pak region. It is now well-known that the Taliban does enjoy the support of rogue elements within the Pakistani establishment which complicates the situation further. In the wake of the American decision to withdraw from Afghanistan by the end of 2014, the Taliban and its sympathisers hope to stage a comeback by any means and this is likely to reverse the process of democratisation of the political system in Kabul. In all likelihood, the ongoing negotiations among the US, the Taliban, the Afghan government and Pakistan will indirectly legitimise the return of Taliban in Kabul. Given the Taliban's insistence on a Sharia-based system in Afghanistan and its past record characterized by *Amr-bil-Maroof-wa-Nahi-anil-Munkar* (promotion of virtue and prohibition of vice) it is anybody's guess as to which direction Afghanistan will go beyond 2014. The West-backed democratic experiment in Afghanistan seems too young and unprepared to face the Taliban assault. Pakistan's determined efforts to retain its so-called strategic depth in Afghanistan by any means will have a destabilizing impact on Afghan politics in the post-withdrawal period and strengthen the prospects of a civil war. While the non-Pashtuns may not be able to put up a unified front against the Taliban, they are likely to resist its march towards the north.

A Taliban-ruled Afghanistan is bound to influence Islamist assertions in Pakistani tribal areas, especially when Pakistan is passing through intense political and economic crises. The Pakistani temptation to divert the attention of these forces to neighbouring countries is likely to pose critical security challenges for countries in the neighbourhood. Investigations by security agencies in India reveal that intelligence activities are afoot to establish linkage among terrorist outfits in the region in a bid to direct the attention of the homegrown terror in Pakistan towards neighbouring states. There is a reluctance to take adequate law-enforcement and security measures to tackle this menace and the dialogues with insurgent/terrorist groups seem to be an apology for the inaction. There is a need to take a fresh look at the security situation against this backdrop and evolve ways and means of countering the threats in a collective manner. The continuing dialogue on these issues amongst law enforcement agencies and Interior/Home Ministers of the countries within SAARC is a welcome mechanism to discuss issues of mutual concern on a regular basis and to evolve common approaches on these issues.

Any regional effort to counter the threat of terrorism, drug and human trafficking and transnational organised crime, has to draw upon the positive examples of effective security and cooperation among states in the region. The bilateral understandings India has had with Bhutan, Bangladesh and Myanmar on flushing out terrorists/insurgent groups taking shelter in these countries in recent years provide excellent examples in this regard. The steps taken by the governments in these countries to address one another's security concerns have had a positive impact on the internal security situation in these states. The Bangladesh government's security cooperation with India has had a dramatic influence on the insurgency situation in India's north eastern states. Similarly, the busting of terror networks within Bangladesh after the serial bomb blasts of August 2005, has reduced the threat of Islamist militancy in this country and minimised the influence from the Af-Pak region. Likewise, India's security cooperation with Bhutan and Myanmar has also had a sobering impact on the situation in northeastern India. However, sustaining these gains will depend on the evolving political dynamics within these states, the willingness of the political elite to act against these forces in the days to come and to initiate political process to address the grievances of the people. This will erode the support structure. Along with this, enforcement of law and order would prevent these groups from extorting money and compelling people to support them with money and material.

Apart from the threat of terrorism and its associated manifestations, there are other common non-traditional security issues like climate change, energy, water, pandemics and cyber-security which are common to all states. These threats cannot be dealt with individually. The South Asian states have recognised the need to work together on many of these issues. However, differences among SAARC states at the political level have inhibited the process of effective operation of many of the SAARC resolutions on these issues.

Need for multi-level Dialogue

Keeping in mind the above discussion it is imperative that the South Asian region must evolve a cooperative regional security system to ensure that the states develop a common perspective on security issues based on shared concerns, and create an atmosphere of trust to deal with more difficult issues that divide them. India needs to works with its neighbours and convince them of the imperatives of forging a common approach to security issues. It should exhibit its genuine interest in regional prosperity by facilitating trade and investment within the region. As the dominant power in the region and a state sharing its border with each of the South Asian countries the need for India to play such a role arises from its geographical setting and the power distribution in the region. Other countries in the region will have to recognise the change in India's approach and forsake their old prejudices about India as a hegemon or regional bully. Today's India is more intent to create a "network of dependencies"[10] than to exercise its coercive might to be recognised as a regional power. Fortunately, the overall global and regional political environment is conducive for such a change of mindset at the regional level, especially when the people, if not the governments, of the region are yearning for peace and prosperity. The time now is ideal for building a positive environment for change.

In order to create such an environment, engagement amongst the countries in the region at various levels is absolutely essential. Such initiatives should better not be left to the governments alone. Any exercise at trust and confidence building must involve dialogues at multiple levels— people to people, media houses, business forums, academic institutions, think-tanks, technocrats, artists, and sportsmen. Such discussions and dialogues will bring people together, dispel any mutual sense of distrust and create the condition for regional cooperation. The governments will have to take measures to facilitate such exercises. They should also identify common challenges and work together to overcome them effectively. Think tanks and academic institutions should talk to each other, develop ideas, expose the machinations of those with vested interests who have stakes in war and conflict, establish the benefits of cooperation or the price of non-cooperation and suggest frameworks to the government to shun the path of hostility and embark on the path of friendship. Only then can South Asians have an assured future.

Notes

1. See for details http://siteresources.worldbank.org/SOUTHASIA EXT/Resources/223546-1296680097256/7707437-1300119933024/ SAR_Strategy_2011.pdf
2. Kenneth Katzman, "Afghanistan: Post-Taliban Governance, Security, and U.S. Policy", Report of the *Congressional Research Service,* November 22, 2011, Report no RL30588, available at http:// fpc.state.gov/documents/organization/178228.pdf
3. For an overview on Pakistani Taliban see "Who is who in Pakistani Taliban", http://spaces.brad.ac.uk:8080/download/attachments/748/ Brief+49B.pdf and Simon Ross Valentine, "The Tehrik-i-Taliban Pakistan: Ideology and Beliefs", *Pakistan Security Research Unit* (PSRU) Brief Number 49, September 8, 2009, available at http:// spaces.brad.ac.uk:8080/download/attachments/748/Brief+49B.pdf.
4. Khaled Ahmed, "Keeping Mum about about Punjabi Taliban", *The Express Tribune*, February 19, 2012, at http://tribune.com.pk/story/ 338400/keeping-mum-about-the-punjabi-taliban/, Also see S. R. Mehboob, "Governance and Militancy in Southern Punjab Region", *CSIS Paper*, December 2011, available at http://csis.org/files/ publication/120312_Mehboob_SouthernPunjab_Web.pdf
5. For a thought-provoking discussion on how Pakistan is slowly inching towards a hybrid theocratic state see Ayesha Siddiqa, "Towards a New Pakistan", *The Friday Times*, Vol. XXIV, No. 04, March 09-15, 2012, available at http://www.thefridaytimes.com/beta2/ tft/article.php?issue=20120309&page=2
6. For details see, http://www.unhcr.org/refworld/country,,WRITE NET,,BTN,,3ae6a6c08,0.html. Also see Smruti S Pattanaik, "Ethnic Identity, Conflict and Nation Building in Bhutan", *Strategic Analysis*, Vol 22, July 1998.

7. For a detailed discussion on neighbourhood policy see Ashok K. Behuria and Smruti S. Pattanaik and Arvind Gupta, "Does India have a Neighbourhood Policy", *Strategic Analysis*, 36(2), March-April 2012, pp. 229-246.
8. See C. Christine Fair, "The Militant Challenge in Pakistan", *Asia Policy* 11, January 2011.
9. For details see http://www.saarc-sec.org/areaofcooperation/detail.php?activity_id=21
10. Shyam Saran, "India and Its Neighbours", Talk at India International Centre on February 14, 2005, available at http://idsa.in/node/1555

5

India-Bangladesh Cross-border Connectivity

Sreeradha Datta

Fragmented and inadequate transport networks, because of historical, political and economic reasons; and the lack of cooperation among member countries have been the bête noire of border trade in South Asia. In a significant move, in early 2010, India and Bangladesh decided to open up their borders to facilitate trade and commerce. This breakthrough came about with the Bangladeshi prime minister Sheikh Hasina's four day visit to India in January 2010. The meetings between the leaders of the two countries were marked by a goodwill that had been singularly lacking in the bilateral context until very recently. Apart from the positive atmospherics that this landmark visit generated, the two sides have set out a bilateral agenda that - if well implemented - will ensure that the process continues and India and Bangladesh can benefit from the uninterrupted flow of trade and transport as was the case before the division of the subcontinent.

Most of the surface trade (about 70 per cent) between the two countries takes place across the Benapole-Petrapole border in West Bengal. This is a highly congested Land Custom Station (LCS) and has a road that is not much broader than 5.5 metres. The alternate route is through the Northeastern states. Despite the over 54 rivers that criss-cross the two countries, waterways have not been utilised to further Indo-Bangladeshi trade. This is particularly surprising since water transport plays an important role in Bangladeshi domestic trade. The Indo-Bangladesh joint communiqué signed in January 2010 primarily sought to address the issue of connectivity and remedy this anomalous situation.

The importance of the communiqué has to be seen within the context of other developments that were taking place both on the bilateral front and within India's Northeastern region. This chapter attempts to essentially examine the various infrastructure projects that have been undertaken by India to improve its transport connectivity with Bangladesh and its Northeastern states. It examines the ongoing cross-border projects, spanning different sectors, including roads, rails and ports.

The Northeast: Transport Connectivity

The measures seek to improve India's border connectivity with two of its eastern neighbours - Bangladesh and Myanmar - which when fully implemented will transform the nature of bilateral trade and commerce. The decision to facilitate border trade and connectivity will not only enhance its economic ties with the neighbours, but will also engage India's Northeastern region. This is also likely lead to a spurt of greater economic activity in this region that will eventually enable it to be a large trading partner of Bangladesh. Bangladesh already enjoys a growing trade gap with Tripura which is in favour of the former.

At first, it will be useful to enumerate the number of projects being planned by India and Bangladesh.

Bangladesh: New Trade Routes and Measures

- As part of its efforts to expand rail network in the region, the railway line is to be extended up to Sabroom in southern Tripura, 135 km from Agartala, and Akhaura in western Tripura, six kilometre away from agartala railway station[1]. The Sabroom-Ramgarh link would be completed by March 2014.
- India is to construct a bridge over Feni River in southern Tripura which would provide direct access to the Chittagong port thereby enabling the easy passage of goods and heavy machineries from the land-locked region.
- India has agreed to finance the construction of the 14 km Akhaura-Agartala rail link. This combined with the transit rights, will reduce the distance between Kolkata and Agartala by 550 km from the current distance of 1,200 km via Guwahati.
- Furthermore, the proposed railway station would be just 75 km from the Chittagong port. As a result, goods from Tripura which

currently take the 1,645 km route to reach Kolkata port through the 'chicken's neck' would now have to traverse only 400 kilometres through Bangladesh to reach Kolkata.

- The on-going broad-gauge line would reach Udaipur, the south Tripura district headquarters, by December 2012.
- Fifty-eight per cent of the broad gauge conversion of the track from Assam's Lumding to northern Tripura's Kumarghat has been completed.

In view of these developments, there are suggestions that Silghat in Assam and Ashugunj in Bangladesh could be designated as ports of call to facilitate trade movement from the Northeastern region of India to Bagabarlin in Bangladesh as well as to Kolkata. This would be in addition to the existing inland waterway protocol between Rajshahi (Bangladesh)-Dhulian (southern Assam) which could be linked further to the Aricha-Dhaka route which is one of the important national highways that connect the north-western and northern regions of Bangladesh with Dhaka. The four inland water routes via eastern Bangladesh in which the vessels of both the countries can ply are Kolkata-Pandu (in southern Assam), Kolkata-Karimganj (in southern Assam), Rajshahi (in Bangladesh)-Dhulian (in southern Assam), and Karimganj-Pandu. There are four ports of calls in both the countries: Narayanganj, Khulna, Mongla and Sirajganj in Bangladesh and Kolkata, Haldia, Karimganj and Pandu in India.[2]

In addition, India could use the Mongla and Chittagong ports for movement of goods to and from India by road and rail.[3] Bangladesh has already agreed to provide port facilities to India, Nepal and Bhutan. It is expected that goods from Assam could reach Europe through the Chittagong port which would mean 1,000 km less than if they were to be transported through Kolkata. The benefits of these small steps are immeasurable. For example, a container from New Delhi to Dhaka is transported via the Mumbai-Singapore/Colombo-Chittagong maritime route and then is transported by rail to Dhaka. This normally takes 35 days. The same container would take just five days, if it were to be transported directly through a new Delhi-Dhaka rail link.[4] According to some estimates the distance of 2,000 km between Delhi and Dhaka could be covered in two to three days by rail.[5]

Conscious of these benefits, both countries signed a few agreements including an MoU on the Standard Operating Procedures for monitoring of the entry and exit of vehicles at the land custom station (LCS) on the Indo-Bangladeshi border and agreed on the modalities for border-haats. On January 22, 2011 the finance minister of India and the agriculture minister of Bangladesh jointly inaugurated the bilateral trade at the Fulbari-Banglabandha LCS.[6]

In addition to these bilateral measures, India took some steps for improving border trade and connectivity by agreeing to the long standing demand of Nepal and Bhutan for direct land trade links with Bangladesh through India. In the past both India and Bangladesh had used transit rights as bargaining chips for extracting political concessions from the others.[7] As landlocked countries, the Himalayan states are heavily dependent upon India for their trade and economic development. The alternative trade route through China has to overcome the natural barrier of the Himalayas.[8]

The following measures are also part of the new move to further cross-border trade:

- India agreed to allow movements of trucks from Bhutan and Nepal being and to enter about 200 metres into the Zero Point at Banglabandh at the Banglabandh-Phulbari LCS.
- Bangladesh would be allowed to use the Rohanpur-Singaband broad gauge rail link for transit to Nepal. Towards this end Bangladesh has plans to convert the Radhikapur-Birol line into broad gauge.
- Nepal and Bhutan would be given access to Mongla and Chittagong ports.

In the past, while providing transit routes to Nepal and Bhutan India had been reluctant to expand these facilities to facilitate their extra regional trade. As part of its new desire to expand intra-regional trade cooperation, it has agreed to grant trade routes for Bangladesh's trade with the Himalayan states. India agreed to allow Bhutan to use the Phuentsholing (Bhutan) and Changrabandha (India) roadlink to extend further to Burimari (Bangladesh) to facilitate Bhutanese trade with Bangladesh. In the past, India did not allow the route to be used for third-country trade, citing security concerns. The same shift is noticeable vis-à-vis Nepal. Earlier Nepalese trucks were allowed only on specific routes and the Indian trucks which entered Nepal had to depart within 72 hours.

India is also committed to upgrading the railway projects connecting Nepal with Bangladesh through the Birgong-Rauxul-Katihar-Singhabad line and the Partbatipur-Birol-Radhikapur-Jugabani-Biratnagar line. The railway link through Rohanpur (Bangladesh)-Singhabad (India), Kathihar-Raxaul (Nepal) to Birganj in Nepal is 1,000 km from Khulna in Bangladesh. Currently, there is no railway route for Assam and Meghalaya. In January 2011 India assured Bangladesh of the speedy implementation of the Rohanpur-Singhabad link from Bangladesh to Nepal through India.

Since Nepal currently imports raw materials for its handicrafts industry, Bangladeshi cotton, chemicals and processing equipments would have been cheaper for its industries. Similarly, Bangladeshi producers of packed foods are also losing out by not importing cheap and high-quality grains, lentils and fruits from Nepal.[9] Rather, three-fourths of Nepali exports continue to exit Nepal through the Birganj border and on to the Kolkata port. Bangladesh has offered Nepal a 50 per cent fee discount for its use of the Mongla port.

In the absence of an Indo-Nepal agreement on the use of transit routes to Bangladeshi ports, Nepal cannot access the Bangladeshi market, let alone effectively use Mongla and Chittagong ports. It is up to India to implement the recent agreements. In principle, India has opened up the Fulbari route in Dinajpur, but its position on the use of Indian territory from Birgunj and Biratnagar towards Bangladesh remains unclear.[10] However the above is refuted by India and Bangladesh on the grounds that no agreements or protocol are required for usage of this transit that will be presently proposed for Nepal and Bhutan.[11] Bangladesh and Nepal have signed an 'Agreement on operating modalities for the carriage of transit/trade cargo between Nepal and Bangladesh'[12].

Conceding Long Standing Demands

The two land locked countries of South Asia – Nepal and Bhutan- are now part of India-Bangladesh effort at establishing road network and connectivity. Indeed Bhutan is now using the new transit route through Northeast India on the Dwaki- Tamabil route in Meghalaya as against the much longer route through Siliguri in West Bengal state for transporting goods to Bangladesh.[13] Earlier India had provided transit to Nepal and Bangladesh for their overland bilateral trade, but not for their extra-regional transit trade.

These agreements and connectivity corridors need to be viewed in the context of transport infrastructure that is being developed at both domestic and regional levels. For instance, regional organisation initiatives, SAARC and the South Asia Sub-regional Economic Cooperation (SASEC) initiative involving Bangladesh, Bhutan, India, and Nepal have been simultaneously working on projects for improvement of cross-border vehicular traffic, and other cross-border issues. Likewise in the Bay of Bengal Initiative for Multi-Sectoral Technical and Economic Cooperation (BIMSTEC), a regional study (BIMSTEC Transport Infrastructure and Logistic Study) was completed in 2008. An agreement for the implementation of BIMSTEC trilateral highway linking India-Myanmar-Thailand was signed by member countries in 2005 for improving physical connectivity in the sub-region. But progress on all fronts has been slow. Indeed the Asian Development Bank supported Asian highway and Asian railway projects will also supplement some of the routes designated by India and Bangladesh.

Border Trade

In an attempt to encourage Bangladeshi exports to India, the latter is in the process of streamlining the tariff and non-tariff barriers. Towards this India has also offered to support the upgradation of the Bangladesh Standard Testing Institute to help in the certification of Bangladeshi exports of processed food. India has also decided to build seven Integrated Check Posts (ICPs) at the following locations:

ICPs on Indo-Bangladesh border[14]

No.	*Location, State Border*	*Estimated Cost Rupees Crores*
1.	Petrapole, West Bengal	172
2.	Dawki, Meghalaya	50
3.	Akhaura, Tripura	60
4.	Hili, West Bengal	78
5.	Chandrabangha, West Bengal	64
6.	Sutarkhandi, Assam	16
7.	Kawarpuchiah, Mizoram	27

- Land customs stations at Sabroom (India) - Ramgarh (Bangladesh) and Demagiri (India) - Thegamukh (Bangladesh) are also going to be operationailsed soon.
- The inauguration of a new LCS at Muhurighat in the Belonia subdivision of Tripura connecting with the Feni land port in Bangladesh. Cement is a prime commodity of trade at this border land port. India is also building a bridge over Feni river to provide easy access to Sabroom.
- More border haats would be set up at selected areas. For the present these are operationalised at Baliamari in Kurigram district (Bangladesh)- Kalai Char (Meghalaya) and Lauwaghar in Sunamganj district (Bangladesh) - Balat (Meghalaya).

India is undertaking feasibility studies for the setting up of a few other border haats. It has been decided to revive the five traditional border haats at Dawki, Borsora, Shella and two others in Garo hills. A border haat in Meghalaya was inaugurated in July 2011 by the union commerce minister Anand Sharma and Col (retd) Faruk Khan his Bangladesh counterpart. Twenty-five vendors who will trade in 13 locally produced items in this haat have been identified. All items would require a certification from the magistrate that these were locally produced. Currently traders and products from within a five kilometre radius are allowed at these haats. Bangladesh wants this to be increased to 10 kilometres.

The two sides decided to ease the movement of exports to India by increasing the number of custom stations thus enhancing the opportunities for mutual investments in each other's economies. India has withdrawn its earlier decision on restriction on private investment from Bangladesh. With the flow of private investment from Bangladesh there has seen several developments on both sides of the border. India and its Northeast region without a doubt offer a huge market but that hinges upon Bangladesh increasing its export basket. Bangladeshi industries like PRAN have shown interest to invest in Tripura.

Future Possibilities: Energy grid

The most tangible and immediate benefit that is likely to accrue from the Indo-Bangladesh bilateral decisions is trade in the energy sector.[15] This sector is a priority for the Sheikh Hasina government as the shortage of power in summer is a big problem for any government in Dhaka. As per the two agreements related to purchase of electricity and expansion of trade and commerce, signed during Sheikh Hasina's visit to India, Bangladesh has allowed India to utilise the Ashuganj port for transporting over dimensional cargo (ODC) for building the power plant at Agartala. India has further agreed to sell 250 MW of electricity to Bangladesh. This agreement can also be extended to road transit whereby goods from Ashuganj port can be offloaded and then taken by road to Agartala. These agreements to buy power from India will entail the establishing of an energy grid by Bangladesh on either side of the border. The Palatana project which is being built by India would supply electricity to Bangladesh. This project could be speedily implemented because of the transit accorded to India through the navigable Ashugunj port, by Bangladesh. Initially, 250 MW of power will be made available from the power plant in Tripura, which is expected to start generation in 2012. Two grids - one at Binodpur on the Indian side and Bheramara on the Bangladesh side – a distance of about 125 kilometres - will need to be connected with the switching arrangements on the Bangladeshi side. The ADB has already approved a loan of $100 million for the construction of this cross border transmission line. The two countries have already signed power purchase agreements. The Bangladesh Power Development Board and the National Thermal Power Corporation of India have also inked a joint venture to set up a 1,320 MW coal-based power plant in Bagerhat district of Bangladesh.[16]

India and Bangladesh are also working out the modalities for the exchanging of energy. India will sell to Bangladesh any surplus power it has in the areas close to Bangladesh, while India will draw a similar amount from Bangladesh for power deficit areas in India. India and Bangladesh have signed a 35 year deal to this effect. The Bangladesh Power Development Board (BPDB) will buy 500 MW of power from different power plants in India and India will import its share through the Power Grid Corporation of India Ltd (PGCI) regional transmission system. The power will be transmitted through a 400 KV switching station and a 400 KV single circuit line. The PGCI will also construct a 400 KV double circuit line stretching from India's Bahrampur to Bheramara in Bangladesh. At present the two sides are building a connecting supply line from Bahrampur in West Bengal to Bangladesh's Bheramara and by establishing a substation. The terms and conditions as well as the tariff will be determined by the Central Electricity Regulatory Commission of India. The Bangladeshi prime minster has committed to buying 500 MW of power from India over the next two years.

Thirdly, Bangladesh has enlisted India's support for developing its energy sector. The Bangladesh Power Development Board (BPDB) and the Indian state-run National Thermal Power Corporation (NTPC) have signed an MoU for improving and developing the power sector in Bangladesh. The NTPC will not only assist in establishing coal-based power stations in Bangladesh, it will develop power generation projects through joint ventures. The NTPC and BPDB had earlier agreed to set up 1320 MW joint venture coal fired power plant at Khulna and Chittagong. However now the two countries want to concentrate on Khulna power plant which is to be built at the cost of 1.5 billion USD on the basis of 50:50 equity. India is also building a coal terminal at Jogighopa in Assam. The coal that comes from Meghalaya though rail and road will now be transported by the waterways. The protocol on Inland transit and trade is going to expire in March 2012. The meeting in January 2012 has ended in a deadlock creating further uncertainty.

The immediate and effective implementation of the bilateral agreements will translate into enhanced trade and the economic development of both India and Bangladesh. The engagement would be long drawn as most of the projects would require four to five years time for feasibility studies and implementation. Already India and Bangladesh have signed an agreement to utilise $750 million of the billion dollar credit line extended by New Delhi for various infrastructure projects that have already been identified. If this momentum can gather strength and substance, bilateral relations between the two would have truly turned the corner.

Notes

1. Bangladesh and India Eye Greater Connectivity", *Daily Star*, August 13, 2010.
2. "Bangladesh Keep to up Trade with North East", *Meghalaya Times*, 13 January 2010. http://meghalayatimes.info/index.php?option=com_ content&view=article&id=6266:bdesh-keen-to-up-trade-with-ne&catid=44:front-page&Itemid=28

3. Between India and Bangladesh there are three major seaports namely Kolkata, Haldia and Chittagong. The Mongla Port has about 80 per cent and Chittagong port around 40 per cent spare capacity at the present level of efficiency and technology. It has also the potential for developing a "deep sea port", but its development needs sub-regional patronage. India was going to support Bangladesh government with its dredging of rivers for flood control, navigation and access to ports.
4. M Rahmatullah, "Transport Issues and Integration in South Asia in beyond safta", 'in Sadiq Ahmed, Saman Kelegama and Ejaz Ghani,,(ed.) *Promoting Economic Cooperation in South Asia : Beyond SAFTA,* Sage,,2010, New Delhi.
5. Uma Subramanian and John Arnold, "South Asia Subregional Links in Transportation and logistics in South Asia" in *World Bank Report,* 2001, The World Bank Washington, D.C.
6. "India Bangladesh Relations", High Commission of India, Dhaka http://www.hcidhaka.org/br_politics.php, http://meaindia.nic.in/meapsite/foreignrelation/bangladesh.pdf
7. Prabhu Ghate, "South Asia Towards Greater Connectivity"? *Economic Times*, 8 November, 2010.
8. Bhutan uses Kolkata port; Nepal uses Kolkata port and Haldia port.
9. Mallika Shakya, "Trilateral agreement for Nepali trade," *Himal,* February,2011 at http://www.himalmag.com/component/content/article/3604.html
10. Ibid.
11. "Transit to benefit four countries", *Daily Star*, 9 August 2010 at http://www.thedailystar.net/story.php?nid=150000
12. The route identified for road communication is Banglabandha - Panchagarh-Thakurgaon-Sayedpur-Rangpur-Bogra-Natore-Dasuria-Pakshey-Kushtia-Jhenaidah-Jessore—Khulna-Mongla and the rail route is Rohanpur (Rajshahi)-Rajshahi-Iswardi-Khulna-Mongla. Dhaka has proposed two more routes Benapole-Petrapole and another is Chihati-Haldibari. http://www.thefinancialexpress-bd.com/more.php?news_id=106072
13. "Bhutan sends oranges to Bangladesh via new India route," *BDnews*, 23 February 2010 at http://bdnews24.com/details. php?id =152739 & cid=2

14. Ministry of Home Affairs, India, Report, "Detailed Quarterly Reports On Landports for the Month of September" September, 2010 at http://www.mha.nic.in/pdfs/BM_status_icp.pdf; the rough estimate for 7 ICP and 8 LCS , is $125 million.

15 Arguably Bangladesh has a demand of over 5,000 MW energy while its present supply hovers around 3646 MW. The deficit has led to cuts in its industries affecting its quantity of export. Incidentally Bangladesh government has plans to generate 7,000 megawatts of electricity by 2013 and 20,000 by 2021; 7,0000 MW electricity by 2015 *Daily Star*, April 6, 2010.

16 http://www.mea.gov.in/mystart.php?id=100018210&pid=2290

6

Bangladesh-India Connectivity: A Focus on Transit

Ishtiaque Selim

Poor transport and connectivity between Bangladesh and India, the two close neighbours in South Asia, have cost their economies dear. The poor connectivity raises the cost of transportation and hinders inter-state trade as goods become unnecessarily expensive. As any debate on Indo-Bangladesh connectivity usually boils down to the issue of transit that will connect mainland India with its Northeastern states through Bangladesh territory, this chapter attempts to analyse the challenges that confront the issue of connectivity.

Over the past few years, there has been a general scepticism in Bangladesh regarding transit due to certain concerns and these often dominate any argument in favour of transit. Nonetheless, in recent times a few positive developments lead one to assume that the current government in Bangladesh is more positive about granting transit rights to India. In this context, this chapter will seek to answer the following questions. What is the current status of the Indo-Bangla transit issue? Is infrastructure in Bangladesh in place to facilitate transit? And, what could be the areas of cooperation in this regard?

The chapter is structured as follows: It begins with a brief survey of the Bangladesh-India transport connectivity issue. The next section offers a rationale for Bangladesh-India connectivity with special focus on transit. The third section of the paper discusses the recent developments in issues related to transit and attempts to shed some light on the Bangladesh-India transit issue.

Bangladesh-India Existing Transport Connectivity: A Brief Profile

Bangladesh-India connectivity has thus far remained largely fragmented, even though the two neighbours were well connected by road, rail and waterways in the pre-partition era. These connections remained operational till the 1965 war after which they were completely closed. Trade via waterways was resumed after the creation of Bangladesh, and road and rail links were subsequently re-established between the two countries. The connectivity issue has always been at the forefront in Bangladesh-India bilateral discussions. A brief overview of Bangladesh-India transport connectivity follows:

Road Links

Transportation by road plays a most dominant role in Bangladesh-India trade relations although this mode of communication is not cost effective. A significant proportion of freight and passenger traffic is carried by road. Benapole (Bangladesh) and Petrapole (India) border points are the two most important land ports for the overland trade between the two nations. Near about 70 to 80 per cent of bilateral overland trade passes through these ports.[1]

Passenger traffic between Bangladesh and India started only in 1999 with the launch of the Dhaka-Kolkata direct bus service. Bus services between Dhaka-Agartala, and Dhaka-Siliguri commenced in 2003 and 2005 respectively.

Rail Links

Railways were the most important mode of transportation, during the pre-1947 period. However, in the present day cross-border movement by rail has dwindled significantly as a number of routes have become dormant. Only three broad gauge rail corridors, namely, Darsana-Gede, Rohanpur-Singhabad and Benapole-Petrapole are operational now. These routes are used for export and import of goods.

The Bangladesh-India passenger train service was restored on April 14, 2008. A Bangladesh-India friendship train service –the *Moitri* Train was launched on this day. But the service so far is too time consuming because of long delays in customs and immigration clearance. It takes nearly half a day to travel a distance of only 400 kilometres. Therefore in spite of a much fanfare launch this route is not very popular.

Waterways

Bangladesh and India are the only two South Asian nations connected by inland water transport (IWT), which happens to be the cheapest mode of transportation. Bangladesh and India signed a protocol in 1972 to ensure waterway transit for India through Bangladesh to the Northeastern states of India. To date no passenger movement takes place between the two nations through the waterways and even for trade purposes the water links are not being used extensively due to a number of problems. These problems include among other things the navigability crisis causes by siltation and the shortage of ports of call.[2] The two countries are also reluctant to designate certain port as ports of call as there is divergence of opinion regarding their capacity to handle large scale cargo. Due to lack of infrastructure development some of the ports are underutilised.

Why Connectivity between Bangladesh and India? The Case for Transit

The economic benefits of regional connectivity are well recorded. Both theory and popular rhetoric provide a strong case for connectivity. But the Bangladesh-India connectivity issue, is in general, bogged down by political debates and arguments and thereby becomes a sensitive political matter in Bangladesh. The recent discussions on connectivity have literally focused on the question whether granting transit facilities to India would be beneficial for Bangladesh. While many analysts in Bangladesh have argued for granting transit facility to India, politically it has been opposed by the major opposition party, the BNP, and others who perceive it as being a security issue. In fact, transit, which is more or less only an economic issue, has virtually been overshadowed by political interests.

It is worth mentioning that a trade treaty between Bangladesh and India signed on October 4, 1980 mentioned the granting of transit facility to India.[3] The treaty stated that:

> This [transit] also provides for trade in freely convertible currencies, according most favourable nation treatment, making mutually beneficial arrangements for use of waterways and railways for commerce between the two countries and for passage of goods between two places in one country through the territory of the other.[4]

The treaty was never implemented as the political landscape changed with the deaths of President Zia-ur-Rahman in Bangladesh and Prime Minister Indira Gandhi in India.[5]

Nevertheless, it is geographical proximity that brings the transit issue to the fore in the Bangladesh-India relationship. The Northeastern states of India (comprising the seven states of, Assam, Manipur, Meghalaya, Mizoram, Nagaland, Tripura and Arunachal Pradesh) are connected to the mainland by a narrow strip of land called the 'chicken neck' It is surrounded on the three sides by Bangladesh territory. Detached from the main territory, the seven states face considerable development challenges. India also incurs excessive economic cost as it sends goods to the Northeastern states through a much longer route. For example: a consignment from the Kolkata port to the Northeastern states has to pass through the Siliguri Corridor (popularly known as the "Chicken Neck") between Nepal and Bangladesh, but the consignment travels a total distance of between 1400 to 1600 kilometres. If Bangladesh allows the transit of Indian goods to the Northeast through its territory, the distance would reduce drastically to between 350 and 700 kilometres.[6] This is then the Indian compulsion to improve physical connectivity with Bangladesh which would also facilitate trade. Furthermore, transit through Bangladesh would bring India closer to attaining the much broader objective of connecting with the South East Asian nations.[7] Consequently, India has been seeking transit facilities from Bangladesh.

Bangladesh, at the same time, has its own interests in strengthening physical connectivity with India. The subsequent parts of this chapter will elaborate on these interests.

Politically Bangladesh can use the transit as a leverage to settle some unresolved issues with India.[8] From the economic point of view, the country's trade is likely to benefit from trade with Nepal and Bhutan. India has already allowed Bangladesh to conduct its trade with Nepal and Bhutan through its territory. If Bangladesh allows Indian traffic to go through its territory[9] the physical connectivity with landlocked Nepal, Bhutan and Northeast India could turn Bangladesh into a regional transportation hub. Further, a transit facility to India might open up new avenue for the country to import natural resources from Northeast India and convert them into exportable commodities. A number of studies have recorded the economic benefits that Bangladesh can reap from granting transit to India.

Probable Benefits for Bangladesh

- Bangladesh can earn revenue by trading in transport services. It could then bridge its trade deficit with India.[10]
- According to a study conducted by RIS (Research and Information System, New Delhi) in 2007, the transit revenue for Bangladesh was estimated between $ 660 million to $1060 million, and $110 million to $180 million respectively for two different corridors.[11]
- The markets of the Indian Northeast states would become more easily accessible for Bangladeshi products if transit is provided. Bangladesh can import raw materials and export finished products to the Northeast which would be cheaper because of the physical proximity.
- Transit to India could create employment opportunities for Bangladeshi nationals. According to a 1999 estimate, transit to India would create 2.5 million jobs in Bangladesh in the transport sector and in form of small business opportunities in the areas around the transit routes.
- Transit could lead to the development of transport sector in Bangladesh. For instance, an otherwise fragile railway infrastructure in Bangladesh could be strengthened immensely. The extensive use of railways to facilitate smooth transit could bring the badly needed investment into the Bangladesh railway infrastructure. It may be noted that a recent study by Murshid recommended that railways should be the premier mode of transportation for Bangladesh-India transit.[12]
- Chittagong and Mongla ports could earn good revenue for Bangladesh, if the country accords transit to India. Currently, both Chittagong and Mongla ports have excess capacity to handle additional cargoes and containers. For example, 43 per cent of container and 46 per cent of cargo handling capacity remains unutilised in Chittagong port. Bangladesh may earn an additional $200 million annually by opening up its port facilities for handling Indian cargo.[13]

The Concerns

The most common concern amongst a fourth of the Bangladeshi population is that transit to India might hamper Bangladesh's security.

The perception is that India could use the transit facility to curb insurgency in its Northeastern states which could in turn threaten the security of Bangladesh.[14] According to a Bangladeshi security expert, transit to India could drag the country "into India's internal security matrix".[15] Further, some analysts are of the view that transit might spur arms and drugs trafficking through Bangladesh territory. All these security concerns have created an opinion that is against providing transit to India. However, the grant of waterway transit to India has not threatened the security of Bangladesh. Hence, the concerns might not be justifiable.

The Recent Developments in Bangladesh-India Connectivity

There have been some positive developments on the issue of India-Bangladesh connectivity since the Awami League (AL) came into office with an absolute majority at the end of 2008. First, the Bangladesh premier visited India in January 2010 and some decisions related to connectivity were taken- the details of which are mentioned in the joint communiqué issued at the end of the visit. Secondly, an Asian Development Bank (ADB) study favours transit between the two countries. And, third, another report on transit came out in April 2011, which states the official position of Bangladesh government with regard to this issue.

The 2010 India Visit by Bangladesh Prime Minister

The joint statement made during the visit emphasised the need for connectivity between Bangladesh and India. Apart from the decision to allow India to use Bangladeshi sea ports, namely, Chittagong and Mongla, some other areas of cooperation were identified with regard to waterway and rail communication. Among other things, the two countries agreed to include Ashuganj and Silghat as the two new ports of call. It may be noted that in 2007 India had requested Bangladesh to allow it to use the Ashuganj port as it is only 62 kilometres from Tripura.[16] It is also worth mentioning that India has already started using the transit facility through Bangladesh. For the first time, four consignments of heavy equipment for the Tripura power station went through the Ashuganj port of Bangladesh. India has also given a soft loan of a billion dollars to Bangladesh to build infrastructure to facilitate transit between the two countries.

The Asian Development Bank (ADB) Study Report[17]

The eminent Bangladeshi transport expert Dr. M. Rahmatullah conducted a study on transit for the Asian Development Bank (ADB). The study among other things quantified the benefits that would accrue to Bangladesh from the transit. According to the report, Bangladesh would earn $50 million per annum in the first five years which could go up to a billion dollars in the following years. Further, the study finds that the internal rate of return from transit is 33.46 per cent. The study also reveals that trade in transport services would be economically beneficial for Bangladesh.

The Core Committee Study Report on Transit

On December 2, 2010, the Bangladesh ministry of commerce formed a core committee on transit. It was the very first initiative taken by the Bangladesh government to evaluate the option of granting transit to India in economic terms. Headed by the chairman of the Tariff Commission it consisted of two sub-groups, while the core committee dealt with four issues. These included: probable transit routes, investment for infrastructure development and return from investment, transit fee/charge, and the economic impact of transit.

The report, submitted to the commerce ministry on April 7, 2011, identified seven road routes (See Table I), six rail routes (See Table I) and three new routes for inland water transport to facilitate transit.[18] Three of the seven probable land routes would give Bangladesh access to Bhutan and Nepal across India territory, and one of the six rail routes connects Bangladesh with Nepal (See Table I).

Table I: Recommended Road and Railway Transit Routes

Mode	*Route*
Road (1)	Kolkata-Petrapole/Benapole-Dhaka-Akhaura/Agartala
Road (2)	Agartala-Akhaura-Chittagong
Road (3)	Silchar-Sutarkandi-Chittagong Port
Road (4)	Silchar-Sutarkandi-Paturia Ferry-Benapole-Kolkata
Road (5)	Samdrup Jonkhar-Guwahati-Shillong-Tamabil-Sylhet-Chittagong
Road (6)	Kathmandu-Kakarvita/Phulbari-Banglabandha-Mongla/Chittagong

Road (7)	Thimpu-Phuentsholing-Jaigaon/Burimari-Mongla/ Chittagong
Railway (1)	Silchar-Mahisasan/Shahbazpur-Dhaka ICD-Banglabandha Bridge-Darshana-Kolkata
Railway (2)	Silchar-Mahisasan/Shahbazpur-Chittagong Port
Railway (3)	Agartala-Akahura-Dhaka ISD-Banglabam.ha-Darshana-Kolkata
Railway (4)	Agartala-Akhaura-Chittagong Port
Railway (5)	Kolkata-Petrapole/Benapole-Khulna-Mongla Port
Railway (6)	Birganj-Raxual-Katihar-Singabad/Rohanpur-Khulna-Mongla Port

Sources: *Daily Manbzamin*, 10 April 2011 and *The Financial Express*, 21 April 2011.

The report among other things suggested charging a user fee instead of a transit fee for the use of transit facilities. The report recommended imposing user fees on various services such as transportation and administrative services. For road transit, the user fees include cost of road damage, accident externalities, congestion cost and environmental cost.

To facilitate transit, the report further highlighted the need for substantial investment in Bangladesh to support infrastructure development. It mentioned that Bangladesh would need to invest $11.7 billion to improve transit infrastructure. Roughly 28 per cent of this amount would be needed to develop roads in Bangladesh, while more than 60 per cent will be required to improve railway infrastructure and the rest of the amount, according to the report, will be necessary for the development of sea and land ports.

The report also mentioned that the countries enjoying transit facilities will not be able to purchase fuel from the host country at a subsidised rate for their carriers; rather they will be required to buy fuel at international rates.

Acknowledging all the infrastructural deficits, the report said that India, Nepal and Bhutan would need to wait for at least another three years to avail full transit facilities through Bangladesh territory. The report, alternatively, proposed to provide trans-shipment facilities in the interim. To facilitate this, the report recommended the setting up of a transport company by Bangladesh, India, Bhutan and Nepal in which Bangladesh would have a 51 per cent share.

Infrastructure Deficit: A Threat to Connectivity and an Area of Future Cooperation

Connectivity could be hampered by the lack of good infrastructural facilities in Bangladesh especially given the present state of the road and rail infrastructure. Poor port facilities also would not help the cause as they would have an adverse impact on transit and trade.

Railways are expected to become an important mode of transportation because they are cost effective, environment friendly and safer vis-à-vis the road network - given their poor condition. However, differences of gauge (metre gauge vs. broad gauge) and rolling stock between the nations' rail networks could pose a problem. Also the difference in the levels of the efficiency of the rail networks can also hinder effective connectivity. While the thriving railway network in India has become the lifeline of the country's communication system, in Bangladesh the rail network continues to remain fragile and is hindered by poor infrastructure. Bangladesh Railways have been suffering from shortage of locomotives and lack the capacity to support the required container and freight traffic resulting in the scanty movement of goods.[19]

Another source of concern for Bangladesh is the quality of its roads. To ensure the steady flow of traffic from India and neighbouring nations, wider roads with higher axel-load limits are required. However, Bangladeshi highways have only two lanes with a load limit of 8.2 tonnes against India's axel-load limit of 12 tonnes.

Lack of port efficiency will also impede transit. For example, the custom clearance of imports takes up to 30 days, when it is possible to clear them within 10-12 days.[20] This leads to a virtual procedural deadlock in the ports. Too much checking, excessive documentation or paperwork, and other unnecessary requirements also slow down customs clearance. For instance, as many as 40 signatures are needed to get custom clearances at sea ports.[21]

Areas of Cooperation

However, the lack of infrastructure can open up another avenue for cooperation between Bangladesh and India. India already has given a billion dollar loan to Bangladesh to improve its transport infrastructure. This loan is for developing railway infrastructure, for buying broad gauge locomotives, improving railway workshops and for constructing railway bridges. Further, India has recently agreed to assist Bangladesh to construct a 13 km long rail track for connecting Akhaura with Agartala. The two countries have also decided to operationalise a few land custom stations in Bangladesh–India border by providing appropriate infrastructure.

Recently the Indian commerce minister while visiting Bangladesh announced that India would invest $3.5 billion in Bangladesh in various sectors, such as, telecommunication, food production, chemical and pharmaceuticals. However, there is no Indian investment or participation for developing Bangladeshi transport infrastructure. Although India has given Bangladesh a loan for this purpose as mentioned earlier, the amount is not sufficient to reduce the infrastructure deficit. Hence, India might consider investing in Bangladeshi transport infrastructure, which in turn would facilitate transit.

Concluding Assessment

Over the past few years Indo-Bangla connectivity in form of transit has become a much debated issue. A significant proportion of public opinion in Bangladesh favours the opening up of transit route on account of the economic benefits. But a segment of opinion has opposed transit because of security reasons thereby making the issue a political one. As a result, discussions with India on transit have never gained much momentum.

Lately, however, the issue of granting transit to India is being viewed as a major economic opportunity for Bangladesh. The current discussions on transit in Bangladesh tend to favour the granting of this facility to India. The recent Bangladesh government study on transit may not be regarded as a major breakthrough, but at least it is a significant development. Earlier in 1997 the Dhaka Metropolitan Chamber of Commerce and Industries had commissioned a study on the subject which also had favoured the granting of transit.

It is evident that owing to infrastructural bottlenecks, Bangladesh would only be able to provide full-fledged transit facility to India after a certain period of time. Therefore the report has proposed providing trans-shipment facility in the meantime. But, it is not clear whether India will accept this.

According to sources in Bangladesh government, the core committee report might undergo several changes with both the addition and deletion of some clauses.[22] But no one yet knows what these changes are likely to be. However, in the days to come three issues could prove to be problematic. These are: the transit fee, source of funding and internal costs and the political mindset.

The issue of transit fee created a stir in the Bangladesh media and among the experts. The transit report, as mentioned earlier, only recommended that a fee be imposed for the use of transit facilities by India and other neighbouring countries, but it did not say anything about the transit fee. The report pointed out that Bangladesh should not take advantage, of its geographical situation and charge India a transit fee. Supporting this view, the report argued that, "...transit trade cannot be subject to any customs duties or fees/charges that are purely transit-related unless transit entails some costs for the host country".[23] One policy maker went on to say that as per international convention a country cannot impose transit charge "based on geographical advantage".[24]

On the other hand, some are in favour of imposing such a fee saying India would be transporting goods, not to a third country, but to its own territory, hence Bangladesh can claim a transit fee. One analyst mentioned that the transit facility through Bangladesh would enable India to save INR 70 billion per year, and even if Bangladesh gets half that amount the Indian gains would be quite substantial.[25] Although it is highly unlikely that Bangladesh will receive such an amount as fee. After the submission of the core committee report there is a suggestion from Bangladesh government to impose transit fee. A subcommittee would fix the fee taking into account the concerns of all parties. India, one should note, has always maintained that it would pay transit fee in line with the international convention. However, it is not clear whether the parties involved would agree to take into account the savings on transportation costs while determining the transit fee. Thus the fixing of transit fee is likely to become a contentious issue between Bangladesh and India.

Another concern is related to the huge investments that would be necessary for infrastructure development, before the granting of total transit facility to India. What would be the source of the funds? Will Bangladesh resort to foreign aid? Or, will India come forward with investment proposals in this regard? These are questions to be pondered upon. One suggestion is that India, could take the public private partnership (PPP) investment route. This would enable Indian investors to be involved with transit related infrastructure building activities in Bangladesh.

Last but not least is the political mindset, which is yet another important factor. With a number of bilateral issues at stake, some political parties still remain apprehensive about transit. Nevertheless, the possibility of huge economic gains accruing for Bangladesh from transit can create a consensus in favour of transit across the political spectrum. The Bangladeshi business leaders, for example, are not opposing transit. The recent report did not estimate the tentative benefits to Bangladesh in line with the country's official position regarding transit which argues beneficial effect. The analysts should take the report into account for estimating the benefits for Bangladesh. With no clear understanding of the potential economic benefits, transit can be opposed by a certain political segment. As such both Bangladesh and India would do well to undertake a joint study to evaluate the economic benefits for concerned parties. The economic dividend apart, the two countries should hold consultations to remove the non-tariff barriers on trade, which will multiply the benefits of transit, especially for Bangladesh.

Transit has undoubtedly become a matter of mutual interest and benefit for both countries. The transit facility, would allow mainland India to be connected with its Northeastern states thus enabling it to save on the huge costs of transportation. For Bangladesh, at the same time, transit is economically beneficial as it could be a source of revenue apart from other benefits. Both Bangladesh and India therefore need to discuss ways and means for arriving at a situation that is a win-win for both.

Notes

1. M. Rahmatullah, "Regional Transport Connectivity: Opportunities for Bangladesh", *BIISS Journal,* 31(1), 2010, p. 60.
2. Ibid.
3. Anu Mahmud, *SAARC: APEC: D-8: Eco Anchalik Arthanaitik Forum* (in Bengali), Oitijjhya: Dhaka, 2001, p. 38.
4. Ibid. p. 46.
5. Ibid.

6. Ibid. p. 59.
7. K A S Murshid, "Transit and Trans-shipment: Strategic Considerations for Bangladesh and India", *Economic and Political Weekly*, XLVI(17), April 23, 2011, p. 44.
8. M. Obaidul Haque, "Foreign Policy Perceptions, Regional and Sub-Regional Cooperative Initiatives", in Farooq Sobhan (ed.), *Bangladesh-India Dialogue*, The University Press Limited: Dhaka, p. 27, 2006.
9. Smruti S Pattanaik, "Making Sense of Regional Cooperation: SAARC at Twenty", *Strategic Analysis*, 30(1), 2006, p. 150.
10. For details see, M. Rahmatullah, n. 1, p. 62.
11. Research and Information System for Developing Countries, "Restoring Afghanistan-Pakistan-India-Bangladesh-Myanmar (APIBM) Corridor: Towards a Newsilk Road in Asia", *RIS Policy Briefs*, No. 30, March 2007.
12. K A S Murshid, n.7, pp. 47-48.
13. *Prothom Alo*, 24 April 2011.
14. Sabbir Ahmed, "Transit Issue: Nature and Direction of the Debate", *Quarterly Bangladesh Foreign Policy Survey*, July-September, 1996, p. 8.
15. Abdur Rob Khan, "Transit Issue in Bangladesh Foreign Policy", Presentation at the Independence Day Commemorative Seminar on *Foreign Policy of Bangladesh: Continuity and Change* organized by BIISS on 5 April 2009.
16. Smruti S. Pattanaik, "India, Bangladesh and Southeast Asia: Connecting the Neighbourhood", *IPCS Issue Brief*, No. 113, August, 2009, p. 3.
17. If not mentioned otherwise this sub-section is based on information from *The Daily Star*, 21 April 2011.
18. *The Financial Express*, 11 April 2011.
19. K A S Murshid, n. 7, p. 49.
20. U. Wickramasinghe, "A Multilateral Approach to Trade Facilitation in South Asia", Discussion Paper, *South Asia Watch on Trade, Economics and Environment*, Kathmandu, Nepal, 2004.
21. Ibid.
22. *Prothom Alo*, 20 April 2011.
23. Quoted in *The Financial Express*, 11 April 2011.
24. Ibid.
25. *The Daily Star*, 10 April 2011.

7

India-Bangladesh Trade: Problems and Prospects

Anand Kumar

With the start of a new phase in Indo-Bangladesh relations, which has put the bilateral relations on an upswing, it is only natural that both sides should try to give a boost to bilateral trade. Though the bilateral trade is also not problem free, the issues involved are far easier to resolve than many others. At the same time, closer economic ties could also help in resolving other bilateral issues.

There is significant bilateral trade between India and Bangladesh. India an emerging economic powerhouse caters to many of the needs of Bangladesh. But this has also skewed the balance of trade in favour of India. The imports of Bangladesh are far more than its exports. What is more significant is that even the large volume of informal trade that exists between the two countries is dominated by India. The resultant trade deficit has led to complaints from Bangladesh.

This chapter argues that since - even in informal trade - which is generally undertaken to bypass the high tariff and non-tariff barriers, rules, regulations and enforcement agencies - there are very few products from Bangladesh, it is highly unlikely that a zero-duty regime would change the balance of bilateral trade in any big way. The trade deficit, a major Bangladesh grouse against India would only be reduced if India or some other countries make major investments in Bangladesh thereby enhancing its resource base and consequently its exports.

Beginning of Trade Relations

The bilateral trade between India and Bangladesh started after the latter was liberated from Pakistan in 1971. Immediately after liberation Bangladesh required consumer goods, especially food, which came from India.

Soon after Bangladesh also started opening up its economy. The country introduced economic reforms in 1982. This led to the increase of Indian exports to Bangladesh. The formal and informal exports of India grew because of the appreciation of the real taka/rupee exchange rate by about 50 per cent between the mid-1980s and 1999.[1] At the same time it retarded the growth of Bangladesh exports to India. Though an attempt was made to correct the anomalies, after 1999, but Bangladesh's exports to India continued to stagnate.

In the 1980s the main exports of Bangladesh were basic manufactures, including leather, rubber, paper and chemicals. Gradually, the list has grown and Bangladesh today exports medicines, textiles, iron and steel, metals, raw jute, Jamdani sarees, medical appliances and clothing accessories.

These have found a growing market in India. Bangladesh imports from India include food grains, fabrics, cotton yarn, machinery, instruments, glass and glassware, ceramics and coal.

Trade Agreement

A bilateral trade agreement between Bangladesh and India was signed in 1980 and was later amended and formalised in March 2006. This came into force on April 1, 2006 and was valid till March 2009.[2] This agreement provided for expansion of trade and economic cooperation, making mutually beneficial arrangements for the use of waterways, railways and roadways; the passage of goods between two places in one country through the territory of the other; exchange of business and trade delegations and annual consultations to review the working of the agreement.

Hurdles in Indo-Bangladesh Trade

Two countries start trading with each other when they perceive a clear comparative advantage in exporting products required by each other. India has a 'revealed comparative advantage' in many goods that are required by Bangladesh. This is one reason why Indian exports to Bangladesh have been growing over the years. On the other hand, Bangladesh lacks a similar 'revealed comparative advantage'. As a result, its products have not been able to find an easy market in India.

Trade is also facilitated when two countries have a complementarity in their products. This complementarity has to be both of products as well as quantity. India has the capability to meet the import requirements of Bangladesh. But in most cases, the reverse is not true. Thus, there exists a case of partial complementarity or one way complementarity between the two countries.

In the case of sea-borne trade certain products have to go to specific ports for customs clearance. This has given rise to bootleg smuggling which bypasses customs posts altogether or even "official smuggling" involving bribes to customs and other officials on both sides of the border.

Trade between the two countries has also been constrained by the lack of trans-shipment/transit facilities between Bangladesh and India. Although some policy decisions have been taken in this regard, but progress on ground is still awaited. Trans-shipment through Bangladesh is expected to benefit India by cutting the distance between India's Northeast and the mainland, thus facilitating the transport of goods. These goods can also be exported through Chittagong port. This will also bring in significant amount of revenue to Bangladesh as port fee.

Allegations and Demand Engendered by Trade Deficit

The nature of Indo-Bangladesh relations has created a trade deficit for Bangladesh. To reduce this trade imbalance, Bangladesh wants easy and tariff free access to the Indian market on a non-reciprocal basis.[3] It is also keen to increase trade with Northeastern Indian states.

Bangladesh's exports to India, however, have not been constrained by tariff protection. India has been giving Bangladesh extensive tariff preferences under SAPTA (South Asian Preferential Tariff Arrangement, which was a precursor of SAFTA) and many of the tariff barriers applicable to other countries are not imposed on Bangladeshi exporters. This shows that India's trade policy has not been discriminatory towards Bangladesh and that the slow growth of the latter's exports to India is due to other factors such as a low degree of complementarity and weak comparative advantage.

India has dismantled most of its tariff protection regime for industrial goods. It has also brought down its general tariff levels and Indian markets are full of imported goods from all over the world. Bangladesh will have to compete with the foreign goods in the Indian markets, which could prove difficult even with zero duty access. The protection provided by India to agricultural goods is in accordance with WTO rules.

Over the years, India has taken several policy measures to encourage exports from Bangladesh. At the 14th SAARC summit held in New Delhi in April 2007, India announced that it would grant duty-free access to Bangladeshi imports that are on the 'positive' list. India also agreed to slash import duty on goods on the 'negative' list (Sensitive List) from 45 per cent to 10 per cent. In fact, India decided to grant zero tariff access for products in the positive list to all the Least Developed Countries (LDCs) of SAARC. While India, Pakistan and Sri Lanka are categorised as Non-Least Developed Countries (NLDCs), Bangladesh, Bhutan, the Maldives and Nepal are categorised as the LDCs. This unilateral gesture by India was in keeping with the trade liberalisation and investment enhancing measures as per SAFTA norms with regard to the LDCs of the region, and it came much before the scheduled date of 2009.

Informal Trade

There are two important aspects of informal trade–its size and nature. The volumes, in terms of the informal trade between India and Bangladesh are however quite significant.

The informal trade between India and Bangladesh is essentially a one-way trade wherein goods move from India to Bangladesh. These are marked by the informal trading arrangements which are entered into through friends and relatives.

The traders engaged in informal trade have devised several mechanisms to mitigate risks. They trade through people whom they know. These acquaintances are a guarantee against payment defaults. Secondly, to diversify risk they go for a large number of transactions.

The informal trade between India and Bangladesh is encouraged because of the difficulties faced by the traders in the transacting environment. The Indo-Bangladesh trade is characterised by a plethora of regulations, absence of information transparency, the bureaucratic approach of public agents, infrastructure bottlenecks in transportation, communication, and above all, the rent seeking activities of public servants. All these factors translate into additional costs for traders prompting them to go in for informal trade.[4]

The problems faced by the Bangladeshi traders are in the area of licensing, refunds and custom dealings whereas the Indian traders face more problems with banks and transportation.

Institutional factors are responsible for encouraging informal trade between India and Bangladesh. In informal trade, payment is realised quickly. There is no paperwork or procedural delay. Besides, the transportation costs are also lower. Interestingly, trade policy barriers like tariffs and quantitative restrictions are not factors that lead to informal trade.[5] However, people do resort to informal trade because they do not know much about trade rules due to lack of education.

It has also been found that a large proportion of goods sent from India to Bangladesh are procured from other states in India. This shows that informal trade is at least as – if not better - organised as formal trade. It has also been found that some goods meant for poor people in India that are distributed through the public distribution system are sent to Bangladesh through informal trade. The difference in tariff levels between India and Bangladesh is not much. This is evident from the fact that goods moving from Bangladesh to India are generally not of third country origin.

It is quite obvious that the informal trade between the two countries does not take place because of trade policy distortions. The informal traders engage in illegal trade to avoid the problems they face while transacting through legal channels. Thus it is possible that even in a zero duty regime some informal trade would persist.

Criminal Activities Part of Border Trade

Though all border trade including informal trade is at present illegal some aspects of it include criminal activities like the smuggling of narcotics and contraband substances. Women and children are also trafficked on the border. However, the trade in cattle is a little different. This trade is illegal on the Indian side of the border. But it becomes perfectly legal the moment the cattle enter Bangladesh. This illegal cattle trade has been the cause of several skirmishes on the border. The human trafficking and smuggling in narcotics could be handled by better policing but there is a need to review the cattle trade. At present, around 1.5 million cattle are exported informally to Bangladesh. With the removal of restrictions this trade would increase manifold. Cattle from India are a major source of hides and skins needed for manufacturing export quality finished leather in Bangladesh's more modern slaughterhouses and tanneries.

The annual value of informal exports to Bangladesh from India in the year 2000 was estimated at between $1 billion and $1.5 billion. Consumer goods of international quality are also informally traded at the border.

Trade in Services

Trade in services is problematic from the Indian point of view. This is because it is often difficult to keep track of these services. Health and education constitute a major part of the services sector. Other important constituents are foreign travel, transportation, insurance, investment income, transfer payments and so on. The trade in health and education services goes unrecorded because it hardly ever takes place through official channels. If all these were properly accounted for then possibly one would get a better picture of bilateral trade.

Trade in Health Services

A large number of people from Bangladesh come to India for medical treatment. The reason for this lies in the pattern of wealth creation in Bangladesh which has placed private hospitals in their own country out of the reach of most people.

In terms of health infrastructure, Bangladesh does not fare too well. The ratio of doctors and nurses to patients is one of the worst in the region. A 1999 survey indicates that as many as 57 per cent of Bangladeshi patients seeking treatment abroad went to India, followed by Singapore, the US and UK. Besides the cost and quality of medical treatment, the other factors that influenced the decision of Bangladeshi people was the cost of travel and accommodation, language, alternative medicine options and so on. Bangladeshi patients not only go to hospitals in West Bengal but even to far off places like the All India Institute of Medical Sciences (AIIMS), New Delhi, the Tata Memorial hospital in Mumbai and Escorts Hospital in Chennai. They also go to establishments in Bangalore, Vellore, Pune, Chandigarh and so on.

Most of the patients travelling to India are on a tourist visa, hence the amount paid by them for medical treatment is not reflected in the import of health services account in the official BOP but in the service account of tourism. Often money is also paid through informal channels or *hundis* as they are called in Bangladesh. Development of the health services infrastructure in Bangladesh could help improve the situation.

Trade in Education Services

The problem area for Bangladesh has been higher education. In the absence of sufficient technical colleges and specialised institutions a considerable number of students come to India to study business management, computer science, engineering and medicine. Around 30 per cent of students also study humanities and social sciences or related subjects in India.

Interestingly, a considerable number of Bangladeshi students studying in India assume an Indian identity. Most of them do not have a no-objection certificate from the education department of the government of Bangladesh.

The per capita average expenditure incurred by Bangladeshis for medical treatment in India comes to about $600. The average annual expenditure of a Bangladeshi student in India was estimated at $1400. The number of patients in 1998-99 was estimated to be 40,000 while the number of students was estimated at 53000.

FTA Seen as a Way to Stimulate Two Way Trade

India is very keen to sign an FTA with Bangladesh, particularly to curtail the large volume of illegal trade that takes place through porous border between the two countries. Bangladeshi exporters as well as the government essentially perceive the bilateral FTA as being the bigger economy's ploy to grab the smaller economy's market, although some are willing to admit that it is not really the non-tariff barriers imposed by India but Bangladesh's lack of comparative advantage that is the real hurdle in the way of Bangladesh's access to the Indian market.

India has been highlighting the grand success of the India – Sri Lanka FTA which has catapulted Sri Lankan exports to India from a dismal $45 million (much less than the current exports of Bangladesh) to $194.78 million in 2003-2004. The balance of trade which favoured India 15 to one when the agreement was signed was soon reduced to five to one. India has also emerged as Sri Lanka's third largest investor with nearly 30 per cent of Sri Lankan exports to India accounted for by Indian investments - ever since the FTA was operationalised. The two countries have also been exploring the possibility of entering into a Comprehensive Economic Partnership Agreement, which will not only expand the list of goods covered under the FTA, but also promote cooperation in services, investment and trade facilitation.

An unfavourable balance of trade may not always be bad. For a developing economy it is important to strengthen all the sectors of its economy, if need be by importing from comparatively cheap sources. Bangladesh often imports intermediate goods from India for exports. If it tries to produce them the economies of scale may not favour the country and the resultant increase in costs would only make their exports less competitive.

Recent Developments

After the India visit of Sheikh Hasina in January 2010, there has been a genuine effort to boost Indo-Bangladesh relations. This was also seen in the area of trade and commerce. In the joint communiqué of this visit both sides agreed to intensify discussions at official and technical levels to provide further impetus to trade and economic exchanges.

When India's commerce and industry minister Anand Sharma visited Bangladesh a number of important developments took place. India offered a tariff-free quota of 10 million pieces of apparel from Bangladesh, marking an increase of 25 per cent over previous years, while countervailing duties were lifted on all jute exports from Bangladesh.

India also indicated its desire to bring in more investments and informed Bangladesh that about $3.5 billion worth private investment was in the pipeline. This investment is expected to provide employment to people in Bangladesh. It might also become a value addition for the neighbouring country's exports to the rest of the world.

In July 2011 border haats (markets) were inaugurated. Though mostly for the convenience of the local people these might also boost bilateral trade. Both nations have strengthened the infrastructure at the borders, including construction of land custom stations and integrated check posts, particularly at Petrapole and Agartala, to facilitate trade.

India has offered assistance for the construction of the bridge over river Feni, and the construction of the connecting road on the Bangladesh side. On the other hand, India has welcomed the offer for use of Chittagong and Mongola ports that would greatly benefit the trade and development of Bangladesh and the Northeast of India.

Trade Concessions during Indian Prime Minister's Visit to Dhaka

Bangladesh exports received a major boost when the Indian Prime minister, Manmohan Singh, visited Dhaka in September 2011. Manmohan Singh announced duty-free access to 46 textile items from the country. Bangladesh had been pressing to get a duty waiver on 61 products. Of the total products, 47 were apparel items including pants, shirts, blouses, skirts, kids wear, cotton nightwear, jeans, swimwear and tracksuits.[6] This decision has boosted exports from Bangladesh.

Prospects

Bangladesh has put forward tariff barriers as being the main hinderance to exports from that country. However, even in a duty free regime the volume of trade between the two countries would depend on various factors, including better transport facilities and other additional trade facilitation measures. Much will also depend on whether Bangladesh's exports have a real comparative advantage and whether there is trade complementarity between the two countries.

Lack of proper transportation facilities and infrastructure are major handicaps for trade between the two countries. The problem of congestion at the land ports could be handled by ensuring expeditious clearance. Plans to create integrated check-posts are underway. The check-posts will clear goods, services and even people. These steps would also lead to a reduction in transaction costs.

Since at present there are few complementarities from the point of view of Bangladesh, India can help by encouraging its private sector to make investments in that country. Efforts are already underway to this effect but a lot would depend also on Bangladesh which needs to provide an environment that is conducive for Indian businesses.

Notes

1. Jayshree Sengupta, "Time to Boost India-Bangladesh Trade and Economic Relations," Observer Research Foundation, Issue Brief No. 10, August 2007, at http://www.orfonline.org/cms/export/orfonline/modules/issuebrief/attachments/jayshree_1188277048570.pdf
2. Please see the text of "Trade Agreement Between India And Bangladesh" at http://commerce.nic.in/trade/India_Bangladesh_Trade_ Agreement.pdf
3. Anand Kumar, "Indo-Bangladesh Trade Ties: Free Trade vs. Duty-free Access," Institute of Peace and Conflict Studies (IPCS), #1013, 15 April 2003, at http://www.ipcs.org/article/india-the-world/indo-bangladesh-trade-ties-free-trade-vs-duty-free-access-1013.html
4. Sanjib Pohit, Nisha Taneja, "India's Informal Trade with Bangladesh And Nepal: A Qualitative Assessment", Indian Council For Research On International Economic Relations, Working Paper No. 58, July, 2000
5. Ibid.
6. "Bangladeshi garment makers welcome duty waiver", *The Hindu Business Line*, 7 September 2011, at http://www.thehindu businessline.com/industry-and-economy/economy/article 2431845.ece

8

Bangladesh-India Trade and Investment: Bangladesh Perspectives

Mahfuz Kabir

Introduction

Bangladesh and India have long shared the common objective of fostering closer economic integration in South Asia. Bilateral trade and investment relations are currently of special interest to both countries. Bangladesh made substantial changes in its economic policies in the 1980s and 1990s, which resulted in an increased degree of integration with the global economy.[1] Still, the country is characterised as one that has the least liberal trade policy regimes in the world. The tariff overhang is very high indicating Bangladesh's reluctance to fix the trade policy regime at rates close to the Most Favoured Nation (MFN) rates.[2] On the other hand, after nearly four decades of de facto autarchy, India moved towards a market-driven trade regime in the early 1990s, which encompassed a significant series of reforms in industrial policy, the removal of most of the licencing and other nontariff barriers, domestic deregulation of private industry, and simplification of the trade regime.[3] Its tariff protection has been substantially reduced in recent years. Large tariff reductions took place in 2004-05 and 2005-06 for most industrial products, which led to a significantly lower and more uniform industrial tariff structure. The country's trade has been significantly liberalized over time. Due to geographical proximity and enhanced trade liberalization measures, bilateral trade between India and Bangladesh has been growing steadily since the early 1990s. However, imports from India have been much higher than exports to India, resulting in a yawning trade gap. Although

India's trade and investments in Bangladesh are less significant for it than for Bangladesh, closer economic integration with Bangladesh through increased trade and investment is perceived to be a very important means of reducing the economic and political differences, and ultimately ensuring greater economic prosperity and welfare for their citizens as both countries have long shared the common objective of closer economic integration.[4]

In this context, the objective of this chapter is to analyse the major trends and features of the Bangladesh-India bilateral trade and investment over the years, assess the barriers and the potential, and suggest policy recommendations for furthering trade and investment relations from the Bangladesh perspective. The paper has been organised as follows: after this brief introduction, section two discusses the volume and commodity composition of trade between the two countries. Section three briefly surveys and analyses India's direct investment in Bangladesh. Section four studies the issue of the trade deficit, prospects of a bilateral FTA, and the problems of tariff and non-tariff barriers (NTBs) which have been constraining trade. The conclusion offers some recommendations to strengthen trade and investment relations between the two countries.

Trade Volume and Composition

Imports and Exports

Bangladesh's volume of trade with India has witnessed significant growth in the last three decades. From a total trade of $63.6 million in 1980, it rose to $3.02 billion in 2009. The annual trade peaked at $3.82 billion in 2008. Bilateral trade has been dominated by mounting imports from India, from $55.59 million to $2.75 billion, with an exponential trend during this period that was marked by some fluctuations.

Exports to India have also witnessed a rising trend. From a meagre $8.01 million in 1980 they touched $268.23 million in 2009 - thus going up 32.5 times during this period. However, imports went up 46.43 times, which clearly outpaced the growth of exports (Figure 1).

Since the early 1980s, Bangladesh has become more dependent

Figure 1: Trend of Imports and Exports (million US$)

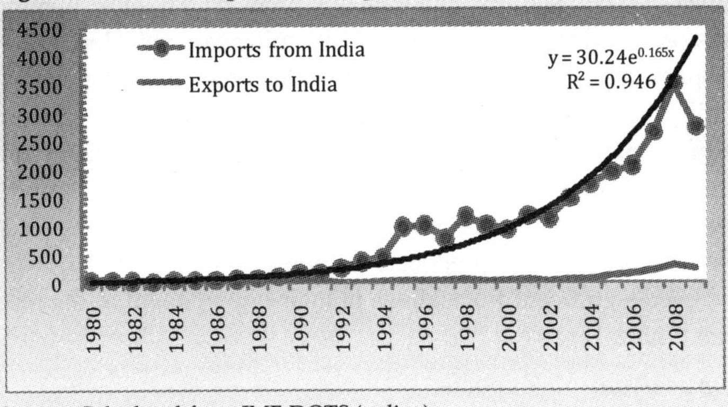

Source: Calculated from IMF-DOTS (online).

on imports from India. In the first half of 1980s, the ratio of imports from and exports to India and Bangladesh's imports from and exports to the world was almost equal. After this period, the share of Bangladesh's exports to India continued to decline compared to imports from India. From a scant 2.13 per cent in 1980, imports from India went up to 15.99 per cent in 1998, witnessing a slight decrease to 12.6 per cent in 2009 (Figure 2). At present India is the second-highest exporter of goods to Bangladesh after China.

Composition of Imports

Figure 2: Share of Bangladesh's Trade with India (%)

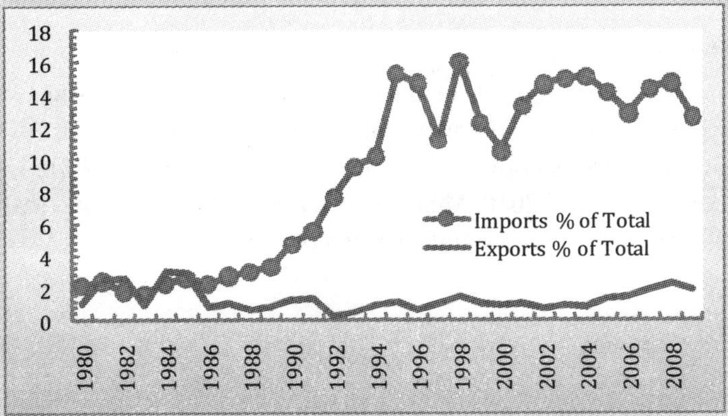

Source: Calculated from IMF-DOTS (online).

The top two commodity groups among imports from India are textiles and textile articles, and vegetable products. The other important items are machinery and mechanical appliances; vehicles, vessels, transport equipment, etc.; mineral products; products of the chemical or allied industries; and plastics, rubber and articles. Amongst these products, textiles and textile articles had the highest share in the recent past (24.98 per cent in fiscal year 2009-10), which was around a quarter of the total merchandised imports in the last five years. It was followed by vegetable products (15.26 per cent in 2009-10), which witnessed significant fluctuations in their import share in the recent years (Table 1).

Composition of Exports

The commodity composition of exports to India, however, presents a different picture in which the top two commodity groups are textiles and textile articles; and live animals and animal products. The other important export items are machinery and mechanical appliances; raw hides and skins; mineral products; products of the chemical or allied industries; prepared foodstuffs; and vegetable products. Amongst these exportable, textiles and textile articles had the overwhelmingly highest share in the recent past (56.16 per cent in fiscal year 2009-10), which was more than half of total merchandised exports in the last five years. This was followed by animals and animal products (10.31 per cent in 2009-10). Base metals and articles of base metal have acquired significant export share in the recent years (Table 2).

Investment

India's direct investment in Bangladesh has been increasing over the years. From a small amount of $2.73 million in end-June 2000, the stock of India's Foreign Direct Investment (FDI) reached $114.46 million by end-June 2010. Although increasing in magnitude and share, it has remained at an insignificant two per cent.

Table 1: Composition of Imports from India (per cent)

Items	*2005-06*	*2006-07*	*2007-08*	*2008-09*	*2009-10*
Live animals; animal products	0.71	0.54	1.22	0.93	1.26
Vegetable products	21.32	17.22	30.80	18.54	15.26
Animal or vegetable fats and oils and their cleavage products; prepared edible fats; animal or vegetable waxes	0.26	0.26	0.30	0.16	0.06
Prepared foodstuffs; beverages, sprits and vinegar; tobacco and manufactured tobacco substitutes	5.04	8.62	9.00	9.51	7.56
Mineral products	9.17	11.89	6.50	5.77	6.20
Products of the chemical or allied industries	9.05	8.80	7.74	10.19	9.57
Plastics and articles thereof; rubber and articles thereof	3.82	4.09	3.33	3.91	3.98
Raw hides and skins, leather fur skins and articles thereof; saddlery and harness; travel goods, handbags and similar containers; articles of animal gut (other than silk-worm gut)	0.06	0.06	0.10	0.06	0.08
Wood and articles of wood; wood charcoal; cork and articles of cork; manufactures of straw, of esparto or of other plaiting materials; basket ware and wickerwork	0.17	0.10	0.07	0.12	0.09
Pulp of wood or of other fibrous cellulosic material; recovered (waste and scrap) paper or paperboard; paper and paperboard and articles thereof	0.97	0.91	0.94	0.91	0.83
Textiles and textile articles	23.44	25.17	21.84	25.92	24.98

Source: Calculated from Export receipts of Bangladesh Bank (various issues)

Items	*2005-06*	*2006-07*	*2007-08*	*2008-09*	*2009-10*
Footwear, headgear, umbrellas, sun umbrellas, walking sticks, seat sticks, whips, riding crops and parts thereof; prepared feathers and articles made there with; artificial flowers; articles of human hair	0.10	0.15	0.11	0.11	0.17
Articles of stone, plaster, cement, asbestos, mica or similar materials; ceramic products; glass and glassware	0.38	0.35	0.31	0.46	0.44
Natural or cultured pearls, precious or semi-precious stones, precious metals, metals clad with precious metal and articles thereof; imitation jewellery; coin	0.08	0.03	0.03	0.03	0.01
Base metals and articles of base metal	7.71	6.79	5.18	6.95	9.08
Machinery and mechanical appliances; electrical equipment; parts thereof; sound recorders and reproducers, television image and sound recorders and reproducers; and parts and accessories of such articles	10.60	8.21	6.21	7.19	7.72
Vehicles, aircraft, vessels and associated transport equipment	5.75	5.78	5.55	7.91	11.52
Optical, photographic, cinematographic, measuring, checking, precision, medical or surgical instruments and apparatus; clocks and watches; musical instruments; parts and accessories thereof	1.04	0.65	0.47	0.82	0.81
Arms and ammunition; parts and accessories thereof	0.04	0.00	0.00	0.00	0.00
Miscellaneous manufactured articles	0.28	0.37	0.31	0.52	0.39
Works of art, collectors' pieces and antiques	0.00	0.00	0.00	0.00	0.01
Total	100.00	100.00	100.00	100.00	100.00

Source: Calculated from Import Payments of Bangladesh Bank (various issues).

Table 2: Composition of Exports to India (per cent)

Items	*2005-06*	*2006-07*	*2007-08*	*2008-09*	*2009-10*
Live animals; animal products	11.05	7.26	8.01	13.15	10.31
Vegetable products	5.53	2.36	4.39	4.45	0.86
Animal or vegetable fats and oils and their cleavage products; prepared edible fats; animal or vegetable waxes	2.19	2.58	1.12	0.00	0.00
Prepared foodstuffs; beverages, sprits and vinegar; tobacco and manufactured tobacco substitutes	1.86	1.68	1.92	3.75	3.27
Mineral products	1.10	6.87	15.84	9.89	8.94
Products of the chemical or allied industries	1.98	21.93	21.92	23.24	3.03
Plastics and articles thereof; rubber and articles thereof	3.06	2.00	0.16	0.60	0.75
Raw hides and skins, leather fur skins and articles thereof; saddlery and harness; travel goods, handbags and similar containers; articles of animal gut (other than silk-worm gut)	2.07	2.08	1.31	3.04	3.14
Wood and articles of wood; wood charcoal; cork and articles of cork; manufactures of straw, of esparto or of other plaiting materials; basket ware and wickerwork	0.25	0.41	0.82	0.62	0.35
Pulp of wood or of other fibrous cellulosic material; recovered (waste and scrap) paper or paperboard; paper and paperboard and articles thereof	0.06	0.04	0.04	0.03	0.06
Textiles and textile articles	61.90	39.22	34.29	33.92	56.16

Items	*2005-06*	*2006-07*	*2007-08*	*2008-09*	*2009-10*
Footwear, headgear, umbrellas, sun umbrellas, walking sticks, seat sticks, whips, riding crops and parts thereof; prepared feathers and articles made there with; artificial flowers; articles of human hair	0.20	0.21	0.14	0.09	0.12
Articles of stone, plaster, cement, asbestos, mica or similar materials; ceramic products; glass and glassware	0.17	0.90	1.14	2.36	1.38
Natural or cultured pearls, precious or semi-precious stones, precious metals, metals clad with precious metal and articles thereof; imitation jewellery; coin	0.00	0.00	0.02	0.00	0.00
Base metals and articles of base metal	3.56	7.69	5.98	2.75	10.12
Machinery and mechanical appliances; electrical equipment; parts thereof; sound recorders and reproducers, television image and sound recorders and reproducers; and parts and accessories of such articles	4.63	4.16	2.32	1.51	0.88
Vehicles, aircraft, vessels and associated transport equipment	0.19	0.40	0.36	0.39	0.21
Optical, photographic, cinematographic, measuring, checking, precision, medical or surgical instruments and apparatus; clocks and watches; musical instruments; parts and accessories thereof	0.02	0.02	0.00	0.02	0.00
Miscellaneous manufactured articles	0.19	0.18	0.22	0.19	0.42
Total	100.00	100.00	100.00	100.00	100.00

Source: Calculated from Export Receipts of Bangladesh Bank (various issues).

Table 3: India's FDI Stock in Bangladesh

Period	*FDI in million US$*	*Percentage of Total*
End-June 2000	2.73	0.14
End-June 2001	10.68	0.51
End-June 2002	12.44	0.53
End-June 2003	12.25	0.47
End-June 2004	18.84	0.66
End-June 2005	18.72	0.56
End-June 2006	23.20	0.61
End-June 2007	27.25	0.62
End-June 2008	41.26	0.86
End-June 2009	47.37	0.92
End-June 2010	114.46	1.92

Source: Foreign Direct Investment in Bangladesh, Survey Report, January-June, 2010. Bangladesh Bank.

India's FDI in Bangladesh is mainly in financial services, textiles and readymade garments (RMG), chemicals and pharmaceuticals, telecommunications and information technology. During January-June 2010, Bangladesh received $32.68 million FDI from India of which the banking sector got almost nearly 92 per cent, followed by textiles (3.5 per cent) and agriculture (1.6 per cent).

Figure 3: Sectors of India's FDI in Bangladesh, January-June 2010

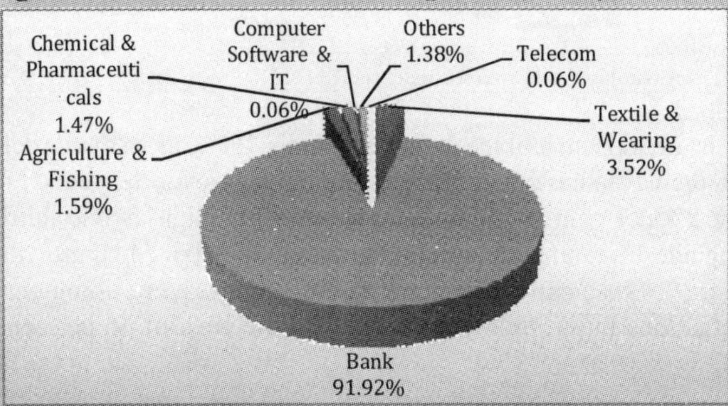

Source: Foreign Direct Investment in Bangladesh, Survey Report, January-June, 2010. Bangladesh Bank.

During his visit to Bangladesh, the commerce minister of India Anand Sharma said that the Indian private sector has plans to invest $3.5 billion in Bangladesh mainly in the telecommunication, pharmaceutical, food processing and household appliances sectors. Indian mobile company Airtel, which has already invested $300 million, plans to invest an additional $500 million.[5]

Issues Related to Bilateral Trade

Trade Deficit

The huge trade deficit is a most important concern for Bangladesh with regard to bilateral trade. The annual deficit shows a rising trend. It went up from $166.69 million to $2.48 billion in 2009 with some major fluctuations during the second half of 1990s. It, however, peaked in 2008 at $3.18 million. Apart from an exponential trend in the annual deficit, the cumulative trade deficit has touched $24.79 billion over the last three decades.

Figure 4: Trade Gap with India

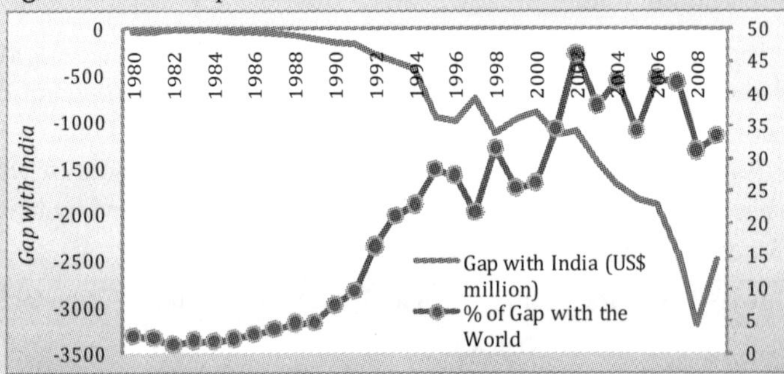

Source: Author's calculation based on IMF-DOTS.

In addition, to its trade deficit with India, Bangladesh's trade deficit with the world has also increased significantly over the years. From only 2.6 per cent in 1980, it increased to as high as one-third of Bangladesh's total trade deficit. However, an exponential growth up to mid-1990s, can be observed while there were some major fluctuations in the following years with the peak of 46 per cent in 2002.

Recently some initiatives have been taken by India to reduce the huge trade imbalance. During his recent visit to Bangladesh, the Indian commerce minister said that India has agreed to increase the import of readymade garment products from the existing 8 million to 10 million pieces. Bangladesh, however, demanded that this be increased to 20 million pieces.[6]

Free Trade Area

There have been some strong arguments for regional economic integration in South Asia, as it will generate significant intra-regional trade and welfare gains for South Asian countries. The potential benefits expected from the South Asian Free Trade Area (SAFTA) and other regional trading arrangements in South Asia are minimal because there are limited complementarities in the region as the main trading partners of individual South Asian countries are in the West. It is also alleged that a Regional Trading Arrangement (RTA) in South Asia will lead to substantial trade diversion rather than trade creation and it may become a stumbling bloc for multilateral trade liberalisation. Keeping these in mind, it is imperative for Bangladesh to look for some other alternatives in order to reduce its mounting trade deficit with India. One of such options would be to go in for bilateral Free Trade Agreements (FTAs). Two scenarios can be considered in this regard:

(i) FTA with India to reduce trade imbalance.

(ii) FTA with another major trading partner in South Asia to reduce trade deficit with India.

However since the trade deficit is most prominent with India and Pakistan, the possible impact on the trade balance can be examined by the following hypothetical scenarios of FTA with these countries.

As per Hossain and Kabir (2011), the application of the partial equilibrium model in the case of Bangladesh-India FTA, would lead to a substantial increase in exports between them, while Bangladesh's imports from its other neighbours would decrease to some extent[7]. The trade gap would still grow against Bangladesh but the additional trade gap would be proportionately very small (only 0.31 percent). However, FTA would help reduce trade gap with the other neighbours, the proportion would be insignificant (highest with Sri Lanka by 8.15 percent). The result would be significantly different in the case of the Bangladesh-Pakistan FTA; the trade gap with Pakistan would on the one hand substantially increase by such an FTA (57.71 percent), and

Table 4: Changes in Trade through Bangladesh-India and Bangladesh-Pakistan Bilateral FTA (Million US$), 2007

Direction of Effect	*Change due to FTA*	*Trade Gap with Bangladesh*	*Impact on the Gap - % Increase (+)/Decrease (-)*	*Direction of Effect*	*Change due to FTA*	*Trade Gap with Bangladesh*	*Impact on the Gap - % Increase (+)/Decrease (-)*
Bangladesh's Exports To India	452.416	-2,413.65	0.31 (+)	Bangladesh's Exports To Pakistan	4.034	-123.38	57.71(+)
India's Exports To Bangladesh	459.842			Pakistan's Exports To Bangladesh	75.235		
Others' Exports to Bangladesh				Others' Exports to Bangladesh			
Bhutan	..	-5.57	..	Bhutan	..	-5.57	..
Maldives	..	0.00	..	India	-3.733	-2413.65	0.15 (-)
Myanmar	-0.189	-23.89	0.79 (-)	Maldives	..	0.00	..
Nepal	-0.556	-11.19	4.97 (-)	Myanmar	-0.142	-23.89	0.59 (-)
Pakistan	-3.600	-123.38	2.92 (-)	Nepal	..	-11.19	..
Sri Lanka	-0.269	-3.30	8.15 (-)	Sri Lanka	-0.030	-3.30	0.91 (-)

Source: Hossain and Kabir. "Export Peromotion and External Issues : Present status and Future Developments" Sixth Five Year Plan of Bangladesh 2011-2015, Background Papers, 1, BIDS and Planning Commission, Dhaka, 2011.

on the other hand, the gaps with the other neighbours would decline marginally as compared to the Bangladesh-India FTA.

Table 5: Trade Balance Effect of Bangladesh-India FTA (Million US$)

Sectors	*Bangladesh*	*India*
Grains Crops	129.53	-172.51
Meat	-0.88	16.49
Extraction	18.61	45.19
Processed Food	4.53	0.99
Text and Wearing Apparel	-174.74	-32.07
Light Manufacturing	57.27	85.85
Heavy Manufacturing	58.53	-14.51
Utility and Construction	0.07	6.66
Transport and Communication	4.23	42.82
Other Services	11.32	117.94
Total	108.47	96.85

Source: Author's GTAP simulation.

The potential effect of Bangladesh-India FTA can also be studied by using a CGE model. The results of the Bangladesh-India FTA in Global Trade Analysis Project (GTAP) model reveal that by entering into a bilateral FTA, Bangladesh would come up with an overall positive trade balance effect of $108 million while for India it would be about $97 million. It indicates that an FTA would exert a positive influence on the trade balance of both countries. For Bangladesh, most of the positive trade balance would come from grains and crops, light and heavy manufacturing and extraction sectors. For India, most of the positive effect would come from light manufacturing, extraction, transport and communication and other services, based on the results of GTAP simulation.

Table 6: Changes in Value of Industrial Output (Million US$)

Sectors	*India*	*Sectors*	*Bangladesh*
Meat	11.74	Grains Crops	154.49
Extraction	40.73	Meat	6.98
Processed Food	12.45	Extraction	20.47
Light Manufacturing	106.30	Light Manufacturing	76.87
		Heavy Manufacturing	80.59
Transport and Communication	4.02	Transport and Communication	33.50
Other Services	96.70	Other Services	28.95

Source: Author's GTAP simulation.

Both countries would also get increased value for their industrial outputs in majority of the sectors. Most of the increased value for India would come from light manufacturing, extraction and other services. For Bangladesh, most of the value increase would come from grains and crops, light and heavy manufacturing, and transport and communications.

Tariff and Non-Tariff Barriers

In Bangladesh there is a general perception that tariff and non-tariff barriers (NTBs) imposed by India significantly restricts the market access of Bangladeshi products to India compared to that of Indian products in Bangladesh. It has been calculated that India imposes a higher average tariff on Bangladeshi products compared to the tariif imposed on Indian products in the Bangladesh market. Out of the ten broad product groups (according to harmonised system 1 level), six product groups of Bangladesh attract higher applied average tariffs in the Indian market. These are (i) meat, fish, dairy products, etc.; (ii) cereals, oil, sugar, etc.; (iii) edible preparations, beverage, tobacco, etc.; (iv) pharmaceuticals, fertilisers, plastics; (v) glass, metal products, etc.; and (vi) mechanical and electrical products (Table 7).

Table 7: Bilateral Applied Average Tariff, 2007

	On Indian Products	*On Bangladeshi Products*
Meat, fish, dairy products, etc.	20.01	35.50
Cereals, oil, sugar, etc.	15.52	43.25
Edible preparations, beverage, tobacco, etc.	10.73	27.77
Pharmaceuticals, fertilisers, plastics	13.09	13.20
Leather, wood and paper products	16.81	12.25
Silk, wool, cotton products	17.98	12.89
Apparel, footwear, umbrella, etc.	22.78	12.50
Glass, metal products, etc.	14.83	14.87
Mechanical, electrical products	10.89	13.29
Ship, optical, toy, furniture	14.04	12.50
Average	**14.20**	**16.75**

Source: Author's calculation from TRAINS database.

With regard to the demand for duty free entry of 61 Bangladeshi products India allowed duty-free access to 46 products during Prime Minister Manmohan Singh's visit in September 2011 and to another 15 products in November 2011. Amongst these products, 47 are textiles, and the others are leather and leather products.[8] This initiative has been a major milestones in the bilateral trade relations.

However, the imposition of strong NTBs has long been one of the major obstacles to bilateral trade. NTBs prevail in the forms of tariff rate quotas, restricted ports of entry, import bans, and the excessive use of health, sanitary and phyto-sanitary measures. The use of NTBs is justified by India under GATT Articles II-2(b), XVII-1(b), XX, etc.[9] For long, Bangladesh's complaints against India have included the excessive documentation requirements, varying methods of assessing duties, expensive mandatory certificates for meeting technical and health standards that need to be collected from distant locations such as Kolkata and Delhi, non-recognition of Bangladeshi certification and testing laboratories, etc. India's NTBs also include ad hoc change of policies regarding various tariff quotas, limited designated ports of entry and administrative procedures.

Table 8: Non-Tariff Barriers[10]

Country	*Non-Tariff Barriers*
Bangladesh	Health, religious, environmental and balance of payments purposes: ▪ Quantitative restrictions ▪ Quasi- QRs ▪ Import through state trading enterprises ▪ Restricted port of entry
India	▪ Tariff rate quotas ▪ Import through state trading enterprises ▪ Health and sanitary regulations (quarantine fees) ▪ Restricted ports of entry and inland customs ports ▪ Anti-dumping and countervailing duties ▪ Customs valuation

Conversely, there is a corresponding lack of information regarding NTBs as well as lack of common definitions and methodologies, inadequate quantity and quality of data, and ways and means of quantifying the impact of NTBs on trade. Problems also arise in trying to identify NTBs because of conflicting perceptions of individual firms across different sectors. Sanitary and phyto-sanitary (SPS) certifications and laboratory testing results are not universally recognised among SAARC members. Health and safety standards and regulations are often applied in a discriminatory manner and supporting scientific evidence is often not available to justify the imposition of SPS.[11]

Very recently, India has agreed to withdraw the non-tariff barriers on two jute products from Bangladesh. Besides, certification by Bangladesh Standards and Testing Institution for 15 imported products has been approved by the Indian authority.[12]

Trade Facilitation Measures

Both India and Bangladesh are reluctant to implement trade facilitation measures. One of the key areas for trade facilitation is to improve the efficiency of customs authorities to facilitate efficient management of cross border trade. Customs clearance procedures are generally cumbersome and time consuming[13]. However, some changes have taken place because of customs automation, which has improved the overall state trade facilitation.

Table 9: Gain in Bilateral Trade from Capacity Development[14] (US$ millions)

Country	*Customs Mode-rnization*	*Regulatory Reforms*	*Port Efficiency (Air and Marine)*	*Services Infra-structure*	*Total Gain*
Bangladesh	144	71	228	339	782
India	193	123	314	519	1,149

Source : J. Wilson and T. Otsuki, "Regional Integration in South Asia: What Role for Trade Facilitation", Policy Research Working Paper No. 4423, Washington: World Bank 2007.

The countries also suffer from inefficient ports (sea and land based) and airports, which lead to severe congestion and delays. Most of the land customs stations have been found to be inefficient; only one station in India (Raxaul) has recently been found to be efficient. Bangladesh also suffers from congestion and inefficiency at major ports, especially Chittagong (sea) and Benapole (land), which affects its trade with India and other parts of the world.[15]

Table 10: Efficiency of Land Customs Stations: DEA Scores

DMU (land customs stations)	*Country*	*2001*	*2002*	*2003*	*2004*	*2005*	*2006*
Petrapole	India	0.510	0.490	0.500	0.570	0.550	0.620
Benapole	Bangladesh	0.040	0.020	0.030	0.030	0.040	0.050
Raxaul	India	0.330	0.170	0.400	0.590	0.690	1.000
Jaigaon	India	0.320	0.830	0.610	0.740	0.560	0.520
Burimari	Bangladesh	0.010	0.000	0.010	0.010	0.010	0.010
Bangla-bandha	Bangladesh	0.000	0.010	0.010	0.010	0.010	0.000

Source : P. De, S. Chaturvedi and A.R. Khan "Transit and Border Trade Barriers in South Asia" In S. Ahmed, S. Kelegama and E. Ghani (eds.), *Promoting Economic Cooperation in South Asia : Beyond SAFTA*, India/California/London/Singapore: Sage, pp. 139-173

There is also inefficient coordination and an institutional deficit across three major ministries dealing with transport, commerce, and customs administration. There is rampant in efficiency in the port and customs administration in India. State-level (provincial) border crossings are run inefficiently; there are frequent complaints of rent seeking and harassment in the name of security. There are also problems of: overlapping jurisdictions in the implementation of border-related procedures, which leads to delays; discretionary powers of the officials that provide them with the opportunity of rent-seeking, and lack of transparency. 'Redtapism' is also a prominent reason for the inefficiency that prevails at the Indo-Bangladesh border.[16]

Table 11: Trade-Related Governance/Institutional Indicators, 2009[17]

Indicators	*Bangladesh*	*India*
Trade Policy Ranking (out of 125)	**97**	**102**
Non-tariff measures frequency ratio (%)	9.8*	..
Institutional Environment Ranking (out of 183)	**119**	**133**
Ease of Doing Business (out of 183)	119	133
WGI - Regulatory Quality (-2.5 to +2.5, best)**	-0.82	-0.21
Rule of Law**	-0.70	0.12
Trade Facilitation Ranking (out of 155)	**79**	**47**
Efficiency of customs and other border procedures (1 to 5 best)	2.3	2.7
Quality of transport and IT infrastructures (1 to 5)	2.5	2.9
Timeliness of shipment (1 to 5)	3.5	3.6
Doing Business - Trading Across Borders (rank out of 183)	107	94
Other Indicators		
Average time to clear exports through customs (days)	8	15&
Average number of times firms spent in meetings with tax officials	1	3&
Business entry rate (new registrations as % of total)	8$	3&

Note: * data for 2000-04; ** data for 2008; *** data for 2007; $ data for 2005; & data for 2006; ^ data for 2004.

Conclusion

This chapter captures the salient features of Bangladesh-India bilateral trade and investment over the years from the Bangladesh perspective. The major traded items are textiles and RMG, vegetables and animal products, prepared foodstuffs, and chemical and chemical products. The major sectors of India's FDI in Bangladesh are banking, textiles, agriculture and chemicals and pharmaceuticals. The bilateral trade figures reveal that both exports to and imports from India show a rising trend of the balance of trade going against Bangladesh. In order to reduce trade deficit, a bilateral FTA would be a preferred option for both the countries since it would create a positive trade balance and increases value of their output in a majority of the sectors. The chapter, however, reveals that there are many trade constraining factors such as cumbersome and inefficient port and customs procedures, tariff and NTBs and trade related governance problems. In order to overcome these problems and facilitate trade and investments, the following recommendations can be taken on board:

Trade

- Tariff on Bangladeshi products in Indian market is higher than that of Indian products in Bangladesh. In order to facilitate Bangladesh's exports to Indian market, India's tariff rate should be reduced.
- Vis-à-vis the South Asia Free Trade Agreement (SAFTA) and BIMSTEC FTA, Bangladesh and India should opt for a bilateral FTA to address prominent trade deficit. However, careful attention should be paid to the industries and sectors which may be adversely affected.
- The two countries should commit to eliminate NTBs to facilitate better trading relations between them. The following steps could be taken to make this happen:
    - better cooperation in identifying and classifying trade restrictive measures
    - creation of NTB notification systems and online inventories for better monitoring
    - human and institutional capacities should be strengthened for collecting and analysing data on NTBs

- technical assistance should be extended to firms to help meet technical standards

However, one way to minimise the use of NTBs is to follow rules and regulations that needs to be clearly laid out. Simplification of border crossings, better trade facilitation and development of efficient infrastructure including introduction of modern technology could bring much of the NTBs to a minimum level.

- International standard multi-agency testing laboratories should be established at major land customs stations where ever it is feasible, or authorise nearby laboratories to conduct testing.
- The "behind-the border" constraints must be overcome. This includes transparency and accountability of public institutions, improving services at sea and airports, and ending red tapism.

Investment in Bangladesh

- Diversification of FDI is required in order to promote industrial growth, employment and efficient use of resources available in the country.
- The Bangladesh government needs to reduce infrastructural constraints, e.g., roads, railways, and waterways, and increase the capacity and efficiency of sea and airports.
- Increase supply of electricity to promote industrial production, especially in the Export Processing Zones (EPZs).
- Streamline the process of FDI registration, connection of basic utilities, and reduce bureaucratic hurdles.
- Make land acquisition easy for foreign investment.

Notes

1. M.A. Hossain and N.D. Karunaratne, "Trade Liberalisation and Technical Efficiency: Evidence from Bangladesh Manufacturing Industries', *Journal of Development Studies*, 40, 2004, pp. 87-114; R. Jenkins and K. Sen (2006), "International Trade and Manufacturing Employment in the South: Four Country Case Studies", *Oxford Development Studies* 34, 2006, pp. 299-322.
2. M. Kabir, *Trade Response to Preferential Liberalization: Evidence from Some Emerging Asian Countries*, Lambert,, Germany, 2010.
3. K. Sen, "Trade Policy, Equipment Investment and Growth in India", *Oxford Development Studies*, 30, 2002, pp. 317-331; World Bank,

"India-Bangladesh Bilateral Trade and Potential Free Trade Agreement", Bangladesh Development Series Paper 13, Dhaka: World Bank, 2006; and R. Hasan, D. Mitra and K.V. Ramaswamy, "Trade Reforms, Labour Regulations, and Labour-Demand Elasticities: Empirical Evidence from India", *Review of Economics and Statistics*, 89, 2007, pp. 466-481.

4. World Bank (2006), Ibid.
5. See, for details, *Daily Sun*, Dhaka, 24 April 2011.
6. *Daily Sun*, Dhaka, 24 April 2011.
7. M.I Hossain and M. Kabir, "Export Promotion and External Issues: Present Status and Future Developments". *Sixth Five Year Plan of Bangladesh 2011-2015: Background Papers* (Volume 1: Macroeconomic Issues), Bangladesh Institute of Development Studies (BIDS) and Planning Commission, Dhaka, 2011, pp. 189-257.
8. *Daily Sun*, Dhaka, 24 April 2011; Holiday, Dhaka, 18 November 2011.
9. GATT Article II-2 mentions, "Nothing in this Article shall prevent any contracting party from imposing at any time on the importation of any product ... (b) any anti-dumping or countervailing duty applied consistently with the provisions of Article VI". Article XVII-1(b) states, "(b) The provisions of subparagraph (a) of this paragraph shall be understood to require that such enterprises shall, having due regard to the other provisions of this Agreement, make any such purchases or sales solely in accordance with commercial considerations,* including price, quality, availability, marketability, transportation and other conditions of purchase or sale, and shall afford the enterprises of the other contracting parties adequate opportunity, in accordance with customary business practice, to compete for participation in such purchases or sales.", Article XX says, "Subject to the requirement that such measures are not applied in a manner which would constitute a means of arbitrary or unjustifiable discrimination between countries where the same conditions prevail, or a disguised restriction on international trade, nothing in this Agreement shall be construed to prevent the adoption or enforcement by any contracting party of measures: ... (b) necessary to protect human, animal or plant life or health.
10. U. Wickramasinghe, "Operationalizing SAFTA: Issues and Options", in *South Asian Yearbook of Trade and Development,* 2006, pp. 389-414.
11. ADB and FICCI, *Key Proposals for Harnessing Business Opportunities in South Asia*, ADB, Manila.

12. *Daily Sun*, Dhaka, 24 April 2011.
13. J. Roy and P. Banerjee, "Connecting South Asia: The Centrality of Trade Facilitation for Regional Economic Integration", in S. Ahmed, S. Kelegama and E. Ghani (eds.), *Promoting Economic Cooperation in South Asia: Beyond SAFTA*, Sage Publications, India/California/London/Singapore, 2010, pp.110-138.
14. J. Wilson and T. Otsuki, "Regional Integration in South Asia: What Role for Trade Facilitation", *Policy Research,* Working Paper No. 4423, World Bank, Washington 2007.
15. P. De, S. Chaturvedi and A.R. Khan, "Transit and Border Trade Barriers in South Asia" in S. Ahmed, S. Kelegama and E. Ghani (eds.), *Promoting Economic Cooperation in South Asia: Beyond SAFTA*, Sage Publications, India/California/London/Singapore, 2010, pp. 139-173.
16. N. Banik and J. Gilbert, "Regional Integration and Trade Costs in South Asia", Working Paper No. 127, Asian Development Bank Institute, Tokyo, 2008.
17. World Bank, *World Trade Indicators*, World Bank, Washington, 2010.

9

Cooperation on the Water Issue: Bangladesh Perspectives

Segufta Hossain

Introduction

Water is a vital resource for Bangladesh. The life and living of her people as well as the eco-system are totally dependent on it. For Bangladesh water is a means of survival. Human civilisation in the deltaic region of the sub continent has been sustained by the three major rivers – the Ganges, the Brahmaputra and the Meghna (GBM) - and their countless tributaries and distributaries. The entire life support system of the country is built around these rivers and wetlands. The rivers of Bangladesh impact both the physiography of the nation and the life of the people. The rivers serve as the main source of water for cultivation and as the principal arteries for transportation. Rivers also provide food for the people of the country. The fisheries sector provides 65 per cent of the country's animal protein.[1] The flooding of the rivers during the monsoon causes enormous hardship and hinders development, but fresh deposits of rich silt replenish the fertile the soil. The rivers also drain the excess monsoon rainfall into the Bay of Bengal. All these facts are indicative of the dependence of Bangladesh on its water resources. Rain water in Bangladesh accounts for only 7 per cent of the total fresh water flow and the remaining 93 per cent comes from trans-boundary river sources that are rain and ice-melt fed and flow into the riverine system of Bangladesh.[2]

The two primary sources of water are the local rainfall, mainly between July and October; and trans-boundary inflows mainly from the Ganges, Brahmaputra and Meghna rivers, which have maximum flows between July and October. Low-lying and riverine Bangladesh is situated on a delta plain at the confluence of the Ganges-Brahmaputra-Meghna (GBM) river systems. The country is criss-crossed by these three rivers and their innumerable tributaries and distributaries. The GBM river basin covers an area of about 1.75 million sq. km. stretching across Bangladesh (7.4 per cent), India (62.9 per cent), Nepal (8.0 per cent), Bhutan (2.6 per cent) and China (19.1 per cent). The country is faced with the dual problems of the shortage of water during the dry season and its abundance during the monsoon. Being the lowest riparian of the GBM river system, this country bears the brunt of floods, discharging over 80 per cent of the GBM basins wide run off within the five months of the rainy season and receives residual flows from the trans-boundary rivers during the lean season.[3]

Water determines the performance of a number of economic sectors in Bangladesh, including agriculture, fisheries, industry and commerce, navigation and health. Water scarcity in Bangladesh is creating havoc in every sector. The inland capture of fisheries has been declining because of lack of water in the dry season caused by the loss of perennial wetlands, irrigation abstractions, encroachment and pollution. Inland water transport has also been adversely affected by siltation, declining flows and a deteriorating water management infrastructure. These problems have not been addressed due to lack of adequate financial assistance. Against this backdrop, the present chapter seeks to discuss the water scarcity scenario in Bangladesh, challenges to cooperation on water issues and offers some solutions to overcome these problems. This chapter is divided into five sections including introduction and conclusions and recommendations. The second section discusses water as a security issue; the water scarcity scenario of Bangladesh is discussed in the third section and the fourth section deals with the challenges to cooperation on water issues.

Water: A Security Concern

Water is considered to be one of the most crucial security issues as it affects the life of common people and is linked to the economy of the country. Water security is essential for human health, well being, economic and political stability and it is thus essential to limit risks posed by water related issues. A complete and fair valuation of the resource, the sustainability of the ecosystem at all stages of the hydrologic cycle and an equitable and cooperative sharing of water resources is very necessary. It is ironic that our planet that has 70 per cent of its surface covered with water is facing an acute water crisis. More than 97.5 per cent of this water is ocean which is salty. The remaining 1.725 per cent is in the form of glaciers, snow and permafrost. Ground water accounts for 0.075 per cent while lakes, swamps and rivers have 0.025 per cent water.[4] The United Nations Environment Programme (UNEP) reported in 1999 that 200 scientists in 50 countries identified water shortage as one of the most worrying problems for the new millennium. We use about 70 per cent of this water in agriculture. The World Water Council believes that by 2020 we shall need 17 per cent more water than is available, if we are to feed the world.[5]

For over five millennia water has been South Asia's most critical resource.[6] Today throughout South Asia water has assumed even greater economic and political significance. Current trends show that the scarcity of water is on the increase and in the distant future this scarcity would take on a grievous form. In Asia, the per capita availability of water has declined by 40 – 60 per cent between 1955 and 1990.[7] It is estimated that over the next 40 years, the world will need to double its food production to meet the growing population – set to increase by around 50 per cent in next 50 years.[8] The South Asian region, which is home to 40 per cent of world population, will have a greater need for water than today. The water issue has therefore begun to figure prominently in term of human security. Water is a central factor in the world's developmental challenges. Whether it is food, energy, health, climate change, pollution and socio-economic development – water is a necessity.

The Himalayan river basins in China, Nepal, India and Bangladesh are home to about 1.3 billion people i.e. almost 20 per cent of the world's population and almost 50 per cent of the total population of these countries. About 10-20 per cent of the Himalayan rivers are fed by glaciers – and are an important source of water in the lean season. According to some studies, the glaciers will be seriously affected by global warming by 2350.[9] Bangladesh will bear the brunt of the melting of glaciers as her main rivers originate in these Himalayan glaciers. According to media reports, about 80 rivers are going to vanish in Bangladesh, while 100 have already lost their natural characteristics due to the upstream withdrawal of water by building dams and barrages.[10] Water availability on a per capita cubic metre basis is estimated to decline from 7320 to 5700 in the case of Bangladesh.[11] In addition to shrinking rivers, all countries will face the problems caused by the loss of permafrost[12], deforestation and the disappearance of lakes. The cumulative effect of water scarcity, glacial melting, disruptive precipitation patterns, flooding, desertification, pollution and soil erosion will lead to a massive reduction in the production of rice, wheat, maize and fish. Water scarcity, decline in food availability, reduction in livelihood opportunities in rural areas, desertification, soil erosion, sea-level rise and construction of dams will lead to displacement and migration of 50-70 million people in four countries by 2050.[13] Bangladesh as one of the world's largest and dynamic deltaic countries is particularly vulnerable to this threat.

Water Scarcity: Bangladesh Scenario

The main sources of water in Bangladesh are rivers and ground water. Bangladesh is called the land of rivers as it has about 700 rivers including tributaries.[14] The total length of all the rivers, streams, creeks and channels is about 24,140 km.[15] There are 57 trans-boundary rivers that Bangladesh shares with her neighbouring countries: 54 with India and 3 with Myanmar. In terms of catchment size, river length and volume of discharge, some of these rivers are amongst the largest on the earth. Being an agrarian and riverine country, Bangladesh in particular is heavily dependent on water for human consumption, crop irrigation, transportation and conservation of biodiversity. This great river system is the country's principal resource as well as its greatest hazard. As of now the insufficient water flows in rivers, depletion of ground water levels, and rapid population growth have made the region highly vulnerable to water stress. The gap between demand and supply is likely to further worsen because of the impact of climate change on weather patterns. The impact on precipitation is likely lead to erratic and uncertain rainfall patterns influencing the flow of the rivers.

With a growing population, Bangladesh is facing more and more difficulties in managing her limited water resources. An average Bangladeshi uses roughly 40 litres of water per day for household use and the demand for irrigation water is gradually increasing.[16] The growing population increases the demand for food. This has led Bangladesh to grow more crops which in turn mean more water for irrigation. Rice production for every individual requires over 800 m^3 of water[17] which multiplied by the population of Bangladesh, means that water demands can become enormous. As the demand for water increases, the share of water per person will decrease, gradually resulting in a greater demand for water.

The water scarcity of Bangladesh has two dimensions. The internal dimension of water scarcity is the contaminated ground and surface water. Ground water supplies 80 per cent of the water that people use. This source is depleting because of the shortage of surface water and inadequate tree plantation. This leads to increased arsenic levels in under-ground water. Waterways have been the principal mode of transportation in riverine Bangladesh over the ages. However, since the completion of the Farakka barrage, Bangladesh's waterways have been severely affected and some of them have been put out of service. About 685 km of waterways were available in the pre-diversion era, which are now reduced to only 230 km now. Pre-diversion, the Ganges could be navigated by large steamers even in the dry season. Bangladesh received only 261 cusecs of water at the Harding Bridge in March 1993 compared to the 1980 cusecs which used to flow through this point the same month in the pre-Farakka years.[18] The Gorai, the Madhumati, the Bhairab, the Arial Khan, the Kapotakkhya and the Mathabhanga have also lost their flow due to the decreasing flow of the Ganges. Fish stocks are declining in rivers and wet lands. Many people have been forced to give up fish cultivation. One study shows that a large number of people are now involved in non-river based activities like rickshaw pulling. The number of fishermen in the south west of Bangladesh dropped from 6 per cent to only 0.5 per cent while rickshaw pullers increased from 1.3 per cent to 5.9 per cent.[19] Jobless and landless village people migrate to cities and towns, swelling the ranks of internal migrants and staking a claim to the limited urban amenities.

The external dimension has also contributed to the water scarcity. Being a lower riparian, Bangladesh faces the negative consequences of the withdrawal of water by the upper riparian countries like India, China and Nepal by the building of dams and embankments. Thus there are various reasons for the water scarcity in Bangladesh which are as follows:

Water Sharing of the Trans-boundary Rivers

Bangladesh faces the problem of flooding during every monsoon (June-September). During each monsoon one-third of the country is affected by flood and the remaining two-third areas are also vulnerable to flood. As the country is lower riparian and the sources of the major rivers are in the Himalayan glaciers, the country is totally dependent on the neighbouring upper riparian countries for the proper flow of water in its rivers. The main causes for problems in the sharing of the waters of trans-boundary rivers include the:

- Farakka Barrage
- River Linking Project (RLP)
- Tipaimukh Dam

Water diversion at Farakka has severely affected the natural flow in the downstream of the Ganges. The Ganges and most of its distributaries have a major surface water deficit. Some of them are almost dying while some others get dried up during the dry season.[20] Agriculture, navigation, irrigation, fisheries, forestry, industrial and economic activities have all been impacted by this. At the same time salinity intrusion in the coastal rivers, ground water depletion, riverbed silting, coastal erosion and sedimentation are also on the rise.

The Farakka Barrage has so far been the most pressing issue for Bangladesh not only in terms of the sharing of the waters of the Ganges but also in respect of the entire relationship spectrum of the two riparian states. The withdrawal of water at Farakka has wrought significant changes in the hydrological system of the Ganges basin in Bangladesh. Up to 40 per cent of the dry season flow of the Ganges has been diverted upstream following the completion of the Farakka Barrage in India in 1974.[21] It is also observed that the groundwater sinking rate is at least 0.5 m/year and the total drop in the water table is about 10 metres in the south-western districts of Bangladesh.[22] The decreased supply of water in the Gorai river due to the diversion of water at Farakka, is by and large, responsible for the increase of salinity in the south-western region of Bangladesh. Reduced freshwater flows cause increased saline intrusion, particularly in the dry season. The salinity front has travelled up to 280 km upstream from sea.[23]

River Linking Project (RLP)

India's river linking project includes both the Himalayan and peninsular rivers of India. It is proposed that the Brahmaputra would be linked with the Ganges to carry waters to Orissa and eventually to South India. The project will divert water from the Brahmaputra towards the Ganges, thereafter driving it into the Mahanadi and Godavari. The Godavari will be linked to the Krishna and then to the Pennar and Cauvery. The Narmada will flow into the Tapti and the Yamuna into the Sabarmati.[24]. The left tributaries of the Ganges would also be linked at several places and the increased volume of water in the Ganges would then be channelled to Rajasthan, Gujarat and Maharashtra. The eastern peninsular rivers would be linked with western peninsular ones and water would also be transferred to southern Karnataka and Kerala.[25] The project also envisages the construction of water reservoirs at many places throughout the length and breadth of India. The RLP will connect 38 rivers through 30 links, 9000 km long canals, 74 reservoirs and several embankments by 2016. The project is estimated to cost between $112 billion to $ 200 billion.[26] If the project is implemented, the Brahmaputra's flow will be reduced to 40,000 cusecs from its normal flow of 1,40,000 cusecs while the combined flow of Padma and Brahmaputra at Maowa point will also be reduced to 30,000 – 40,000 cusecs from the normal flow of 2,00,000 cusecs. There will be no flow in the Dharla, Dhudhkumar, Teesta and Mahananda rivers even during a normal monsoon. Flows in Madhumati, Nabaganga, Ichamati, Mathabhanga, Kapotakhya and Betna will also be reduced substantially.

Tipaimukh Dam

India, in violation of its commitment made in the 36th Joint Rivers Commission (JRC) meeting in Dhaka, has floated an international tender for the construction of a dam at Tipaimukh on the Barak river in the state of Manipur to produce hydro-electricity despite dire warnings by experts regarding the dangers of such a project for the area and for lower riparian Bangladesh.[27] The proposed Tipaimukh dam is to be located 500 metres downstream from the confluence of Barak and Tuivai rivers at the south western corner of Manipur. The dam was originally conceived for containing only the flood waters of the Cachar plains of Assam but later on, the focus shifted to hydroelectric power generation. A high capacity dam with a height of 162.8 metres would thus be built in Tipaimukh. Two hundred and twenty six big dams would be built in suitable places in the south east of India to produce 99,000 megawatt electricity within the next 50 years.[28] It would be built parallel to the border of Karimganj in Assam above the river Barak which is the main stream of the branch rivers Surma and Kushiyara. Both these rivers conjointly create the river Meghna in Bangladesh. This river has a high speed stream and has a better capacity to contain sand than the River Padma. India has set a target of producing 50,000 megawatt of electricity by 2012. The Tipaimukh High Dam is situated very close to the Bangladesh border.[29] As a result Bangladesh would have less water in three rivers – the Meghna, Surma and the Kushiyara. This project would increase the rate of sedimentation as a result of less water low in the river which would gradually decrease the water carrying capacity of the river. This situation would aggravate the rate of sudden and frequent loods in the region. All these effects will be seen in the Northeastern region and especially in the *Haor* area of the country which would totally change the existing scenario in this area. The fertile land of the *Haor* would turn to desert. Agriculture would be destroyed. Rice varieties like Boro, Shail and Aman would be lost as well as the regional biodiversity.

Other Factors

Another matter of major concern to Bangladesh relates to the sharing of the waters of Teesta river, which is of vital importance to the people in northern areas of Bangladesh. According to the JRC, Bangladesh was supposed to get 2700 cusec of water, though the country is receiving a very small amount during the dry season. Bangladesh has been claiming an equal share of the water of the Teesta for long because it is anticipated that if the water is not shared proportionately and if India is not generous in sharing Teesta water, a number of districts (Nilphamari, Rangpur and Dinajpur, etc.) of Bangladesh might turn into deserts.[30]

Arsenic contamination is another serious problem, in Bangladesh. The depletion of ground water table has increased the risk of arsenic contamination in the ground water and it has increased the risk of arsenic poisoning through out the country. At present water in 61 out of 64 districts of Bangladesh is arsenic contaminated. About 1.5 to 2.5 million tube wells are estimated to be affected and 35 million people are at risk.[31] Arsenic contamination of groundwater is due to the withdrawal of freshwater upstream in India. A survey conducted by Ground Water Task Force has reported that 7 out of the 12 most arsenic contaminated districts are located in the Ganges basin where water of more than 70 per cent tube-wells exceeds the permissible limits of arsenic.[32]

Cooperation and Constraints in Water Sharing

All the countries of South Asia are already facing increasing stress and resource depletion due to environmental factors, and a primary challenge is water scarcity. Experts have identified water scarcity in emerging economies as one of the most challenging problems now and in the future. The Himalayan river basins that feed Bangladesh, India and Nepal are seriously threatened by water stress, and this has implications for internal and cross-boundary development and security. According to a UNEP study, among the South Asian countries, Bangladesh is the downstream and deltaic portion of a huge watershed, and is thereby naturally vulnerable due to the quantity and poor quality of water that flows into it from the upstream.[33] All the major rivers flowing through the country originate outside her borders. Thus any intervention in the upper riparian regions has a significant impact on Bangladesh.

The withdrawal of Ganges water by India has severely affected the natural flow of the downstream rivers and its distributaries, with adverse effects on agricultural production, fisheries, forestry, industrial activities, inland navigation, biodiversity, wetlands and so on. The soil fertility has considerably deteriorated and the crop yield has decreased. The annual loss to the agricultural sector is estimated to be about $650 million. It is also estimated that Bangladesh today could have been in a position to produce an additional 3.6 million tonnes of food grains annually if there had been natural flow in the Ganges and its distributaries.[34]

The 1996 Ganges water sharing treaty outlined a flow regime under varying conditions. But it did not contain any guarantee clause for the minimum amount of water for Bangladesh, nor did it contain any provision of equal sharing of flows in the case of shortage of water. The agreement did not take future hydrological parameters into account, ignoring the fact that the water flow at the Farakka point had declined drastically since 1988 as Uttar Pradesh and Bihar in India started drawing water much ahead of the Farakka Barrage.[35] Bangladesh has reportedly been receiving only half of the Ganges flow, compared to what it used to receive before the construction of the Farakka barrage.[36] Due to continuous withdrawal through the Farakka Barrage over the last 31 years, a significant number of rivers of the Padma basin of Bangladesh have already turned into dead rivers. The Gorai, a mighty pre-Farakka river is now almost dead. According to the Bangladesh Water Development Board, 17 rivers in Bangladesh are already dead.[37]

India's gargantuan river linking project that envisages the inter-basin transfer of water aims to addressing the water scarcity in the drier zones in the country. What concerns Bangladesh the most is the proposed diversion of the waters from the Brahmaputra to the Ganges for onward transfer. The resultant reduced flow of the Brahmaputra into Bangladesh and many other common rivers is likely to spell disaster for the lower riparian. As a matter of fact, India's river-linking project is a tremendous security threat to Bangladesh, both in the traditional and the non-traditional sense. The proposed River Linking Project would further reduce the inflow of freshwater from upstream which would gradually lead to a reduction of ground water.[38] The decreased water flow in the river will increase sedimentation as well as salinity intrusion in the rivers. The impact of the Indian river-linking project on Bangladesh will be multi-dimensional affecting agriculture, fisheries, navigation, environment, geomorphology, etc.

Apart from the river-linking project, the Indian authorities' decision to build a hydroelectric power plant at Tipaimukh will inflict huge damage on its downstream neighbour's economy, ecology and will mean disaster for its population. Experts argue that the completion of the project will hit Bangladesh fatally, and with no less a magnitude than the Farakka Barrage across the Ganges in the north-west of Bangladesh. The total ecosystem of this region would be jeopardised. If the rivers Surma and Kushiara lose their flow of water, the river Meghna would also lose its flow. Thus it is not only Sylhet and the *Haor* area that are in danger but also the areas around Meghna are at huge risk. The economy of the country and the normal life of the people of Bangladesh would be seriously impaired.

The river-linking projects will not only severely affect the people and the ecology of Bangladesh, but also that of the four states of India

– Assam, West Bengal, Orissa and Bihar. Besides this, the Tipaimukh Hydroelectric Project will affect, along with Bangladesh, a vast number of people in the state of Manipur in India. The Indian authorities, however, have proceeded with both the projects without even informing Bangladesh, let alone seeking its consent as a lower-riparian country, which is an obligation for the upper-riparian under international laws and conventions that bar building of any structure blocking natural flow of waters at any point before a confluence.

Apart from the management of the Ganges, the sharing of the water of 53 other international watercourses has remained unresolved for years. It is necessary to settle disputes over the water sharing of at least seven of the rivers – Teesta, Dharla, Dudhkumar, Manu, Muhuri, Khowai and Gumti – on a priority basis, with Teesta having the top priority. A Joint Technical Group (JTG) was formed to look into water availability in both countries and to work out interim India and Bangladesh shares. India constructed the Gazoldoba barrage a few months after Bangladesh started constructing the Teesta Barrage in 1983. India made Gazoldoba barrage operational after two years while Bangladesh made her barrage operational after seven years. India keeps the Gazoldoba barrage closed during winter and it has affected the river flow downstream and disrupted the navigability of Teesta river and the ecology of the northern districts of Bangladesh. There was some progress on this issue when the two countries agreed to sign a 15 years interim accord on sharing the waters of common rivers Feni and Teesta at a secretary-level meeting in January 2011.[39] The agreement was expected to be signed during the scheduled visit of Prime Minister Dr. Manmohan Singh to Bangladesh in September 2011. The countries have exchanged drafts of the interim agreement on the 'Principles of the Sharing of Teesta waters During the Dry Season' at the 37th meeting of India-Bangladesh Joint Rivers Commission in New Delhi in March 2011.[40] Both sides reportedly agreed to a 50-50 sharing of the water of Teesta river that originates in the Indian state of Sikkim and runs through West Bengal and Bangladesh.[41] But unfortunately all the efforts failed and India postponed the proposed Teesta water sharing deal when the Chief Minister of West Bengal, Mamata Banerjee, refused to accept the water sharing formula agreed upon by the Indian government saying that it would harm her state's interests. Although Prime Minister Manmohan Singh said that India would continue to work hard to arrive at a viable formula for sharing the water of Teesta river with Bangladesh, it is still not clear how long it will take for the two countries to reach an agreement on the matter. The failure of the Teesta deal also affected agreement on sharing Feni river water.

About 93 per cent of the catchment areas of the Ganges, Brahmaputra and the Meghna (GBM) rivers are located outside Bangladesh. It is estimated that the catchment area of the Ganges, Brahmaputra and Meghna rivers is 12 times the size of Bangladesh.[42] India, being economically and militarily more powerful and technologically more developed, tends to play an influential role in South Asia. The sharing of the waters of these international watercourses and common rivers has been the most persistent bone of contention between Dhaka and New Delhi, owing mainly to the unilateral upstream withdrawal of waters and structure-building by India with disastrous consequences for Bangladesh which affects the entire gamut of her relationship with India. Some analysts suggest that "water" is the determining factor of Bangladesh-India relations. India has sometimes been insensitive to the rights, needs and concerns of Bangladesh with regard to the fair sharing of common river resources. Bangladesh finds itself in an unenviable and helpless situation on the management of her water resources.

5. Conclusion and Recommendation

Water is essential not only to life, it is also an integral part of the economy, society and ecology. Diversion of water from major rivers causes immense sufferings to society as a whole. Water resources dominate the natural system of Bangladesh. Indeed, water is the key natural resource of the country. Bangladesh will face a severe water crisis within next couple of decades. The major sources of water for the country are trans-boundary rivers (76.5 per cent), rainwater and groundwater accounting only for 23 per cent and 1.5 per cent respectively.[43] Water withdrawal by the upper riparian countries, particularly in the dry season, makes the problems for Bangladesh critical and pervasive. According to water experts, as the origin of the main rivers of Bangladesh is outside the country, its river's depend on upstream water for their flow and the country will not be able to address water related problems without an integrated initiative with the neighbouring countries. As such, Bangladesh's response to the water issues must be developed and coordinated within the framework of the country's national security. It must receive highest priority, as it is a threat and the suggestions of the civil society organisations working on this issue should also be taken care at various levels such as to deal with the environmental and legal dimensions of the problem.

The trans-boundary rivers of pose a variety of water related challenges to the water sharing countries encompassing floods in the monsoon, water shortages in the dry months, sedimentation and erosion in the rivers and associated flood plains, drainage congestion in low-lying areas and environmental and water quality problems associated with human activities in the region. The fundamental objective of the countries is to secure vital national interests including people's survival, ecological sustainability and protection of socio-cultural stability. Multilateral cooperation regarding harnessing the vast water resources in the GBM basin is, therefore, a development challenge and constitutes a security imperative for the impoverished millions of the sub-region. Better management in the GBM basin is the way to achieve a water secure region. A multilateral water resource management initiative demands the involvement of all the five countries of the GBM river system – Bangladesh, India, China, Nepal, and Bhutan. The establishment of consultative bodies on the different aspects of river management will also facilitate the basin-wide management of the water resources of this region. Joint water management offers the scope for people-to-people and expert-to-expert connections, thus creating a channel for peaceful dialogue.

The current formal negotiation structures between the riparian countries of the region such as the Joint Rivers Commission do not seem to function as an effective platform for constructive and innovative dialogue on all the technical, managerial and political aspects of the issue. Civil society dialogue between the riparian countries on the subject of trans-boundary rivers could be a solution for this problem. A Track-3 approach (civil society – civil society) of the respective countries can strengthen the local voices which will ultimately reach the politicians and get reflected at the various international forums.

The water sharing practices of other trans-boundary rivers of the world can be taken as example to solve the water related crisis of this region. The Mekong River Commission (MRC)[44] and the Nile Basin Initiative (NBI)[45] can be taken as example of trans-boundary water sharing. SAARC, as a regional body, has not yet found any satisfactory way to solve the problem. The water issue of South Asia has a regional characteristics and the water crisis should be solved regionally by making it a collective effort under the SAARC umbrella.

Notes

1. The World Bank, *Bangladesh Country Water Resources Assistance Strategy*, Bangladesh Development Series - Paper No 3, December 2005, at:http://www-wds.worldbank.org/external/default/WDSContentServer/WDSP/IB/2006/03/21/000160016_ 20060321180655/Rendered/PDF/355520BDS30Water1 CAS01PUBLIC1.pdf
2. Qazi Kholiquazzaman Ahmad, "Water Water Everywhere, How Much Do We Have To Drink", *The Daily Star*, February 19, 2006.
3. Sufia Khanom, "Tipaimukh Dam: Likely Environmental Consequences for Bangladesh", *BIISS Journal*, Vol. 27(3), July 2006, pp. 223 - 249.
4. Ainun Nishat, "Climate Change Programme", IUCN - Asia Region, August 25, 2008.
5. Alex Kirby, "Dawn of a Thirsty Century", *BBC News*, at: http://news.bbc.co.uk/2/hi/science/nature/755497.stm
6. Rober W. Bradnock, "The Geopolitics of water sharing in South Asia: New Approaches to Old Problems?", Paper presented in the international Seminar on *Sharing of Water Resources in South Asia: A Case of Bangladesh* organized by Bangladesh Institute of International and Strategic Studies (BIISS) on November 26, 1995.
7. Spurgeon, 2000 cited in Yue Choong Kog, "Water Security in Southeast Asia", available at http://www.unesco.org/water/wwap/pccp/zaragoza/speakers/doc/Keynote_Speech_Kog.pdf
8. "Global Water Partnership, The Urgency of Water Security", at: http://www.gwp.org/en/The-Challenge/The-Urgency-of-Water-Security/
9. "The Himalayan Challenge: Water Security in Emerging Asia", available at: http://www.strategicforesight.com/Himalayan%20challenge% 20ES.pdf
10. Tarequl Islam Munna, "Bangladesh Among Countries Most hit by Climate Change", *The Daily Star*, December 20, 2008.
11. "The Himalayan Challenge: Water Security in Emerging Asia", n. 9.
12. In geology, permafrost, cryotic soil or permafrost soil is soil at or below the freezing point of water (0°C or 32°F) for two or more years.

13. "Himalayan Challenge: Water Security in Emerging Asia", n. 9.
14. "River and Drainage System", *Banglapedia*, Vol. 8, Asiatic Society of Bangladesh, March 2003, pp. 434 - 437.
15. Ibid.
16. Haroun Er Rashid and Babar Kabir, Case Study: Bangladesh - Water Resources and Population Pressures in the Ganges River Basin, Alex de Sherbinin and Victoria Dompka (eds.), *Water and Population Dynamics: Case Studies and Policy Implications*, at: http://www.aaas.org/international/ehn/waterpop/bang.htm
17. Ibid.
18. "Farakka Barrage", *Banglapedia*, Volume 4, Asiatic Society of Bangladesh, March 2003, p. 56.
19. See more details in Tajkera Khatun, "The Ganges Water Withdrawal in the Upstream at Farakka and Its Impact in the Downstream Bangladesh", M. Feroze Ahmed et.al. (ed.), *Regional Cooperation on Transboundary Rivers: Impact of the Indian River-linking Project*, BAPA *et. al.*, Dhaka, 2004, p. 243.
20. Ainun Nishat and F.K. Pasha, "A Review of the Ganges Treaty of 1996", the paper presented at the seminar in the *International Specialty Conference on Globalisation and Water Resources Management: The Changing Value of Water*, University of Dundy, 6-8th of August 2001, on http://www.awara.org/procedings/dundeed01/Documents/Pashafinal.pdf, (accessed on 12 March 2007).
21. A. K. Azad and J. Sultana, "Potential Impacts of Indian River-Linking Plan on Ecosystem of the Sundarbans", M. Feroze Ahmed *et.al.* (ed.), n. 19, p. 175.
22. Tajkera Khatun, 2004, n. 19, p. 231.
23. During 1975-1992, in the Khulna region, compared to pre-Farakka average, salinity has increased as much as 1800 percent for some months of dry season, see more in A.K. Azad and *et. al.*, "Potential Impacts of Indian River Linking Plan on Ecosystem of Sundarbans", Ibid., p. 176.
24. Mohammad Monirul Azam and Md. Saiful Karim, "Indian River Linking Project: Making Bangladesh a wasteland", *Dhaka Courier*, October 3, 2003.
25. Working Paper of the Brainstorming Session on "India's River Linking Project: Implications for Bangladesh" organised by Bangladesh Institute of International and Strategic Studies (BIISS), April 12, 2004.

26. Mohammad Humayun Kabir and Sufia Khanom, "India's River Linking Project: Possible Implications for Bangladesh", *BIISS Journal*, Vol. 29, No. 2, April 2008, pp. 177-209.
27. Sufia Khanom, Ibid.
28. K. Maudood Ealhi and M. Tajuddin Sikder, "Mega Dams in the Himalayas: An Assessment of Environmental Degradation and Global Warming", available at: http://www.benjapan.org/iceab10/1.pdf, p. 15.
29. Prof. Tareque Shamsul Haque, cited in Ayreen Khan, "Water Security: The Threat Facing Bangladesh", *Issue Brief*, Bangladesh Institute of Peace and Security Studies (BIPSS).
30. *The New Age*, May 13, 2009.
31. Department of Public Health and Engineering, Government of Bangladesh, "Arsenic Contamination of Ground Water in Bangladesh", *Final Report 2001*, 1: Summary, , Dhaka, pp. 1-15.
32. Mohammad Humayun Kabir, Neila Husain and Segufta Hossain, "Non-Traditional Security of Bangladesh", in Mufleh R. Osmany (ed.), *Whither National Security Bangladesh 2007*, Bangladesh Institute of International and Strategic Studies (BIISS) and The University Press Limited (UPL), 2008, p. 261.
33. Mukand S. Babel and Shahriar M. Wahid, "Freshwater Under Threat - South Asia: Vulnerability Assessment of Freshwater Resources to Environmental Change", United Nations Environment Programme and Asian Institute of Technology, 2008, at: http://www.unep.org/pdf/southasia_report.pdf
34. Ainun Nishat, "Impact of Water Dispute on Bangladesh in Asian International Waters", A.K. Biswas and T. Hasimoto (ed.), *Ganges-Brahmaputra to Mekong*, Oxford University Press, Bombay, New York 1996, p. 70.
35. Nurul Kabir, "Water Sharing Between Bangladesh and India", paper presented in the *Bangladesh-India Dialogue for Young Journalists* organized by Bangladesh Enterprise Institute (BEI) on September 7-8, 2004.
36. Ibid.
37. Ambassador (Retd.) Muhammad Zamir, "Bangladesh-India Relations: Sharing of Waters of Common Rivers", Paper presented in a Roundtable Discussion on *Bangladesh-India Relations: Exploring New Horizons* on January 09, 2010.
38. Mohammad Humayun Kabir and Sufia Khanom, n. 26.

39. "India and Bangladesh Finalise Deal on the Sharing of Teesta and Feni River Water", *IAS Current Affairs*, at: http://iashunt.blogspot.com/2011/03/india-and-bangladesh-finalise-deal-on.html
40. "India, Bangladesh exchange drafts of Teesta Water-sharing Agreements", available at: http://articles.timesofindia.indiatimes.com/2010-03-21/india/28145156_1_teesta-waters-ramesh-chandra-sen-tipaimukh-dam-project
41. "Teesta Failure Unfortunate", *The Daily Star*, September 8, 2011.
42. Severe water crisis within next two decades, say experts, *The Daily Star*, August 22, 2010.
43. NWMP, "National Water Resources Management Plan", *Bangladesh, Main Report*, Vol. 2, July 2001.
44. The Mekong River Commission (MRC) was formed on 5 April 1995 by an agreement between the governments of Cambodia, Lao PDR, Thailand and Viet Nam. The Agreement on the Cooperation for the Sustainable Development of the Mekong River Basin came about as the four countries saw a common interest in jointly managing their shared water resources and developing the economic potential of the river. The four countries signed The Agreement on the Cooperation for the Sustainable Development of the Mekong River Basin and agreed on joint management of their shared water resources and development of the economic potential of the river. The MRC supports the Mekong Programme, a Regional Cooperation Programme for the Sustainable Development of Water and Related Resources in the Mekong Basin owned by its member countries, The Mekong River Commission, available at: http://www.mrcmekong.org/
45. The Nile Basin Initiative (NBI) is a partnership initiated and led by the riparian states of the Nile River through the Council of Ministers of Water Affairs of the Nile Basin states. The NBI seeks to develop the river in a cooperative manner, share substantial socioeconomic benefits, and promote regional peace and security. The NBI started with a participatory process of dialogue among the riparians that resulted in their agreeing on a shared vision-to "achieve sustainable socioeconomic development through the equitable utilization of, and benefit from, the common Nile Basin water resources, Nile Basin Initiative, available at: http://www.nilebasin.org/newsite/index.php?option=com_content&view=article&id=71%3Aabout-the-nbi&catid=34%3Anbi-background-facts&Itemid=74&lang=en

10

Water Problems in Bangladesh: Internal and External Dimensions

Medha Bisht

> There is a new geography of conflict – a reconfigured cartography in which resource flows rather than political and ideological divisions constitute the major fault lines. Just as a map showing the world's tectonic faults is a useful guide to likely earthquake zones, viewing the international system in terms of shared water systems provide a guide to likely conflict zones in the twenty-first century.

Michael Klare, *Foreign Affairs*, 2000[1]

While the aforementioned statement belongs to a school which perceives the water-conflict nexus to be inevitable, in view of the strategic weight that water holds in the 21st century, it would be no exaggeration to state that water is likely to become a potential political flashpoint between South Asia riparians. This was visible during the much awaited visit of Manmohan Singh to Dhaka in September 2011, when the expectations of inking the Teesta agreement were high. With the West Bengal chief minister Mamata Banerjee opting out of the Indian delegation and her publicly expressed reservations about the sharing of Teesta waters, the euphoria over the Manmohan-Hasina visit ended. Clearly water emerged as the favourite media byte, and became an important rider for bilateral relations. The Teesta episode also reveals that domestic constituencies are becoming important actors in transboundary issues. Also, as water is a state subject in India, such patterns are likely to become more visible in the coming years.[2]

Given these developments, wherein resolving the water dispute has become an important litmus test for bettering bilateral relations, it would be appropriate to cast a fresh look on the water diplomacy between India and Bangladesh. Often the discourse on India and Bangladesh water issues is couched within the broad rubric of 'water security'. Various reports and expert forums have argued that water security in Bangladesh is an urgent issue which should be addressed by the government.

In this context, it would be appropriate to disaggregate the term 'water security' in India-Bangladesh relations. This paper identifies three pillars of water security—water reliability, water quality and water quantity. It is argued that operationalising these three pillars in the Indo-Bangladesh consultations on water can help diffuse tensions and enhance understanding between both countries. However, before one undertakes a discussion of the three pillars, it would be appropriate to assess the broad framework under which Bangladesh-India water issues operate.

India-Bangladesh Water Engagement

The present India-Bangladesh water engagement revolves around the sharing of Ganges and Teesta waters and addressing concerns apropos the Tipaimukh dam. Though the two countries share 54 common rivers, problem pertaining to these three rivers have been the moot point between both the countries at various points of time with India preferring a bilateral framework and Bangladesh insisting on a multilateral framework to resolve various differences. Differentiated national positions primarily stem from the geographical location as occupied by these countries in the subcontinent—with India being the upper riparian and Bangladesh, the lower riparian. Around 54 rivers flow from India into Bangladesh and both countries are part of the larger GBM basin.

The negotiations between Bangladesh and India over the River Ganges have resulted in number of understandings. For instance, in 1977, they signed an agreement and in 1982 and 1985 they signed MoUs. In 1996 the two countries signed a 30 year Treaty on Ganges water sharing. An Indian scholar pointed out "understandably and necessarily, it was a political rather than a technocratic settlement"[3]. Allocation of river waters and augmentation of flows in the dry season has been the central point of dispute between both the countries. Though many have considered the Ganges Water Treaty of 1996 between Bangladesh and India to be a success story, many others claim that the treaty lacks the flexibility of the 1977 agreement, which assured a minimum guarantee or an alternative water agreement in case of reduced river flows. Also it is claimed that the treaty does not offer remedies for a long term solution in the event of potential water scarcity. However, there are provisions within the treaty that guarantees water between March 1 and May 10 and also guarantees 90 per cent of the water flow pending review each five years[4]. In particular, one of the main concerns of Bangladesh is that the treaty does not explore means to engage other co-riparians. This is considered to be the major shortcoming of the treaty.[5] However, since it is a bilateral treaty the scope to involve other co-riparian was not possible. In the past Bangladesh proposal to store water in Nepal for augmentation was not acceptable to the Nepalese[6].

However, some positives, which made the treaty acceptable to both the sides need reiteration. First the treaty is an exceptional example of a need based approach rather than an interest based one. The treaty also provides for minimal guaranteed flow during the lean season. For instance Article 3 prohibits India from reducing Bangladesh's share of water without "valid reasons." If New Delhi is compelled to do so, this article, like the 1977 agreement, provides that India will be allowed to reduce Bangladesh's share by only 200 cusecs - in very specific cases. Under paragraph 3 of Article 2, the two signatories are to meet if the amount of water available at Farakka drops below 50,000 cusecs.[7] Further Article 4 creates a joint committee, consisting of an equal number of members from both countries, to oversee implementation of the treaty. The joint committee is also empowered to settle any differences of opinion on treaty implementation. Meanwhile Article 7 provides that if the joint commission is unable to settle differences, the issues will be sent to the Joint Rivers Commission for settlement. If that fails, the two governments are to meet on an urgent basis to try to sort out the differences.[8] This reflects the willingness of both countries to pro-actively resolve any differences.

Article 10 stipulates that the treaty is to be reviewed every five years. Also that when the new treaty expires India must provide Bangladesh with not less than 90 per cent of the water promised in the treaty until a new agreement is negotiated (Article 11).[9]

Further, uncertainties on water allocation are addressed in Annexure 1 which lays down a formula for the sharing of water if the volume of available water at Farakka drops below 70,000 cusecs. In such a situation, both countries are advised to share the available water equally. If the amount of water at Farakka is between 70,000 and 75,000 cusecs, Bangladesh will receive 35,000 cusecs and India the rest. If the amount of water available is over 75,000 cusecs, then India gets 40,000 cusecs and Bangladesh the rest. Bangladesh, however, has been guaranteed at least 35,000 cusecs of water every three cycles - each consisting of ten days - from March 1 to May 10, if the amount of water drops below 70,000 cusecs. The 1996 treaty also gives Bangladesh 52 per cent, compared with India's 48 percent, of the total water available at Farakka during the dry season.[10] The Ganges Water Treaty thus successfully resolved issues that are proving to be quite controversial in Teesta discussions.

The sharing of Teesta waters has become one of the most contested issues in India-Bangladesh relations. The Teesta river flows through the state of Sikkim and West Bengal to Bangladesh. India has built the Gazoldoba barrage on the Teesta, 60 km north of Bangladesh to divert water for irrigation purposes in West Bengal. Bangladesh has built Dalia barrage over Teesta 20 km south of the Indian border. Bangladesh has been complaining that India diverts water to the Gazoldoba barrage at the cost of Bangladesh's lower riparian needs. Allegations are also made that water withdrawal upstream have been detrimental to land fertility thus increasing soil salinity as less water is being discharged into the delta. Consultations between countries on water sharing are underway. India meanwhile has plans to generate 3635 MW of power from the hydel projects on Teesta river. However, these plans are being criticised by environmental groups not only in Bangladesh but also Sikkim on account of forest clearances and social costs of human displacement.[11]

Indo-Bangladesh relations are also strained over the issue of Tipaimukh dam which is proposed to be built in the state of Manipur on the Barak river in order to generate 1500 MW of hydropower. While the Indian government has said that Tipaimukh is a run on the river project, some in Bangladesh has challenged this.[12] However there are counter views to this argument[13].

Sections of Bangladeshi population are opposed to the construction of the dam as they argue that this would lead to the drying up of two main rivers, the Surma and the Kusiyara, which cater to the irrigation needs of north eastern Bangladesh. However, there is a conflict of opinion on this. Meanwhile in India the Tipaimukh is being opposed as experts have suggested that apart from displacing the local population, the dam would have an adverse seismic impact on the region. These controversies for long have stalled any decision on the subject and progress has slowed down since March 2007 due to environmental reasons and protests from the locals. Though the issue grabbed attention in late 2011, there has been a growing opposition from some sections within Bangladesh demanding more openness and transparency from India. To address the issue – which has become contentious- it is essential that India share data with Bangladesh.

Demand-Supply Equation in India-Bangladesh Relations

A look at Bangladesh-India water engagement reveals that *equitable water allocation* plays a primary role in shaping the element of reciprocity between both countries. Disputed claims and constraints on water allocation stem from increasing *domestic demands from the concerned states in India, electoral politics in both countries*, and demands by Bangladesh to ensure *a minimum flow* during the lean season. There is thus dissonance between the supply and the demand, where *economic needs* determine the *demand side* and geographical *location* determines the supply side. The supply side often triggers bilateral strains as it is increasingly hampered by potential dam building controversies in India. The debate on dams in the Northeast has also been broadened to include cultural and ecological factors over the last few years. Sediment load, increasing salinity and water contamination is also a cause for anxiety and concern in Bangladesh. To add to the water woes of both countries, the impact of climate change on food security and sea level rise appear as one of the key reasons in aggravating the lower riparian fears of Bangladesh. These concerns are visible in the National Water Policy of Bangladesh[14] of 1999 which emphasises the development of early warning and flood proofing systems to manage natural disasters like flood and drought. Identifying flood risk zones and making contingency plans for each region during flood and drought periods has also been highlighted in this policy report. In fact the Coastal Development Strategy[15] has been elevated to a national economic policy, as it is perceived that much of Bangladesh's economic progress and stability is dependent on the defence of its the coast line. With basin wide development identified as a long term priority, consultation and engagement with India via a multilateral framework has been a priority for Bangladesh's regional water policy.

Given these concerns, it would be appropriate to understand the India and Bangladesh relations through the three pillars identified above, viz. water reliability, water quality and water quantity.

Water Reliability

Water reliability can be defined as the ability of the system to maintain its functions in both routine and unexpected circumstances. Often equated with water quantity, the concept of water reliability often evades discussion. Of late, water reliability in Bangladesh has been questioned by a section of Bangladeshi population on account of growing demographics, river tapping and diversion plans in India, impact of climate change and growing energy demand due to urbanisation and industrialisation in both countries. Notwithstanding the supply dimension, as 93 per cent of the surface water of Bangladesh comes from outside the country, water management would help to address the water scarcity issue. An important criterion for conceptualising and understanding reliability is revisiting the management aspects of the domestic water sector and its relationship to food security in Bangladesh. This is because water and agriculture are the lifeline of Asian societies and Bangladesh exemplifies such a linkage. Adaptation measures in Bangladesh in terms of flood management approaches also need to be factored in while discussing the issue of reliability. This is because crop cultivation takes place in the flood plain agro-ecological zones, which are the backbone of the economy.[16] Also farmers take decisions based on traditional predictive factors related to flooding characteristics. If the decisions are in accord with natural phenomena then the year's production survives and if floods overtake the capacity of the system, food security is often endangered.[17] Bangladesh is the fourth largest rice producer country in the world, but of late has emerged as a major food importers.[18] Water reliability in terms of securing and maintaining food security thus becomes important. Efficient watershed management techniques in the Chittagong Hill Tracts in south eastern Bangladesh, which constitutes about 30 per cent of the Bangladesh's forest area could provide some relieve to ecological health. Rainwater harvesting in Bangladesh could be encouraged to ease water scarcity[19].

The economy of Bangladesh is largely rural-based, and in 2009, 18 per cent of GDP was derived from the agriculture sector. This sector employs about 47 per cent of economically active population and is also the prime source for raw material in many industries.[20] Agriculture also consumes the largest share of water. As per 2008 figures, the total water withdrawal was estimated at about 35.87 km^3, of which about 31.50 km^3 (88 per cent) was for agriculture, 3.60 km^3 (10 per cent) was for municipalities and 0.77 km^3 (2 per cent) was for industries. It is important to note that in Bangladesh 79 per cent of the withdrawal is from ground water and 21 per cent from surface water.[21] The overt use of ground water is primarily because of two reasons — first, the non-availability of surface water supplies during the lean season and second, due to the difficulty of constructing gravity based dams on flat deltaic terrain- an option which is also costly for Bangladesh.[22] Minor irrigation projects, which can lift groundwater are therefore most preferred in irrigation development. As per 2008 Aquastat, FAO figures, small irrigation schemes cover a total area of 4.91 million ha (97 per cent) of land.

However, given the importance of water to food security, no policy or act related to irrigation or water management has been formulated yet.[23] Due to the rapid growth of minor irrigation in the private sector, the Ministry of Agriculture enacted the Groundwater Management Ordinance in 1985 thus controlling the spacing for installation of irrigation equipments. The Ordinance was suspended in 1987 with a view to expand minor irrigation. Due to suspension of space requirements of irrigation equipments, the optimum and effective utilisation of groundwater resources has been impeded.[24] New ways are needed to address the current food security concerns and ground water management in Bangladesh. Also, due to the overt use of water in the agriculture sector there is a growing competition from other sectors which underlines the need for an Integrative Water Resource Management Vision, which would address the demand of other water using sectors.

The main challenge to the reliability of water is therefore posed by the lack of integrative water management practices. This is because while demand for water has been growing rapidly in agriculture, the urban and industrial sectors, fishery, inland navigation and salinity control, the supply of clean uncontaminated water has become a looming challenge due to inadequate surface water supply, pollution caused by the effluents upstream, salinity intrusion in the coastal area and arsenic contamination. As one author puts it; "On the demand side, irrigation has received higher priority than the supply of safe drinking water. On the supply side, the use of groundwater has received more emphasis than surface water. The result is mass scale arsenic contamination."[25] A solution proposed by the same author is that tubewell water should be treated and alternative ways should be explored for collecting water from alternative sources such as surface or rainwater. Contaminated water also raises concerns regarding food safety stemming from irrigating with arsenic contaminated water.

Reliability thus needs to be seen within a comprehensive context of health safety as well as food security rather than just the quantity of water flowing into Bangladesh. Adaptation strategies are as important as food security. This is because Bangladesh is a flood prone country because of the flat deltaic land. According to one study there is a possibility of more frequent flash floods in the next two decades. Some studies even note that increased rainfall in the future is expected to lead to increased surface run-off with severe consequences of flooding in the country.[26]

There has been some cooperation between India and Bangladesh on this front and some substantive progress is underway. A meeting of Indo-Bangladesh experts took place in August, 2000 in which they discussed the issues of strengthening and expanding the existing co-operation for improving the Flood Forecasting and Warning System.[27] In the joint communiqué in 2010, India agreed to provide flood data of Farakkha for Ganga so as help Bangladesh to forecast flood in advance. Bangladesh has also given its consent for joint dredging to facilitate river navigation along the Calcutta-Haldia and Karimganj river routes.[28] This is important as water transport accounts for about 15 per cent of the total transport GDP in Bangladesh. Dredging should be undertaken at the national level on a regular basis[29]. During the September 2011 visit of Prime Minister Manmohan Singh to Bangladesh it came to public knowledge that – dredging of the river Ichhamati along the common reach between Angrail and Kalanchi bridges has been completed and, river bank protection works along the Mahananda, Karatoa, Nagar, Kulik, Atrai, Dharla, Punarbhaba, Feni, Khowai, Surma etc. are being carried out in phases.[30] Given the implications of flood management to food security, cooperation on this front thus needs urgent attention. Regional cooperation on data sharing on rivers has been active. Apart from India, Nepal provides data for the Narayani river and China for the Nugesha, Yangcun and Nuxia and Brahmaputra rivers. China is also providing data on the Brahmaputra from January to October free of cost.

Some of the issues that need to be addressed at the national level are adequate budget allocations and proper maintenance of flood management structures including reducing silt from the rivers. This is important as huge amount of sediment - approximately 200 billion tonnes per year - pass through the main river systems.[31] These reduce the river capacity and increase the frequency of floods. Thus reliability of water should entail focussing on domestic water management as well as effective cooperation on flood management between riparian countries, so that the overall system that is sustained through the water sector is not damaged. Notwithstanding Bangladesh's natural claim as a low riparian country, the management of water within Bangladesh would not make it less dependent on India.

Water Quality

As mentioned above the quality of water is a serious issue between Bangladesh and India and focussed attention is needed to address the same. A study published in 2010 states that 77 million people in Bangladesh are being exposed to toxic levels of arsenic, potentially taking years or decades off their lives.[32] Also termed as mass poisoning, many studies have highlighted that arsenic in groundwater indicates that one in ten people who drink water containing 500 mg of arsenic per litre may ultimately die from various cancers, including lung, bladder and skin cancers.[33]

Though arsenic contamination was first discovered in 1993, geological investigation has revealed that most of the arsenic is occurring in the younger sediments derived from the Ganges Basin. A major reason for the declining quality of groundwater, as stated before, is because of the excessive extraction of water for irrigation and domestic water supply, lack of water management and inadequate recharge of the aquifer.

An important factor contributing to the contamination of water is the discharging and dumping of untreated waste into the water bodies. This practice is prevalent both in Bangladesh and India. For instance, Dhaka is the centre for the leather industry, which is one of the lead foreign exchange earners in Bangladesh. The inadequate development of modern tanneries in Bangladesh has led to a lack of treatment plants. Most of the wastes and effluents are subjected to natural decomposition in the environment, causing serious pollution problems affecting soil, water, air and human life.[34] According to official estimates, the tanneries discharge 22,000 cubic metres of untreated liquid toxic waste daily into the rivers, gutters and canals that run alongside the roads of Hazaribagh. Toxins are also leaching into groundwater.[35] Most of the tanning industry waste ends up in River Buriganga, which receives 25,000 tonnes of untreated waste and 40,000 tonnes of toxic chemicals every day.[36]

The story is much the same in India. While the Indian growth story has been acknowledged world wide, the environmental impact of industrialisation has also not gone unnoticed. A 2009 State of the Environment Report, flags major Indian concerns and costs associated with serious land degradation, loss of biodiversity, deteriorating air quality in cities, increasing water scarcity, and generation of large quantities of hazardous waste from industries. The report states that the share of the most polluting sectors in India's exports has increased dramatically during the last decade, and a growing pollution footprint is negatively impacting human health and development outcomes.[37]

The River Ganga is an important site for environmental pollution and its impact in India. The Ganges basin accounts for 25 per cent of India's water resources, and passes through the five Indian states (Uttarakhand, Uttar Pradesh, Bihar, Jharkhand, and West Bengal) before entering Bangladesh. The treatment capacity in large cities along the mainstream of the Ganga is only 44 per cent of the requirement, and is conspicuous by its absence in small cities. As 90 per cent of the Ganga flows are extracted for irrigation, the high abstraction results in very low in-stream flows, exacerbating the water quality problems, especially in the dry season, which also has an adverse lower riparian impact in Bangladesh.[38]

At the national level, one of the main problems in India, relating to transboundary rivers is that water is a state subject. Although the central government has the powers for the regulation and development of inter-state rivers (such as the Ganga), these have not been used in the recent decades for establishing any river basin organisations.[39] It is pertinent to note that over 12,000 million litres of sewage pours into the Ganga daily – apart from effluents from tanneries, industrial waste and agricultural runoffs.[40] Though the state pollution control boards are responsible for enforcing environmental compliance, most of them are under-resourced and lacks technical know-how and equipments. The Central Pollution Control Board has played an insignificant role in enforcing environmental regulations in the states. While the Clean Ganga Water Campaign (National Ganga River Basin Authority) was undertaken by India and supported by a World Bank loan of a billion dollars, water management in Ganga basin has been identified as the most suitable approach for mitigating the problem. It has been reported that Ganga basin is expected to be the most seriously affected due to imminent water scarcities. Also with supplies close to full utilisation, water deficits are projected to reach 50 per cent of the total implied demand by 2030.[41] A coordinated effort and approach by India and Bangladesh can help address some of the problems of water quality, an issue of imminent concern - environmentally.

Another issue which could well impinge the GBM basin in the coming years is the Brahmaputra river. Some recent studies reveal that exploitation of mineral resources in Tibet is contributing to the contamination of river water through land erosion and ore tailings. Also continued deforestation is a major ecological concern as it is upsetting the 'water run-off regime' and reducing natural habitats and native species.[42] The forests are important as they serve key functions like controlling stream flows and regulate climate to provide a major carbon sink. The Chinese government has been slow in responding to the large scale deforestation and according to some estimates, frequent flooding in Arunachal Pradesh and in Bangladesh has been linked to deforestation in south eastern Tibet.[43] The ecological health of the Brahmaputra is thus emerging as an important concern for the lower riparians.

Given the stakes of the various riparian countries, it is important that Bangladesh, India and China, cooperate on approaches related to joint management of the basin. While South Asian nations have been engaging each other on bilateral basis, a regional forum to discuss issues related to flood management, afforestation, data sharing on river flows, dredging and siltation should be undertaken on periodic basis. Review meetings should be held to monitor the progress in the area. Constituting a regional mechanism on the issue will not be a problem, given that bilateral cooperation between countries on issues such as flood management is in progress and has deepened over the period of time. However domestic efforts need to simultaneously supplement regional coordination on the issue of joint basin management. Such efforts will go a long way enhancing water quality and also ensuring water security for the countries. Ground water should be discussed as an issue of competing importance and priority as it is directly related to issues of water management.

Water Quantity

Water quantity issues primarily relate to surface water resources and have been the most contested topic between both countries. While equitable water allocation is often perceived as a zero-sum game, where the benefit of one is considered as the loss of the other, the Ganges Water Treaty negotiated between both countries in 1996, emphasised a need based approach. Negotiations on the allocation of water between both countries revolves around augmenting flows during the dry season (January 1 - May 31). Many measures to augment the flow during the lean season have been discussed. While the Bangladeshi position underlines the need to utilise the waters of the Ganges either through the construction of dams in Nepal and India, which could release the water to Bangladesh in the lean season, or through construction of link canals in West Bengal, which could also link Nepal rivers with Bangladesh rivers, thus providing Nepal an inadvertent access to the sea; India on its part has rejected these propositions and instead suggested diversion of Brahmaputra waters to the Ganges by construction of a link canal across the Brahmaputra, upstream of Bangladesh to divert waters into the Ganga. Bangladesh has however has rejected India's proposal. Nepal also is not keen to allow construction of dam within its territory as it would submerge land in Nepal.

With regard to the Teesta, both countries have come to an adhoc understanding since 1983, whereby during the lean period, Bangladesh is allocated 36 per cent of the water and India 39 per cent, leaving the remaining 25 per cent to be decided on later. But water sharing has been impeded by implementation issues - primarily stemming from the divergence in data interpretation.[44] It was in 2010, particularly at the 37th meeting of the Joint Rivers Commission in Delhi, that the Bangladesh water resources minister, Ramesh Chandra Sen demanded the 50-50 distribution of the Teesta water at Gazaldoba point.[45] At present the main point of contention relating to the Teesta water is the sharing of water on a 50:50 basis and Bangladesh's demand for a minimum guarantee clause. The minimum guarantee is fixed at 3500 cusecs of water for Bangladesh. This is an issue, because according to Kalyan Rudra, (appointed by Mamta Banerjee to coordinate an expert committee on Teesta waters), in the lean season the total water availability is 3000-4000 cusecs. This means that even after applying the distribution formula Bangladesh would not get more than 2000 cusecs[46], a figure which is unacceptable to Bangladesh. In the coming years any agreement on Teesta would also entail a discussion on the role of dams in Sikkim and the command area under the Teesta irrigation project.

With the impact of climate change and the growing impact of domestic politics on bilateral river sharing agreements, any consensus on the equitable sharing of river waters will be difficult. Given that Bangladesh is a deltaic country, a minimum amount of water should be guaranteed to Bangladesh for the protection of the delta. Suggestions should go beyond traditional approaches such as proportionality and joint studies needs to be carried out by both countries to determine the water flows that need to be maintained for maintaining the ecological health of the system.[47] Perhaps, this as the starting referent point could provide some scope for consensus. So far the joint committee of experts, constituted by the Joint River Commission, has divergent opinions. While India insists that 10 per cent should be set aside for the delta, Bangladesh insists on 20 per cent. Though coordinated research is needed by both countries to reach a common understanding on this front, an enabling environment for cooperation needs to be created by addressing water management and water quality issues, which are important for maintaining the ecological health and hydrological stability of the river system. Domestic consensus is as important as consensus at the bilateral level. River basin organisations—for the Brahmaputra and Ganga should be formed to deal with the issue of water management. At the regional level, a framework for dealing with climate change should be created, to determine the impact of climate change on water scarcity. Such initiatives will help bridge the perception gap which seems to exist at present.

Conclusion

On the basis of the above analysis it would be appropriate to conclude that water reliability, quality and quantity do provide opportunities to cooperate on larger issues of water management which has the potential to take the bilateral relations forward. As the debate on climate change and water consumption have increased uncertainties, and put pressure on the availability of water, it is important that new approaches be followed by both countries. Joint basin management with the overarching objective of maintaining the quality and reliability of water should be the starting point for cooperation. Differences over the Tipaimukh dam need to addressed through consultation and more transparency. At the bilateral level, the issue seems to be overwhelmed by diverging opinions on both sides. Gowher Rizvi, the advisor to the prime minister of Bangladesh, has said that, the hydroelectric plant, being constructed at Tipaimukh, can in fact help Bangladesh. He has argued that the project is estimated to generate 1500 MW of electricity and Bangladesh can also invest in the project.[48] Before undertaking any action on Tipaimukh, the Indian government should have joint consultations with Bangladesh, and records of the meeting should be made public for satisfying lower riparian anxieties. Thus water should not only be looked as a resource waiting to be harnessed by both sides but should be used as an effective tool to facilitate and improve bilateral relations between both countries. Joint efforts to improve the quality of water and R & D cooperation towards developing appropriate technologies to adapt to climate change could facilitate cooperation.

Technological development and cooperation thus could be a major tool for minimising water stress and enhancing the availability and quality of water in South Asia. Facilitating effective use of water through sprinkler and drip irrigation method rather than fixed allocations of water could be an effective antidote for problems pertaining to the supply side of water equation. Technological ingenuity could also help in desalination; and the construction of coastal and flood defence infrastructure in coastal Bangladesh for dealing with the threat of sea level rise.

It is likely that water issue would become increasingly politicised in Bangladesh and India in the years to come. It is time that an integrated approach is adopted. India, by not signing the Teesta agreement at the last minute, due to the opposition of the Paschimabanga chief minister does not inspire confidence. This further politicises the issue of water sharing. In this context, addressing domestic concerns and negotiating with domestic stake-holders is a must before any assurance is given to Bangladesh. This would help India to avoid last minute controversy and loss of credibility. This would prevent building of unnecessary expectation on eitherside. The display of effective leadership by the central government in India while negotiating water issues with the lower riparian Bangladesh is also of extreme importance.

Notes

1. Michael T. Klare, " The New Geography of Conflict," *Foreign Affairs*, May/June, 2001.
2. The Chief Minister of Bihar, Nitish Kumar recently asserted that the Ganges Water Treaty, 1996, was negotiated at the cost of Bihar. He said that during the lean season, Bihar has to release 1,500 cusecs for Bangladesh, leading to water shortages and heavy deposition of silt in the catchment areas of the Ganga. See Amitabh Srivastava, War Over Water, *India Today*, September 30, 2011, at http://indiatoday.intoday.in/story/bihar-cm-nitish-kumar-lalu-prasad-yadav-farakka-water-treaty/1/153252.html
3. Ramaswamy Iyer, "Conflict Resolution: Three River Treaties", *Economic and Political Weekly*, Viol. 34(24), June, 12-18, 1999, p. 1514.
4. For details see Ibid., 1514.
5. M.M. Rahman, "Water Conflict an Cooperation between Bangladesh and India," *Asteriskos,* 1/2 2006, at http://www.scribd.com/doc/13264275/Ganges-Water-Conflict.
6. See B.G.Verghese and Ramaswamy Iyer, "Harnessing the Eastern Himalayan Rivers: Regional Cooperation in South Asia", Konark Publishers, Delhi, 1993, chapter 9. Ramaswamy Iyer, *Water Perspectives, Issues, Concerns.* Sage Publications, New Delhi, 2003,

7. For the text see Phillipe Sands, "Bangladesh and India: Treaty for Sharing of Ganges Water at Farrakka", International Legal Material, Vol. 36(3), May 1997, p. 524.
8. Ibid. p. 525.
9. Ibid. p. 526.
10. Ibid. pp. 527-28.
11. Kanchi Kohi, "Sikkim Dams on Horizon," *Civil Society*, April 2011, at http://civilsocietyonline.com/Archive/apr11/apr1112.asp
12. Some of the objections that Bangladesh experts have raised are: India will hold 15 BCM water out of which 8 BCM is for dead storage, and the environmental study ignores the impact of dam on the Haor region of Bangladesh, Some other objections on the nature of the run of the river project are that the project will hold around 8 BCM of water as dead storage, which amounts to 17,000 cusecs, which is a huge amount for the Surma-Kushiyara-Meghna rivers in dry season. For details see., Md. Khalequzzaman, "Tipaimukh Dam: Bangladesh a Perspectives," *India Water Portal,* at: http://www.india waterportal.org/post/22888
13. Gowher Rizvi, "Tipaimukh: A Please for Rational and Scientific Discussion", *Daily Star*, December 13, 2011.
14. National Water Policy, Ministry of Water Resources, Government of the People's Republic of Bangladesh, 1999, at : http://www.mowr.gov.bd/Documents/National%20Water% 20Policy%20(English).pdf
15. Coastal zones include 19 districts in Bangladesh, facing or in close proximity with the Bay of Bengal and exclusive export zones.
16. Younus *et. al., Climate-induced Flooding, Autonomous Adjustments and Human Security in Bangladesh - A Geographical Assessment. Papers from the International Workshop on Human Security and Climate Change,* 2005.
17. Ibid.
18. Bangladesh food import bill likely to rise by 15 pct, *Daily Financial Times*, January 24, 2011, at: http://www.ft.lk/2011/01/24/bangladesh-food-import-bill-likely-to-rise-by-15-pct/
19. Islan, Kabir and Chau, Feasibility Study of Rainwater Harvesting Techniques in Bangladesh, "Hawaii Rainwater Catchment Systems Programme", at: http://www.ctahr.hawaii.edu/hawaiirain/Library/papers/Islam_Manzurul.pdf

20. Bangladesh FAO, 2010, http://www.fao.org/nr/water/aquastat/countries/bangladesh/index.stm
21. Ibid.
22. Ibid.
23. Ibid.
24. Ibid.
25. N.T. Chaudhry, "Water Management in Bangladesh: An Analytical View," *Water Policy*, 12, 2010, p. 40.
26. Younus *et. al,* "Climate-induced Flooding, Autonomous Adjustments and Human Security in Bangladesh - A Geographical Assessment". *Papers from the International Workshop on Human Security and Climate Change*, 2005.
27. "Indo-Bangladesh Cooperation", Ministry of Water Resources, at http://wrmin.nic.in/writereaddata/linkimages/CHAPTER%20-%2071809012297.pdf
28. Seal on joint dredging of river - Dhaka accepts Delhi offer, *The Telegraph*, December 26, 2008, at: http://www.telegraphindia.com/1081226/jsp/northeast/story_10301807.jsp
29. China Harbor Engineering Company Limited' (CHEC) has entered into an agreement with BWDB for dredging work at Gorai and Jamuna river.
30. "Joint statement on the occasion of the visit of the PM of India to Bangladesh", September 7, 2011, Ministry of External Affairs. at http://www.mea.gov.in/mystart.php?id=100018210&pid=2290
31. K. M. Morshed, "Flood and Sediment Management in Major Rivers in Bangladesh", Ministry of Water Resources, Bangladesh, at: http://www.iwhr.com/zswwenglish/rootfiles/2011/12/08/1321928673258980-1323218419461169.pdf
32. "Study: Millions in Bangladesh Exposed to Arsenic in Drinking Water," *CNN,* June 20, 2010, at: http://articles.cnn.com/2010-06-20/world/bangladesh.arsenic.poisoning_1_arsenic-mass-poisoning-bangladesh?_s=PM:WORLD
33. Smith, Lungas and Rehman, "Contamination of drinking-water by Arsenic in Bangladesh: A Public Health Emergency", *World Health Organisation*, 78 (9), 2000. at: http://www.who.int/bulletin/archives/78(9)1093.pdf
34. S.M. Inamul Haq, "Critical Environmental Issues Related to Environmental Issues in Bangladesh", Department of Soil Sciences,

University of Dhaka, at: http://aciar.gov.au/files/node/319/PRO088%20part%202.pdf

35. Daniel Lanteigne, "Colours of water: Bangladesh's Leather Tanneries", One Word, United Nations University, May 12, 2010, http://ourworld.unu.edu/en/colours-of-water-bangladesh%E2%80%99s-leather-tanneries.
36. Ibid.
37. "India: National Ganga River Basin Project", World Bank, May 4, 2011, at: http://moef.nic.in/downloads/public-information/2011-05-04%20Ganga%20PAD.pdf
38. Ibid.
39. Ibid.
40. Sudha Ramachandran, "Murky realities in Clean Ganges Initiative", *Asia Times,* July 2, 2011, at: http://www.atimes.com/atimes/South_Asia/MG02Df01.html
41. India: National Ganga River Basin Project, World Bank, May 4, 2011, at: http://moef.nic.in/downloads/public-information/2011-05-04%20Ganga%20PAD.pdf
42. Brahma Chellaney, *Water: Asia's New Battleground,* Uttar Pradesh: Harper Collins, 2011, p. 119.
43. Ibid, p. 120.
44. Gargi Parsai, "The Tale of Two Rivers," *The Hindu*, September 6, 2011, at: http://www.thehindu.com/news/national/article2427517.ece
45. M. Inamul Haque, "What Happened to Teesta Waters", *Daily Star*, September 27, 2011, at: http://www.thedailystar.net/newDesign/news-details.php?nid=204060
46. Ibid.
47. Punam Pandey, "Water Sharing between India and Bangladesh: Old Confusion and New Realities", IDSA Comment, December 20, 2011, at: ttp://www.idsa.in/idsacomments/WaterSharingbetweenIndiaandBangladesh_ ppandey_201211
48. "No Harm if Tipaimukh Dam Goes Ahead: Rizvi", *Bangladesh News,* December 5, 2011, at: http://bdnews24.com/details.php?id=212986&cid=2

11

Bangladesh-India Cooperation on Energy Issues: Bangladesh Perspectives

Mahfuz Kabir

Introduction

Energy plays an essential role in any economy. On the demand side, energy is one of the products a consumer decides to buy in order to maximise utility. On the supply side, energy is a key factor of production in addition to capital, labour and materials and is seen to play a vital role in the economic and social development of countries. It is a key factor in increasing economic growth and living standards.[1] Both Bangladesh and India achieved impressive economic growth along with continuous expansion of industrial and export-oriented manufacturing sector over the last two decades or so. The growing size of the economy and rising energy demands go hand in hand with few exceptions.[2]

The two countries are energy-hungry although India has considerable hydrocarbon reserve. Energy security is significant for India since it is gradually emerging as a major economic power.[3] Among the different forms of non-renewable energy resources, Bangladesh has some reserve of dry natural gas, which is expected to get exhausted in the next ten years. Additionally, due to controversies over the method of extraction and utilisation, the potential contribution of coal in the economic development of the country is not yet realised. Uninterrupted and sufficient supply of energy is a prerequisite for achieving double-digit economic growth by 2017 and fulfilling 'Vision 2021', which aims to transform Bangladesh into a middle-income country. Therefore, it is important to understand the potential and mutually beneficial avenues of cooperation between Bangladesh and India on energy issues. The two countries have signed Memorandum of understanding on renewable energy cooperation in September 2011 when the Indian Prime Minister visited Dhaka.

Given this backdrop, the objective of this chapter is to analyse the major trends and characteristics of energy production, consumption, and energy security in the context of Bangladesh, and identify possible avenues of energy cooperation between Bangladesh and India. This chapter has been organised as follows. After this brief prelude, the next section examines the long-term equilibrium and causal relationship between energy consumption and economic growth. It further describes the energy resources situation, production and use of energy in the two countries. It presents the energy security situation in Bangladesh, which has a bearing on greater cooperation between the two countries on energy. Finally, a conclusion and policy recommendations have been suggested.

Energy Consumption and Economic Growth

Economic theory implies that if causality runs from energy consumption to GDP then it implies that an economy is energy dependent and hence energy is a stimulus to growth.[4] On the other hand, if causality only runs from GDP to energy consumption, it implies that an economy is not energy dependent.[5] If there is no causality in either direction ('neutrality hypothesis'), it implies that energy consumption is not correlated with GDP, which implies that energy conservation policies may be pursued without adversely affecting the economy.[6]

Table 1: Maximum Eigenvalue Test of Co-integration between Energy Consumption and GDP, 1980-2009

Country	*Co-integrating Rank*	*Statistic*	*Critical Value*	*P-value**
Bangladesh	None	18.64	14.26	0.009
India	None	3.129	3.84	0.07

* MacKinnon-Haun-Michelis *p*-value.

Table 2: Granger Causality between Energy Consumption and GDP, 1980-2009

Country	*Direction of causality*	*F-Statistic*	*Probability*
Bangladesh	GDP does not Granger Cause ENERGY	4.05	0.05
	ENERGY does not Granger Cause GDP	0.15	0.70
India	GDP does not Granger Cause ENERGY	3.92	0.04
	ENERGY does not Granger Cause GDP	1.35	0.28

Source: Author's estimation, based on data from US Energy Information Administration (EIA) and World Development Indicators.

Evidence reveals that there is long-term and causal relationship between energy consumption and economic growth in Bangladesh and India *i.e.*, energy consumption causes economic growth (Tables 1 and 2).[7] It implies that a shortage of energy may negatively affect economic growth or may cause poor economic performance, leading to a fall in income and employment. Thus, energy is a limiting factor in the economic growth of Bangladesh and India, and therefore there is a strong need for sufficient supply of energy in order to keep the economy growing to achieve the goals of poverty reduction and social development. It strongly implies that shortage of energy may negatively affect economic growth or may cause poor economic performance, leading to a fall in income and employment, which may further lead to social unrest and create disaffection for the government.

Energy Resources and Use

Bangladesh faces many of the same challenges as the rest of the world. Its economy is growing at an impressive rate fuelling energy demand, whereas it has not developed sufficient domestic resources so it is increasingly becoming dependent on imports. State-owned companies lack commercial incentives and tend to be inefficient. Prices for fuel are distorted with subsidies and cross-subsidies that encourage inefficient use of energy, and deter additional investment in energy supply, sometimes resulting in shortages and rationing.[8] Energy consumption of Bangladesh is very low compared to the energy demand in the world. The country, given the size of its population, has the potential to grow its share of world energy demand significantly if its recent economic growth is sustained. The annual average energy consumption per capita of Bangladesh at present is one of the lowest in the world.[9]

Natural Gas

In Bangladesh, domestic natural gas constitutes the highest proportion in the energy consumption mix (nearly 70 per cent of its energy) followed by oil (around 24 per cent). The share of hydroelectricity and coal remains negligible in the energy consumption basket. The share of net energy imports for the country is around 23 per cent. (See Table 3)

Even though India has a higher (though not significantly so) reserve of dry natural gas than Bangladesh, its production is more than double and consumption is around threefold than that of Bangladesh. The gap between domestic extraction and consumption is met by imports, which is currently about half trillion cubic feet per year.

Electricity

Annual electricity consumption per capita was 147 kwh in Bangladesh in 2009, which was almost half of the South Asian average (260 kwh). However, it has currently increased to 236 kwh, which is still below the South Asian average. Furthermore, there are significant technical and non-technical losses in the electricity sector in the country, which is estimated to be 23 per cent of production.[10] However, Bangladesh has achieved significant progress in reforming the power distribution and transmission sector, leading to improved commercial performance. The electrification ratio increased from about ten per cent in 1994 to over 49 per cent in 2011.[11] (See Table 4)

India's net electricity generation is around 24 times higher than that of Bangladesh. Currently India is making significant contribution to the national grid through solar and wind power. It is also importing electricity to meet its galloping demand for power to keep up with its impressive economic growth and living standard.

Petroleum

Bangladesh is heavily dependent on imported oil. It has a very negligible amount of oil reserve and produces only 5.73 thousand barrels per day.[12] Its net oil import is 94 per cent of consumption. The

Table 3: Consumption, Production, Reserve and Imports of Dry Natural Gas

		1980	*1985*	*1990*	*1995*	*2000*	*2005*	*2009*
Production (Billion Cubic Feet)	India	51.00	135.00	399.00	627.55	794.59	1055.92	1424.96
	Bangladesh	50.00	100.00	162.00	260.27	342.56	494.41	697.47
	India % of World	0.10	0.22	0.54	0.80	0.90	1.06	1.34
	Bangladesh % of World	0.09	0.16	0.22	0.33	0.39	0.50	0.66
Consumption (Billion Cubic Feet)	India	51.00	135.00	399.00	627.55	794.59	1269.22	1870.64
	Bangladesh	50.00	100.00	162.00	260.27	342.56	494.41	697.47
	India % of World	0.10	0.22	0.54	0.80	0.90	1.25	1.75
	Bangladesh % of World	0.09	0.16	0.22	0.33	0.39	0.49	0.65
Proved Reserves (Trillion Cubic Feet)	India	9.30	12.00	12.43	14.51	14.83	15.00	16.88
	Bangladesh	8.00	8.00	7.00	7.00	7.00	7.00	11.80
	India % of World	0.36	0.46	0.43	0.48	0.47	0.44	0.49
	Bangladesh % of World	0.31	0.30	0.24	0.23	0.22	0.21	0.34
Imports (Billion Cubic Feet)	India						213.30	445.68
	Bangladesh							
	India % of World						0.67	1.37
	Bangladesh % of World							

Source: US Energy Information Administration (EIA) and author's calculation.

Table 4: Consumption, Production, Installed Capacity and Imports of Electricity

		1980	1985	1990	1995	2000	2005	2009
Net Generation (Billion Kilowatt-hours)	India	119.26	174.93	275.49	396.02	529.12	661.80	785.53
	Bangladesh	2.67	4.62	7.62	10.41	14.87	24.98	32.93
	India % of World	1.49	1.85	2.44	3.14	3.63	3.82	4.11
	Bangladesh % of World	0.03	0.05	0.07	0.08	0.10	0.14	0.17
Net Consumption (Billion Kilowatt-hours)	India	97.90	140.65	219.88	318.28	375.39	483.26	600.65
	Bangladesh	1.83	3.14	5.02	8.62	12.46	23.01	31.24
	India % of World	1.34	1.62	2.12	2.77	2.85	3.07	3.44
	Bangladesh % of World	0.03	0.04	0.05	0.08	0.09	0.15	0.18
Installed Capacity (Million Kilowatts)	India	33.70	53.00	74.69	95.44	112.14	147.58	177.38
	Bangladesh	0.99	1.31	2.52	3.28	3.60	4.71	5.45
	India % of World	1.70	2.21	2.70	3.11	3.25	3.59	3.84
	Bangladesh % of World	0.05	0.05	0.09	0.11	0.10	0.11	0.12
Total Imports (Billion Kilowatt-hours)	India	0.01	0.02	1.00	1.68	1.54	1.76	9.25
	Bangladesh							
	India % of World	0.00	0.01	0.34	0.42	0.31	0.29	1.51
	Bangladesh % of World							
Total Exports (Billion Kilowatt-hours)	India	0.04	0.11	0.10	0.05	0.20	0.21	0.39
	Bangladesh							
	India % of World	0.03	0.05	0.03	0.01	0.04	0.03	0.06
	Bangladesh % of World							

Source: EIA and author's calculation.

country has very little proved reserve and production of natural gas. It is 0.22 and 0.5 per cent of that of the world, respectively. Currently Bangladesh has 28 million barrels of proven oil reserves (as of January 2006). The country produced an estimated 4,000 barrels per day and its low level of reserves and production capacity make it a net oil importer. Petroleum exploration has been unsuccessful. Bangladesh has 33,000 bbl/day of crude oil refining capacity at Eastern Refinery Ltd (ERL) in Chittagong.

Petroleum accounts for about 34 per cent of India's total energy consumption, and has been growing gradually in recent years. Its oil consumption is more than 32 times higher than that of Bangladesh. Its demand for petroleum is sharply increasing and it is looking for extra-regional cooperation in oil fuel in order to sustain its economic growth. (See Figure 1)

Coal

Bangladesh has an estimated coal reserve of 2.7 billion tons. It has very high quality coal reserves at Barapukuria and Phulbari. However, all of the coal needs of Bangladesh are met by import rather than by domestic source.[13] The country expects to reach one million ton per year production, as a result of which the share of imports would decline. This strategy of diversifying its energy source to fulfill domestic demand has made Bangladesh move away from natural gas and begin using domestic coal reserves as well as imports, which can help Bangladesh enhance its energy security. Bangladesh began commercial coal production in April 2003 with the opening of the Barapukuria Coal Mine, which is expected to produce one million tons of coal per year (mmst/year) mainly for electricity generation. Another possible coal mining project at Khalashpir is under consideration.

Coal is the dominant commercial fuel in India, satisfying more than half of India's energy demand. Power generation accounts for about three-quarter of India's coal consumption, followed by heavy industry. India is the world's third largest coal producer (after China and the United States). Nearly all of India's 390 mines are under Coal India Ltd. (CIL), which accounts for about 90 per cent of the country's coal production. (Table 5)

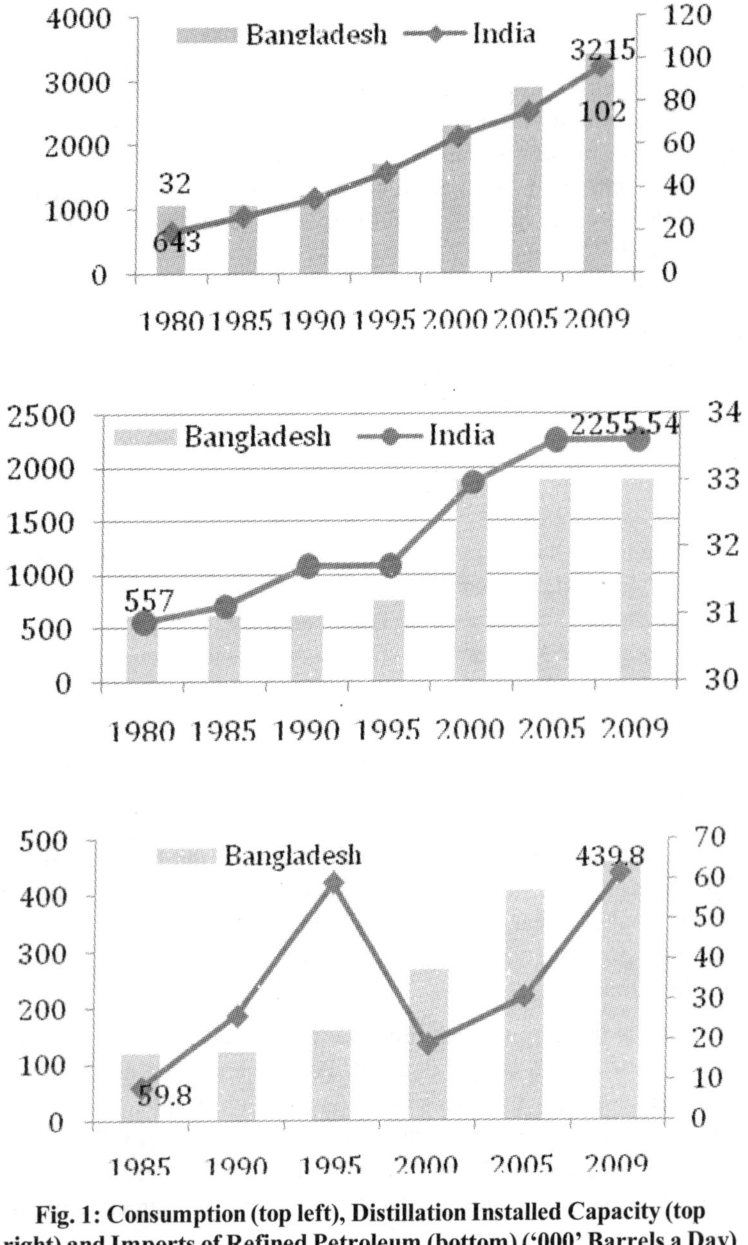

Fig. 1: Consumption (top left), Distillation Installed Capacity (top right) and Imports of Refined Petroleum (bottom) ('000' Barrels a Day)

Source: EIA and author's calculation.

Table 5: Consumption, Production, Reserve and Imports of Coal

		1980	*1985*	*1990*	*1995*	*2000*	*2005*	*2009*
Production	India (million short ton)	125.85	189.93	247.57	320.56	370.02	473.27	611.44
	Bangladesh (million short ton)	0.00	0.00	0.00	0.00	0.00	0.08	0.93
	India % of World	3.01	3.88	4.63	6.31	7.56	7.22	7.96
	Bangladesh % of World	0.00	0.00	0.00	0.00	0.00	0.00	0.01
Consumption (Million Short Tons)	India	122.93	194.07	247.86	329.29	403.41	504.91	685.65
	Bangladesh	259.04	108.03	620.60	707.68	727.53	817.92	1697.56
	India % of World	2.98	3.97	4.71	6.48	7.99	7.77	9.05
	Bangladesh % of World	0.01	0.00	0.01	0.01	0.01	0.01	0.02
Total Recoverable Coal (Billion Short Tons)	India							66.80
	Bangladesh							0.32
	India % of World							7.05
	Bangladesh % of World							0.03
Total Imports (Million Short Tons)	India	0.26	0.11	0.62	0.71	0.73	0.77	0.77
	Bangladesh	0.36	2.24	5.57	11.07	25.74	45.42	76.75
	India % of World	0.08	0.03	0.13	0.12	0.10	0.08	0.07
	Bangladesh % of World	0.12	0.55	1.20	1.93	3.57	4.96	7.38
Total Exports (Million Short Tons)	India	0.12	0.24	0.11	0.76	1.43	2.37	2.55
	Bangladesh							
	India % of World	0.04	0.06	0.02	0.13	0.20	0.25	0.23
	Bangladesh % of World							

Source: EIA and author's calculation.

Primary Energy

Both production and consumption of primary energy have been increasing in Bangladesh and India over the years. From 1.08 per cent in 1980, India's primary energy production has increased to 2.78 per cent of the world production in 2009. The case of Bangladesh is similar in this regard, which increased from 0.02 to 0.14 per cent in this period. However, both the countries demonstrate a positive gap between consumption and production, which are filled in through imports. (Fig. 2 and Table 6)

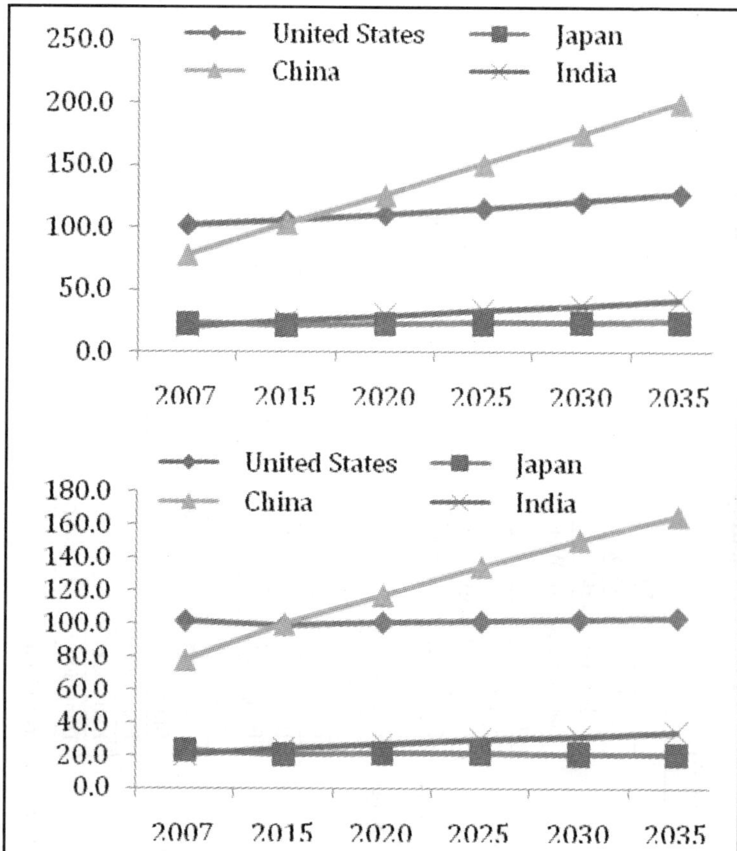

Fig. 2: World Primary Energy Consumption (Quadrillion Btu), High Growth (Left) and Low Growth (Right) Assumptions

Data Source: EIA.

Table 6: Consumption and Production of Primary Energy (Quadrillion Btu)

		1980	*1985*	*1990*	*1995*	*2000*	*2005*	*2009*
Production	India	3.10	5.27	6.82	9.48	9.83	11.76	13.66
	Bangladesh	0.05	0.10	0.16	0.26	0.35	0.53	0.68
	India % of World	1.08	1.71	1.95	2.61	2.49	2.57	2.78
	Bangladesh % of World	0.02	0.03	0.05	0.07	0.09	0.11	0.14
Consumption	India	4.04	5.91	7.88	11.44	13.46	16.36	19.95
	Bangladesh	0.13	0.17	0.25	0.38	0.50	0.71	0.87
	India % of World	1.43	1.91	2.27	3.13	3.39	3.54	4.05
	Bangladesh % of World	0.05	0.06	0.07	0.10	0.13	0.15	0.18

Source: EIA and author's calculation.

It is important to notice that India is one of the significant consumers of primary energy. According the EIA's projection by the year 2035, the average annual growth of primary energy consumption would be 2.6 and 1.9 per cent in high and low growth cases, respectively. It indicates that the consumption would be 41.5 quadrillion btu in 2035 in high growth case. The growth rate would be the third highest, after China (3.4 per cent) and Brazil (2.8 per cent), but the amount of consumption would be the third highest after China (200.5 per cent) and USA (126.7 per cent). Therefore, Bangladesh needs strong ties with India in securing primary energy from the competitive world market in order to reap the benefit of India's high economic growth.

Energy Security

Energy security can be referred to as the state of uninterrupted physical availability of energy at an affordable price keeping in mind environmental concerns. Energy security may also be defined as "the availability of usable energy supplies, at the point of final consumption, in sufficient quantity and timeliness so that, given due regard for encouraging energy efficiency, the economic and social development of the country is not materially constrained."[14] In other words, energy security indicates a state where the risks related to high dependence on energy imports, political instability in producing, and/or transit countries, as well as of other adverse contingencies, are mastered at reasonable economic costs. The dominant understanding of energy security is one of sufficient import diversification – diversification of energy sources as well as supplier portfolio. Other energy security risks include terrorist attacks on individual sites, network risks in the electricity sector, etc. Economically speaking, energy security is a part of "public goods", because it is non-rival (*i.e.*, it can be consumed by several people without loss of utility) and non-excludable (*i.e.*, exclusion of its use is not easily possible).[15]

Energy security is also defined as the ability of an economy to guarantee the availability of energy resource supply in a sustainable and timely manner with the energy price being at a level that will not adversely affect the performance of the economy. Thus, there are three fundamental elements of energy security: *first*, 'physical' energy security, i.e. the availability and accessibility of supply sources; *second*, 'economic' energy security, i.e. the affordability of resource acquisition and energy infrastructure development; and *third*, 'environmental sustainability', i.e. the sustainable development and use of energy resources that meet the needs of the present without compromising the ability of future generations to meet their own needs.[16]

Most energy importers, especially countries with negligible domestic natural resources, developed various strategies to enhance energy security and have pursued them. These strategies include upstream investment in producing countries, long-term contracting at premium prices, diversifying fuels and suppliers of each of them, promoting dual fuel technologies, efficiency and conservation, and building strategic reserves. Environmental considerations also impact energy security calculations. This also encourages development of alternative sources such as non-carbon generating technologies.

Energy security is an integral part of sustainable development for both, the industrialised and developed as well as developing nations. In Bangladesh, security of energy supply is threatened by a number of reasons, including lack of domestic energy resources, high dependence on imported transportation fuels and poor energy infrastructure.[17] Energy security indices[18] reveal that Bangladesh's rank in energy security is very low. In terms of 'net oil import dependency' indicator of energy security, the score of India and Bangladesh are 24 and 23 per cent, respectively *i.e.*, they are not much dependent on oil. It indicates that the country does not seem too vulnerable to oil supply risk as oil represents a relatively small share of their energy mix.

On the other hand, 'net import dependency' indicator of energy security indicates the score of 55 per cent for Bangladesh, indicating moderate vulnerability to shock in import sources. Conversely, it is 26 per cent for India, which indicates that the country is not vulnerable. However, this plain conclusion based on the index score would be misleading because oil products do not have convenient substitutes as transportation, agriculture and household fuels are mostly used by the poor and people of backward regions. Any disruption in oil imports is likely to result in inflation, macroeconomic instability and unrest among people who are poor and live in disadvantaged areas.

Finally, 'diversification of energy supply sources' indicator shows Bangladesh's low score (40 per cent) because of being primarily dependent on one source of energy. The low score is not necessarily a handicap for it is possible to sustain its economic development by managing this lack of diversification with the help of efficiency and conservation programmes among other initiatives. India has diversified energy moderately, as can be seen by its score of 64, but it can still achieve the diversification score up to the levels of very high-income countries like Japan, Canada and the USA.

The main objectives of Bangladesh National Energy Policy (NEP) (1996, 2004) are to provide energy for sustainable economic growth, meet the energy needs of different geographic zones of the country, and ensure sustainable operation of the energy utilities with a rational use of the total energy sources.[19] The revised NEP (2005) aims to "ensure reliable supply of energy to the people at reasonable and affordable price' vis-à-vis encouraging rational use of electricity and removing supply-side bottlenecks, thereby including the notion of energy security".[20] The Final Renewable Energy Policy of Bangladesh (2008) reveals that the major global transition in the energy sector is due to a decline in fossil fuel availability, the need to drastically cut global emissions for mitigating climate change (80 per cent reduction by 2050) and the need for 'energy security'.[21] However, the strategy of achieving energy security is absent in the policy documents.

Energy is linked with security of a country as well. The channels through which energy can generate both traditional and non-traditional security threats can be described as follows. Crisis of energy can reduce output in agricultural, industry and service sectors, leading to food shortage, job loss and an overall crisis in economic activities, which can be ascertained from the causal relationship between energy and GDP in Bangladesh as mentioned above. Such threats of food and economic security may give rise to other security threats, such as deterioration of domestic law and order situation, tension with other countries due to cross-border illegal migration, etc. However, energy crisis is not a security threat at present but it is very likely to be so in the near future.

Avenues of Cooperation

Bangladesh-India energy cooperation can take place in diverse fields. It should not be limited to the trade of some energy resources. It can cover, *inter alia*, stocktaking of knowledge, building mutually beneficial infrastructure, and sharing experience of successes and drawbacks.

Gas export to India from Bangladesh was the major issue a decade back. The current state of Bangladesh's reserve reveals that the country has shortage of gas and it will exhaust reserves by 2025. It needs large imports unless new reserves are found. It is looking forward to importing gas from Myanmar and electricity from India. In the case of the proposed Bangladesh-India-Myanmar gas pipeline project, both Bangladesh and India were in a position to derive benefits in a number of ways. However, Bangladesh put forward three major economic demands as a package with that project:

- transmission of hydro-electricity from Nepal and Bhutan to Bangladesh through Indian territory
- granting of unrestricted and round-the clock transit facilities to and from Nepal and Bhutan through India
- taking necessary measures to address the Bangladesh-India trade deficit

Conversely, India viewed the gas transit pipeline as a purely commercial deal de-linked from other bilateral issues. As a result the tri-lateral pipeline project was abandoned. However, at the advent of the fifth decade of Bangladesh-India relations, there are a number of potential avenues of energy cooperation to explore. Some of the areas are mentioned below:

The energy consumption of the two countries are reflected in the graph below:

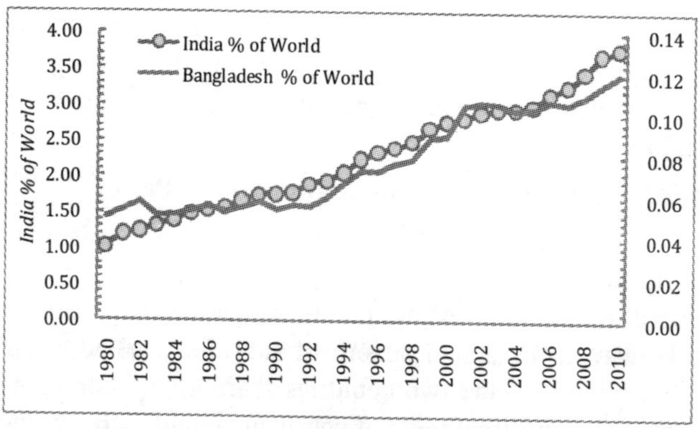

Fig. 3. Total Petroleum Consumption (Thousand Barrels Per Day)

Electricity

Bangladesh, Bhutan, Nepal and India multilateral electricity trade can be a viable option of cooperation in electricity where India has an active role to play. However, absence of interconnecting transmission systems between India and Bangladesh on the Eastern and North Eastern side has to-date hindered the transfer of electricity. Such interconnections at several points along the border can be established immediately if India and Bangladesh agree.

Natural Gas and Oil

Natural gas and crude oil can be brought from North-eastern India (Tripura and Mizoram) to Eastern India through Bangladesh. In addition, Bangladesh can extend cooperation if the pipelines transporting gas/oil either from Myanmar or from North-eastern India go through Bangladesh with the provision of accessibility to the gas/oil from these lines when necessity arises.

Strategic Reservoir

Bangladesh and India can have common strategic reserves of crude oil and petroleum products. Strategic Petroleum Reserve (SPR) can be built over time which could be used during the periods of high prices. Like other regions and regional blocs, an SPR can contribute positively to achieve energy security. It would be exclusively a crude petroleum reserve, not a stockpile of refined petroleum fuels. India has begun the development of a strategic crude oil reserve of 37,400,000 barrels (5,950,000 m^3/day), enough for two weeks of consumption. A joint India-Bangladesh reserve can be established as both the countries are heavily dependent on imported petroleum, and price hike in the world market directly transmits to the cost of production and other everyday living expenses that causes macroeconomic instability.

Joint Monitoring and Harmonisation of Oil Price

Both Bangladesh and India provide subsidy to petroleum aimed to support low income groups to buy petroleum products, as a strategy to support irrigation in the agriculture sector, and to reduce transport cost. However, the actual benefit of subsidies can be eaten up by informal traders — the two countries share a long common border through which informal trade of petroleum could increase due to the price differential. Therefore, regular price monitoring and harmonisation should be institutionalised to curb such informal cross-border oil flow besides increasing vigilance.

Other Areas

The two countries can undertake joint ventures for production of hydroelectricity in the northeast. This type of projects would provide benefit to both the parties if the electricity generated is shared. The northeast region would be developed because of power supply- India would benefit from the power export, and Bangladesh would benefit from higher volume of exports to the northeastern market due to higher import demand in that part of India.

Exchange of views and experience on renewable sources such as bio-gas, wind and solar energy is important. Both the countries have some best cases experiences which can be shared for mutual development of renewable energy resources. Bangladesh is currently undertaking the Roopur nuclear energy project with technical support from Russia. India can extend support by sharing its experience, which would benefit Bangladesh in avoiding nuclear hazards. India has significantly progressed in energy conservation through different pilot projects and strategies. These experiences can also be shared to benefit Bangladesh by helping in adopting energy conservation methods and technologies.

Concluding Remarks

This chapter covers the sectoral overview and key issues relating to energy and energy security in Bangladesh and India. It reveals that both Bangladesh and India are energy-deficient countries and energy consumption has short and long-term implications where their economic growth is concerned. India has been emerging as an economic powerhouse. Being a neighbour to such a big economy with impressive economic growth, Bangladesh can surely benefit through greater energy cooperation to achieve its Vision 2021 of becoming a middle-income country. At the onset of the fifth decade of diplomatic relations, the countries can undertake a range of initiatives, which include facilitating electricity trade and joint venture in the northeast of India, transporting crude oil and natural gas from Northeast to Eastern India through Bangladesh, establishing joint or regional SPR, institutionalising joint monitoring, harmonising of oil prices to curb cross-border informal trade, and sharing information and experience in renewable energy, nuclear energy and energy conservation. These initiatives would help achieve greater energy security in both the countries without causing any harm. Such Pareto-efficient avenues should be explored without delay.

Notes

1. Jaruwan Chontanawat, Lester C. Hunt, and Richard Pierse, *Causality between Energy Consumption and GDP: Evidence from 30 OECD and 78 Non-OECD Countries*, Guildford: Surrey Energy Economics Centre, 2006.
2. Mahfuz Kabir, A.B.M. Ziaur Rahman and Sharif M. Hossain, "BIMSTEC-Japan Cooperation in Energy Sector: Bangladesh Perspective", in Abdur Rob Khan (ed), *Towards BIMSTEC-Japan Comprehensive Economic Cooperation: Bangladesh Perspective*, Kolkata/Dhaka, CSIRD and BIISS, 2007.
3. India is already the 9th largest economy of the world with US$1.7 trillion of GDP in 2011.
4. D. Stern, "A Multivariate Cointegration Analysis of the Role of Energy in the US economy". *Energy Economics* 22: 2000, pp.267-283.
5. A.M.M. Masih and R. Masih, "On the Temporal Causal Relationship between Energy Consumption, Real Income, and Prices: Some new Evidence from Asian-Energy Dependent NICs based on a Multivariate Co-integration/Vector Error-Correction Approach". *Journal of Policy Modeling* 19(4), 1997, pp.417-440.
6. C.B.L. "Jumbe Co-integration and Causality between Electricity Consumption and GDP: Empirical Evidence from Malawi". *Energy Economics* 2004, 26, pp. 61-68.
7. Chontanawat *et al*, n.1, and Q.M.A. Hye and M. Mashkoor (2010), "Growth and Energy Nexus: An Empirical Analysis of Bangladesh Economy", *European Journal of Social Sciences* 15 (2), 2006, pp.51-55.
8. "Energy Security in South Asia", *Energy Security Quarterly*, Issue 1, January 2008.
9. World Development Indicators (Online).
10. "Energy Security in South Asia", n. 8.
11. However, power shortages increased during 2002-2008 due to insufficient public sector investments in power generation and failure to attract new investments from the private sector. See, Asian

Development Bank, *Sector Assistance Program Evaluation for Bangladesh Energy Sector*, Independent Evaluation Department, Asian Development Bank, Manila, October2009.

12. *Bangladesh Energy Profile*, at http://www.eia.doe.gov.
13. US Energy Information Administration (EIA), website: www.eia.doe.gov.
14. UN Economic Commission for Europe (UNECE) Energy Security Forum; cited in "Energy Security in South Asia", n.8.
15. Christian von Hirschhausen, *Strategies for Energy Security - A Transatlantic Comparison*, German Institute for Economic Research, Berlin, 2005.
16. There are several factors that can influence the 'security' of energy supply, such as: (i) the availability of fuel reserves, both domestically and through external suppliers; (ii) the ability of an economy to meet projected energy demand; (iii) the level of an economy's energy resource diversification and energy supplier diversification; (iv) accessibility to fuel resources, in terms of the availability of related energy infrastructure and energy transportation infrastructure; and (v) geopolitical concerns surrounding resource acquisition. For further details, see, *A Quest for Energy Security in the 21st Century: Resources and Constraints*, Asia Pacific Energy Research Center (APERC), 2007.
17. S.K. Noim Uddin and Ros Taplin,, "A Sustainable Energy Future in Bangladesh: Current Situation and Need for Effective Strategies", Paper presented at *the 2nd Joint International Conference on Sustainable Energy and Environment (SEE 2006)*, Bangkok, November 21-23 , 2006.
18. J.C. Jansen, W.G. van Arkel and M.G. Boots, *Designing Indicators of Long-Term Energy Supply Security*, report prepared for the Netherlands Environmental Assessment Agency, January 2004.
19. Government of Bangladesh, *National Energy Policy*, Ministry of Energy and Mineral Resources, Dhaka, 1996 and 2004.
20. Government of Bangladesh, *National Energy Policy (Updated in 2005)*, Ministry of Power, Energy and Mineral Resources, Dhaka, 2005, November.
21. Government of Bangladesh, *Renewable Energy Policy of Bangladesh*, Ministry of Power, Energy and Mineral Resources, Dhaka, 2008, November.

12

Transcending India-Bangladesh Relations: Framing Mutual Security Parameters

Smruti S Pattanaik

Prime Minister, Sheikh Hasina's visit to New Delhi, just after she completed a year in office, set the political tone for taking bilateral relations between India and Bangladesh forward. Five agreements – ranging from energy issues to trade and transit – were signed during this visit which according to many holds the promise of being deemed a watershed in their bilateral ties. The most important factor that generated hope was the change in the political atmospherics in Bangladesh regarding relations with India. The Awami League government headed by Sheikh Hasina made it clear through various statements and policy pronouncements that Bangladesh is ready to play a larger regional role both in regional connectivity and counter-terrorism[1]. It also laid stress on improving its bilateral ties with India. The relations between the two countries witnessed a significant shift in view of the agreement over a larger cooperative framework as per the joint communiqué issued in January 2010 when the Bangladesh prime minister visited India.

Both the countries have travelled a topsy-turvy path in bilateral relations. The 1971 liberation war provided a strong foundation for bilateral relations that were based on close cooperation, historical socio-cultural bonding and shared ideology. However this tempo could not be sustained as Bangladesh went through tumultuous political changes and India got mired in its own political evolution as a democratic state.

Various domestic and international factors impinged on the relations between the two countries. As a result, mutual mistrust and suspicion began to dominate the relationship that had started with shared values. Instead of envisioning a mutual security parameter, given their geographical proximity and porous international border, the two states viewed each other as a threat to their stability and internal order.

After the war of liberation and the emergence of Bangladesh, the two countries decided to sign the Treaty of Peace and Friendship in 1972 to ensure their mutual security interests. within a common parameter of friendship and non-aggression. Instead of providing a platform for further cooperation on issues of security; the 1972 treaty gave rise to suspicions as certain vested interests raised concerns regarding India's intentions and questioned the motives behind the signing of this treaty. The army felt that the treaty was signed to marginalise them. The creation of the India-trained *Jatiyo Rakkhi Bahini* that was supposed to be an 'aid to civil' multiplied the grievances nursed by the army[2]. With the reorientation of foreign policy under Zia's regime[3] Bangladesh gave less importance to its relations with India. India was also critical of the military takeover to begin with. Lingering unresolved problems between the two countries added to the complexity of the relationship. The larger geopolitics of the region also impinged on Indo-Bangladesh relations China which had vetoed Bangladesh's entry into the UN, recognised it as an independent country after the assassination of Mujib. The issue of the sharing of river water led to a further deterioration of relations between the two countries except for the brief period when the Janata government was in power in India. Given the power dynamic, unresolved problems and regime interests; suspicions between the two countries grew and not much attempt was made to address these issues. Ironically India was portrayed as a threat to Bangladesh to the surprise of many in India. India became a important factor in domestic political discourse and the relations between the two countries became so politicised that it was difficult to further normal ties because of too much public scrutiny.

The question that arises here is: How can the two countries with diverse security perceptions forge a parameter of mutual security, especially when they perceive each other to be a factor of instability. However geopolitical developments in the region and menace of terrorism and other non-traditional threats provided the two countries with the opportunity to cooperate.

Emerging Regional Security Scenario: Imperatives for Cooperation

One needs to take into account the regional security scenario to make an argument for how the two countries would benefit by cooperating on security issues. The reasons are as follows: Both the countries confront similar challenges to their security and stability. Problems of terrorism, small arms proliferation, drug smuggling, transnational networks of criminals and terrorists confront the two countries, thus making bilateral cooperation imperative. Guarding the long and porous border that stretches more than 4,000 kilometres is a challenge. Synergy between the border forces will help them to tackle smuggling, human trafficking and the illegal small arm trade that has sustained insurgency and criminal activities in the two countries. Can a single country handle these challenges alone? Offensive defence is no longer considered a prudent policy option for resolving issues and cooperation between states appears to be only alternative. A strong military is relevant only for dealing with threats from another state; however, the challenges that are mentioned above can only be dealt with by mutual cooperation.

States are likely to cooperate only when mutual benefit accrues to them and also to the regimes. It would be important to keep in mind that mutual security cannot be a zero sum game. India and Bangladesh have diverse aspirations as nation states and their perception of security has been different. The partition of the subcontinent in 1947, the liberation of Bangladesh in 1971 and subsequent developments have made a deep impact on the countries' identity construction and their threat perceptions. Though India remain central to the discourse on both these issues the geographical location and the economic aspirations of Bangladesh make the country imperative for it to take a broader view of India. However, in recent times the fragility of its democracy due to lack of strong institutions; challenges to the democratic order has come from radical elements and terrorists who have emerged as major concerns for security and stability of Bangladesh. These resonate with some of the challenges that India also faces such as radicalism, terrorism and problems of the economic and political marginalisation of some communities and groups in spite of the record achievement of its largely uninterrupted democracy.

Global geo-political developments have impacted on regional security. The end of the Cold War revealed the fragility of military might as a guarantor of state stability. The anti-Soviet jihad also unleashed extremist elements that have now acquired sophisticated technology, financial muscle and a global network that challenges the state system from within through subversive activities. They have become globalised in terms of their activities, ideological leanings and have sustained their presence through transnational activities. These non-state actors have emerged as a community with global reach given the revolution in communication network. They see themselves as brothers-in-arms benefiting from each other's networks. While the states, especially the post colonial ones tend to evaluate cooperation as an infringement of their sovereignty and are reluctant to share information and sometimes provide sanctuary to some of these terrorist elements, there appears to be greater cooperation among the non-state actors. Thus it is not surprising that countries have used them as a bargaining tool or instrument of destabilisation to serve regime interest or make them a part of asymmetrical warfare.

Unfortunately almost all the countries of South Asia have become victims of terrorism due to their reluctance to cooperate and use these elements as instrument of state policy. It is increasingly being realised that these elements who acquired prominence in South Asia after the end of Cold War cannot be tackled by any state single-handedly. Given the challenges of terrorism it is not only prudent but it is necessary that India and Bangladesh cooperate to meet the common challenges enumerated above. Security cooperation in terms of real time intelligence sharing is important. Actionable intelligence is likely to help in the arrest of terrorist and criminal elements and is likely to build confidence to further cooperation between the two countries. Reportedly in the recent past India alerted Bangladesh of a likely coup attempt by Islamists that could have threatened democratic stability in Bangladesh[4].

Non-state actors have taken advantage of the mistrust and suspicion that have existed between the two countries and have built their networks and support structures. The inability of the security forces to deal with the challenge, and their reluctance to cooperate in terms of capturing the terrorist or criminals wanted in one another's country has often led to misunderstanding that has served to strengthen these elements. Strained relations between the two countries is good news for non-state actors who thrive in such situations. For example, Indian insurgent groups benefited from the lack of cooperation between India and Bangladesh between 2001 and 2006 when the BNP was in power. Rather then cooperating to flush out Indian insurgents who were sheltering in Bangladesh the previous government insisted that there were no such insurgent groups taken shelter in Bangladesh. Sometimes regime interest has also exacerbated the sorry state of affairs in bilateral relations.

While the end of Cold War brought to the fore the non-traditional threats to security; but India and Bangladesh refused to recognise the post Cold War security dynamic and to forge mutually beneficial relations. Relations between the two countries remained at rock bottom mostly during the BNP regime. Awami League's first stint in power after re-establishment of democracy could not improve the relations between the two countries given the compulsions of electoral politics. The opposition parties led by the BNP continued to accuse the AL of making Bangladesh subservient to India. The 1972 Treaty was given silent burial in 1997. In any case the treaty was a non-starter from the beginning. It was projected as loss of sovereignty since the two countries required to consult each other and lost its purpose after Mujib's assassination. There was no concept of mutual security as the two countries accused each other of harbouring elements that they considered as threats to their national security. However it can be said that the relations between Bangladesh and India have been better during the Awami League's rule given their shared ideological affinity that is based on secularism and liberal democratic values. The BNP's constituency has been the centre right and religious political parties that have been sustained by the pro-Islamists and the anti-India constituency. Speaking at Atlantic Council on May 25, 2011 Begum Khaleda Zia emphasaised that BNP wants good relations with India while arguing that India needs to talk to all political parties to resolve outstanding issues with Bangladesh.

Post Cold War and the 9/11 political dynamics have provided a context for the two countries to address concerns regarding their security through cooperation. This is imperative due to the changing nature of security and the nature of the challenges that India and Bangladesh face. Two factors explain why it is necessary for the two countries to make a shift from a country centre perspective of security to a bilateral framework. These are terrorism and the transnational character of non-state actors; and globalisation and climate change. The issue of terrorism and non-state actors is discussed elsewhere in the paper.

Globalisation has unleashed its own dynamic. It has not only integrated markets but has led to the emergence of forces that have taken advantage of this phenomena and moved men and materials across borders with ease. Moreover, given the inter-dependent economies a crisis in one state is no more confined to that state alone. It has a cascading effect and has the potential to generate instability across the region[5]. The under ground money market, transferring money through *hundi,* proliferation of small arms through smuggling requires that the states cooperate to address the issue of money laundering that funds terrorism and illegal activities[6]. Human trafficking is another issue that has taken advantage of porous border and in this context the children and women have been worst sufferers.

Whether it is the effect of climate change or floods and other natural calamities, all these factors impinge on state security. They can lead to massive internal displacement and may lead to migration creating unnecessary inter-state tension. In such circumstances India and Bangladesh can cooperate for the rehabilitation and resettlement of environmental refugees. Devising flood control mechanisms, setting up advance warning systems and sharing of data are necessary to meet the challenges of natural disasters. While climate change and flood are not important components of hardcore security they do have interstate ramifications in terms creating environmental refugees by displacing population.

Dealing with the Security Challenges

As discussed above, threats from non-state actors are a greater source of insecurity than the military forces of either India or Bangladesh. Bangladesh in the recent past has seen spurt in terrorism due to various reasons. Whether it was the issue of religious extremism that sent shock waves throughout Bangladesh with more than 450 bomb blasts all over the country in 2004 or rise in religious extremism in India that threatens its pluralistic fabric and its democratic antecedents; the two countries need to unite to meet the challenge. Given the fact that the two countries are also evolving democracies they face several threats to their nation building process. Any instability would have cross border ramifications.

It has been observed in the past that the insurgent groups have taken advantage of the porous borders and have moved into each other's territory with much ease. In the past there have been incidents when the RAB (Rapid Action Battalion) had confronted some of these groups but the government of Bangladesh under Begum Khaleda Zia denied the presence of any such groups[7] thereby overruling any cooperation in this regard. While sheltering these elements may give a short term advantage to a country but in the long run these groups may emerge as a threat as has happened in the case of Pakistan. They are likely to set up local networks and establish linkages and can operate independent of state support. If required they can also collaborate with domestic terrorists to target the host country to further their interest or get rid of regimes that are considered ideologically incompatible or threat to their activities. In this respect there is no dearth of fund and rather there is a chance that they may get help from international actors having vested interest in the region.

However, the dynamics of India-Bangladesh relations are different. Intelligence sharing between the intelligence agencies of the two countries and cooperation in arresting these elements is bound to have a salutary effect on bilateral relations. For example unprecedented cooperation in the arrest of Indian insurgents by Dhaka is one of the rare instances of assistance that generate enormous good will and makes one believe that such cooperation is not difficult to achieve.[8]

In spite of difficulties and disagreements in the past over the Indian insurgent hideouts and the number of such camps that have existed in Bangladesh; the handing over of the ULFA leaders by Dhaka gives hope and highlights the fact that given political will the two countries can transcend mistrust and apprehension. Handing over of the insurgents to India was accomplished in spite of the fact that the two countries do not have extradition treaty. To quote the prime minister of Bangladesh:

> They [militants and terrors] will use the land of Bangladesh to conduct their terrorism in another country and we will create enmity by harbouring them — this cannot be... I know there are risks. I also have life threat but for the sake of the country and its sovereignty, I will not allow that.[9]

Thus political will is a pre-requisite even for the sharing of intelligence. The two countries are dealing with the issue of intelligence sharing at the regional level within the SAARC framework as well as at the bilateral level through home secretaries' meets. Both the countries have also exchanged lists of criminals staying in each other countries at various bilateral meetings. The home secretaries of the two countries held talks in January 2010 to discuss cooperation in this matter. India has also sought Bangladesh's help in dismantling 46 insurgent camps which it believes continue to operate in that country[10].

Guarding the Border

Smuggling has emerged as another challenge to the security of the two countries as the border is breached to smuggle goods especially cattle that is rampant in this border. This has resulted in firing across the border and civilian casualties. Smuggling of phensedyl into Bangladesh is common and Bangladesh has often complained about this as it is facing the problem of phensedyl addiction. In a meeting held last year March between the drug control agencies of both sides, Bangladesh has reportedly handed over a list of 51 factories where phensedyl is produced and later smuggled to Bangladesh. Many times children are used for smuggling items which shows how children are increasingly dragged into drug networks as they arouse sympathy and if caught may not face severe punishment. Bangladesh remains a major transit point as it is situated in the middle of 'golden triangle' and the 'golden crescent'. Smuggling of drugs is also a common phenomenon. Illicit arms also find their way into each other's countries and this feeds political violence and insurgency and creates general insecurity among the citizens. The Chittagong arms haul of 2004 also revealed the transnational nature of the network. Terrorist groups can use Bangladesh to transfer arms given the nexus between law enforcing authorities and the arms merchants. There are also chances that pilferage may happen during the transfer of small arms which may fall into the hand of ordinary criminals. There are reports that Indian insurgents are procuring arms from China and Myanmar and using Bangladesh as a transit point. This was revealed in a written statement of India's minister of state for home affairs in the Rajya Sabha[11].

The JMB that was responsible for more than 450 bomb blasts all over Bangladesh was reported to have procured bomb making materials from across the border in India. The porousness of the border has made it difficult to address the issue. Apart from this, the lack of cooperation between the agencies of the two countries has helped the smugglers and terrorists operating in the region. Thus only way this problem can be tackled is through joint patrols. The two countries are discussing the issue of joint patrolling and coordinated patrols by border forces are already taking place. The process requires to be synergised in terms of coordination to make it effective to prevent cross border crime.

Unauthorised border crossing has created tension between the two countries. Given the nature of security threat to the countries of the region it sometimes becomes difficult to distinguish common people from the criminals and anti national elements in the darkness of night. This has led to unpleasant situations. The joint India-Bangladesh guidelines for the border authorities issued in 1975 require the two forces to cooperate as it was realised without such cooperation it would be impossible to guard the border. The riverine features that are prone to mud sliding make it almost impossible to act against the geo-physical dynamics of this border that is prone to heavy rain fall. The 1975 treaty requires that: "between the two border security forces and police there should be close cooperation and everything possible should be done to ensure eradication of trans border crimes, smuggling etc. by mutual and timely exchange of information and intelligence at appropriate level"[12]. However it is clear that such instructions exist only in letter and have not been carried out in spirit as non-cooperation of Bangladesh and its refusal to address the issue of illegal migration forced India to build a fence on its eastern border to address cross border problems[13]. The government of India has sanctioned the fencing of 3,436.59 km of the Indo-Bangladesh border out of which 2,735.12 km has already been completed[14].

At the recent director general level meetings between the BSF and BDR it was proposed to have joint patrols to deal with trans-border crimes. India has also agreed to use non-lethal weapons on the border. India has raised fences on the border to deal with some of the challenges unilaterally. However, with mutual understanding and trust, as both the countries are equally threatened by non-state actors this problem can be addressed to the satisfaction of the two countries. These would perhaps require joint exercises and exchange of officers for training at each others institutes that would not only help them to devise strategies by building on their experience but would also be a major confidence building exercise. Enclaves also add to the problem. Both the countries have already demarcated the border and have taken the decision to exchange enclaves and land under adverse possession. The two countries have held home secretary level meetings to address issues of mutual concern. In January 2010 the two countries agreed on mutual legal assistance on criminal matters and signed a pact for combating international terrorism, organised crime and illicit drug trafficking.

Framework to Address Security Concerns

The two countries have adopted a bilateral, regional and multilateral framework to address the security challenges that they face. Moreover, the post 9/11 dynamics proved how serious the issue of terrorism can be, when the terrorists find sanctuary outside the geographical entity of the nation-state which makes it almost impossible for individual countries to tackle the problem singlehandedly. Individual countries in South Asia have been fighting terrorism for a very long time. Due to mutual distrust the regional framework has not worked as the states remain mired in the debate on the definition of a terrorist. Giving sanctuary to terrorists or tolerating their presence by not taking action against them because of domestic compulsions and to use them as instruments of foreign policy to pressurise opponents has backfired in South Asia. Some countries have learnt the lesson and have changed their policy, but some countries continue to use it as an instrument of state policy. Some of the initiatives in which the two countries are members are discussed below.

(i) Bilateral Initiatives

After the war of liberation India and Bangladesh attempted to enter into a mutual security arrangement to address the common challenges to their security. For example: In 1972 the two countries signed a bilateral Treaty of Peace and Friendship to address their security concerns. The treaty was relevant in the circumstances when Bangladesh was liberated. Many countries had not recognised Bangladesh as an independent country and China had vetoed Bangladesh's entry into UN as an independent nation. The Bangladesh army was still in its infancy. This treaty also needs to be understood in the context of the Cold War[15]. The treaty has now lapsed after 25 years of existence.

The countries have regular bilateral talks at the home secretary level to address issues of mutual concern. The two border forces – the Border Security Force and the Bangladesh Rifles also hold director general level meetings to address border related issues. There are also regular commander level meetings at the local level to address problems arising from the patrolling at the border. These interactions provide an institutional framework to address issues that have larger security implications especially in the context of a porous border.

After Sheikh Hasina who was target of August 21, 2004 bomb blast assumed power, she floated the idea of a South Asian task force on terrorism. However, there has not been must progress in translating this idea into concrete policy. However, the Awami League government has taken several actions against terrorist groups and has arrested leaders of radical groups and has also seized arms and ammunition which would impact on regional security dynamics. These groups are a threat to the Bangladesh state and some of them have links with groups in India. The government realises that it is essential to root out terrorism in all its forms to deal with the issue comprehensively. The AL government's commitment is reflected in its decision to arrest the ULFA leaders and hand them over to India. This has heralded a new chapter in bilateral cooperation.

One can argue that an institutional framework though important, is not necessary if the two countries have the political will to cooperate on the issue of terrorism. Bangladesh which has been a victim of terrorism and tragic suicide bombings has made its battle against terrorism and the ideology that feeds in terrorism, the main pillar of its policy. The bilateral approach to deal with terrorism, however, will triumph given the mutuality of concern. The two countries decided to sign a Framework Agreement on Cooperation and Development during Prime Minister Manmohan Singh's visit to Dhaka in September 2011.

Article 9 of the Framework Agreement on cooperation for development reads, "To cooperate on security issues of concern to each other while fully respecting each other's sovereignty. Neither party shall allow the use of its territory for activities harmful to the other"[16].

(ii) *Regional/global Initiatives*

As members of SAARC and BIMSTEC, the two countries are part of the regional framework for tackling some of the challenges that they are facing. For example: the SAARC convention on terrorism signed in 1987 and additional protocol ratified in 2005 provides a framework for dealing with terrorism – a common challenge faced by the countries of the region. An additional protocol that was ratified in 2005 also addresses the issue of money laundering. Though both, the convention on terrorism as well as additional protocol have the provision for extradition but the criteria for extradition is too ambiguous thus defeating the very purpose of the treaty. For example Article 7 of the convention reads:

> Contracting states shall not be obliged to extradite, if it appears to the requested State that by reason of the trivial nature of the case or by reason of the request for the surrender or return of a fugitive offender not being made in good faith or in the interests of justice or for any other reason it is unjust or inexpedient to surrender or return the fugitive offender.

The Additional Protocol contains a similar provision in Article 17. It also criminalises "the provision, collection or acquisition of funds for the purpose of committing terrorist acts and taking further measures to prevent and suppress financing of such acts".

BIMSTEC the other regional cooperation organisation of which India and Bangladesh are members has also ratified cooperation on terrorism among its member states. In accordance with the BIMSTEC summit declaration a joint working group was set up in 2004 to look into the issue of terrorism and transnational crime. At the 12th BIMSTEC ministerial meeting held in 2009, the regional organisation adopted the convention on combating terrorism and insurgency. Both the regional initiatives – SAARC and BIMSTEC – recognise the transnational character of the threat of terrorism. Unfortunately, in spite of this recognition, the regional initiative has largely been ineffective as the language of the convention remains ambiguous and there are so many conditions for extradition that they defeat the very purpose of the agreement.

India and Bangladesh are part of UN initiative on terrorism. Prime Minister Hasina after assuming power also announced that Bangladesh would take the lead to form a South Asia task force on terrorism. The necessity of forming this task force was explained by Foreign Minister Dipu Moni at a press conference where she said:

> So far as the concept of regional task force to fight terrorism is concerned, already certain regional and international mechanisms exist. All of us are part of U.N. Security Council resolution... to ban terrorist organisations... What is more important is the sincerity to fight against the menace of terrorism.[17]

Her initiative has the support of Western countries but it is yet to garner much support within the region.

Conclusion

As the states of South Asia make their journey as nation-states and recognise that they are multi-cultural and plural societies and promote democracy and inclusive growth which would empower marginal groups to become stakeholders, the security challenges that they are facing from within would reduce. The temptation of groups to take external aid to fulfil their political aspiration would then become less attractive. A self confident nation to some extent will address problem of insecurity between the states that mostly arise from asymmetry in size and aspirations for power in the international system which hinder cooperation. However, in spite of best efforts there will be groups that will resort to terrorism. If states have excellent relations between themselves and recognise the long term threat that these entities may pose to the state itself, the terrorists/insurgents will have less of an incentive. Both India and Bangladesh have been facing the challenge of terrorism. The current prime minster of Bangladesh who survived an attack in August 2004 realises this. Moreover, the 2005 bomb blasts, and the later suicide attacks on judiciary and the emergence of Jamatul Mujaheedin Bangladesh (JMB) and Jagrata Muslim Janata Bangladesh (JMJB) made the people of Bangladesh realise the imminent threat to their way of life. The two countries do not need any other reason for cooperation as whether one likes or not, the terrorists have become truly South Asian in terms of their cooperative endeavours that facilitate their objectives. While regional and multilateral frameworks are essential to deal with various security challenges these countries face, bilateral institutional mechanisms can deal with the issues that fall within the capacity of the two states to meet the challenge. The moot question here is why in spite of compelling reasons for close cooperation the two countries lack synergy on security issues? The reason is regime centricism that has made governments prefer narrow regime interests over the broader well being of their people.

The two countries face common security challenges that range from poverty, illiteracy to small arms proliferation, militancy etc. Though there are many issues on which the two countries differ, nevertheless this could be the beginning of a journey to forge mutually beneficial ties in a globalising world. To quote Prime Minister Manmohan Singh, "India seeks to build a new future with Bangladesh. The time has come to chart a new path. We are ready to pursue a bold vision for our relations, based on mutual respect and mutual benefit". India should not let the opportunity to redefine its relations with Bangladesh be frittered away by getting entangled in the bilateral nitty-gritty. For example the decision of the Awami League government to participate in the Asian highway and to constitute a South Asian task force on terrorism would certainly give Bangladesh a visible regional role. In the past Bangladesh played a pioneering role in creating SAARC and other such decisions therefore would give an edge to the Bangladesh foreign policy given its strategic geographical location. Cooperation on security assumes greater importance as it is security issues that generate mistrust and suspicion that percolates into other areas of bilateral ties.

Notes

1. Haroon Habib, "Hasina Proposes South Asia Task Force to combat Terrorism", *The Hindu*, February 10, 2009. at http://www.hindu.com/2009/02/10/stories/2009021059951200.htm, accessed on June 2011. The government also signed the Asian Highway network that forms important part of inter-region connectivity. To quote Prime Minister Hasina "For rapid socioeconomic development of our country, we need to be linked with Asian Highway", see "Bangladesh Gets abroad Asian Highway Network", http://www.asiaecon.org/special_articles/read_sp/12874

2. For details see "Internal Political Dynamics and Bangladesh's Foreign policy towards India", *Strategic Analysis,* 29(3), July-September 2005, pp. 398-99.
3. Article 25 of the Bangladesh constitution inserted by General Zia emphasized on developing fraternal relations with brother Muslim countries both for political and economic reasons.
4. "Dhaka Tipped off by Delhi", *Daily Star*, January 22, 2012.
5. For example: the war in Afghanistan has impacted the security situation in the entire region. Economic crisis in the US has also affected entire globe.
6. Instance of such cooperation is the decision to facilitate the CHT treaty which saw the return of Chakmas refugees to Bangladesh. In the context of Sri Lanka, India provided critical naval intelligence to Sri Lanka and provided it with radar to enhance Sri Lankan's army's capability to defeat the LTTE.
7. Mohammed Tajuddin, "Countering Terrorism-A regional Perspective", in Farooq Sobhan ed. *Trends in Militancy in Bangladesh: Possible Responses*, UPL, Dhaka, 2010, p. 84.
8. Bangladesh has made several arrests which attest to the commitment of the current government. For example on 10 April BDR handed over Sujit Debbarma of the National Liberation Front of Tripura to the BSF. On 29 May the Rapid Action Battalion demolished the camps of Kamtapur Liberation Organisation but was unable to arrest anyone because they fled before the raid. In recent important development Arabinda Rajkhowa, the Chief ideologue of ULFA was arrested In Meghalaya. In November ULFA's finance Secretary Chitrabon Hazarika and Foreign Secretary Sasha Chowdhury were arrested in Dhaka and were forced to surrender to the Indian security forces in Assam. Similarly, NLFT chief Bishwa Mohan Deb Burman was arrested in Bangladesh. Bangladesh Carries out Raid on Indian Separatist Groups", at <http://www.thaindian.com/newsportal/uncategorized/bangladesh-carries-out-raids-on-indian-separatists-camp_10054258.html>.
9. No Room for Terror:", *Daily Star,* January 6, 2010.
10. "46 insurgent Camps inside Bangladesh", *Daily Star*, December 17, 2011 http://www.thedailystar.net/newDesign/news-details.php?nid=214487
11. http://articles.timesofindia.indiatimes.com/2011-12-09/guwahati/30497585_1_indo-myanmar-border-insurgent-groups-border-areas

12. Avtar Singh Bhasin, *Indo-Bangladesh Documents*, Siva Exim Pvt. Ltd., Delhi, 1996, p. 1903.
13. "India-Bangladesh Border: Flawed inheritance and Problematic Future", *Strategic Analysis*, October-November 2011.
14. Ministry of Home Affairs, *Annual Report* 2010-2011, p. 39.
15. For details see author's article "Internal Political Dynamics and Bangladesh's foreign policy towards India", *Strategic Analysis* 29(3), 2005, pp. 398-401. Also see Shaukat Hasan, "Indo-Bangladesh Relations During the Awami League Government, 1972-1975", unpublished thesis, Australian National University, 1987, p.139. J.N.Dixit, *Liberation and Beyond: Indo-Bangladesh Relations* UPL, Dhaka, 1999, p.138; Mohammad Shahiduzzaman, "Alliance Reliability in the Post Cold War context and Bangladesh's Military Strategy in Bangladesh and SAARC: Issues, Perspective and Outlook", paper presented in a seminar organized by BIISS, August 23-24, 1992, p. 5.
16. http://www.mea.gov.in/mystart.php?id=100018197&pid=2294
17. Harron Habib, "Hasina Proposes South Asia Task Force to Combat Terrorism", *The Hindu,* February 10, 2009.

13

Security Dynamics and Bangladesh-India Relations: Bangladesh Perspectives

Shaheen Afroze

Introduction

Bangladesh's relations with India have gone through several ups and downs over the past 40 years. The relationship has often been marked by occasional setbacks, thereby making the bilateral ties rather lukewarm and uneven. It will not be an exaggeration to say that they plummeted to a low of mutual mistrust and suspicion from the heights of very close friendship that lasted a brief period in the aftermath of Bangladesh's independence in 1971. Neither the warmth or nor the trust in the relationship could be sustained for very long. This uneven relationship appears to be caused by the misperceptions regarding each other in both countries. Recently, there has been a tectonic shift in bilateral relations between the two countries following a series of high level visits that produced some significant outcomes for both Bangladesh and India in the security arena. Against this background, the main objectives of this chapter are to understand the common security challenges and their implications for Bangladesh-India relations by analysing the security dynamics and how can these be dealt with by the two countries. The paper argues that since this is a defining period in Bangladesh-India relations, there is an opportunity for transforming the overall relationship into one that can address each other's sensitivities and enable them to work together to achieve economic prosperity social benefit and development.

Security Concerns of India and Implications for Bangladesh-India Relations

India from the very beginning of its existence has remained sensitive and concerned about peace and stability in its neighbourhood. This is because it believes that political instability and disorder on its periphery may impact its own security directly or indirectly. In this regard, India's policy has been opposed to any external interference in case of a crisis situation in the region. Also, India remains against any sort of alignment among its neighbours, in particular when it, in India's reading, has an anti-Indian underpinning. A brief glance at the region's history would show how concerned India was about the Tamil crisis in Sri Lanka, Nepal's deepening relations with China, the change in Bangladesh's domestic and foreign policy after 1975 etc. It may be mentioned that this pertains mostly to the smaller states on India's periphery, whereas in case of Pakistan, India's policy is guided by completely different geo-strategic and security considerations.

Beginning from the end of the Cold War period, India witnessed changes in its own polity. In particular, the policy of economic liberalisation broadened India's mindset. With the end of the Cold War, the question of alignments and superpower involvement in the region lost ground. India wanted to seize upon all opportunities in post-Cold War period to accelerate its economic and military power. The second nuclear test in 1998 attests to this. With the restoration of democracy in Bangladesh from the early 1990s, India's expectations rose high. But the region again plunged into crisis due to Maoist insurgency in Nepal, increasing tension in Indo-Pak relations (Kargil), and involvement of the outside powers in peace talks relating to the Tamil crisis bypassing India etc.

As far as Bangladesh is concerned, the restoration of democracy in 1991 in Bangladesh was a good sign for India's political and economic development despite the fact that the journey towards democracy begun by a party that was opposed to India's - traditionally favoured party- the Awami League. However, due to globalisation and India's opening up, economic relations between Bangladesh and India started flourishing. Bangladesh's adoption of a free market economy suited India. However, contentious bilateral issues, in particular sharing of the Ganges water and the insurgency in Chittagong Hill Tracts (CHT) (where India was reportedly involved) were not dealt with during the initial period of Bangladesh's democratic transition. Despite this, international relations between the two countries though not cordial were normal.

In 1996, when the Awami League came to power the window of opportunity was further widened to mend the fences. The CHT accord and the Ganges treaty testify to this. The period from 2001-2006 was apparently not very congenial for India. The induction of Islamic parties (four party alliance led by the Bangladesh Nationalist Party) or elements in the then government did not suit India. Disputed issues again remained on the back burner. Increasing acts of terrorism by the Islamic extremists in Bangladesh added to India's disappointment. Issues like transit and trans-shipment kept oscillating to and fro from the table to the cupboard.

Bangladesh-India Border and Related Security Issues

Bangladesh is surrounded on the north, east and west by India. India shares over 4,096 kilometres (km) of a porous land boundary with Bangladesh - the longest among all its neighbours of which 6.5 km are yet to be demarcated. Of these, 1.5 km are in Daikhata in the Panchagarh district; 2 km in the riverine parts of the Comilla-Tripura area and 3 km in Lathitila-Dumabari in the Moulvibazar district remain undemarcated. All these areas remain undemarcated because of differing technical positions taken by Bangladesh and India.

The problem of enclaves is a legacy from the days of British India which Bangladesh inherited in 1971 after its independence. As per an agreed list of enclaves signed in April 1997 at the level of the director general land record and survey (DGLR&S), Bangladesh and DLRS, India, Bangladesh has 51 enclaves inside India measuring 7,110 acres and India has 111 enclaves measuring 17,158.1 acres within the territory of Bangladesh.[1] According to the Land Boundary Agreement of 1974, both Bangladesh and India were required to exchange their enclaves expeditiously. Although Bangladesh handed over the Berubari enclaves to India soon after the Land Boundary Agreement was signed, India is yet to hand over Tin Bigha.

There are about 52 pieces of land measuring about 3,500 acres belonging to Bangladesh which are in the adverse possession of India and about 49 pieces of land measuring about 3000 acres belonging to India that are in the adverse possession of Bangladesh.[2] The issue has remained unresolved for the last 40 years contributing to frequent border incidents. According to Article 2 of the Land Border Agreement of May 1974 between Bangladesh and India, all the areas in adverse possession of each country were to be measured and demarcated at the earliest. Once these are completed, the areas in adverse possession would be exchanged within six months. Although the Bangladesh government was quick to ratify the Agreement in 1975, the Indian government has yet to do it. Through two supplementary agreements signed in 1982 and then in 1992, India instead of agreeing to lease the area in perpetuity to Bangladesh, as was envisaged in the 1974 Agreement, has agreed to allow the common use of the Tin Bigha corridor by both countries.[3] It may be mentioned that some acres of land in Sylhet too reportedly have been occupied by the Indian Border Security Forces since independence.[4]

Apart from these, there are other issues relating to the Bangladesh-India border which act as barriers to trust and confidence building between the two neighbours. India claims that cross border movement of illegal immigrants is causing economic, social and political problems, especially in Assam and the Northeastern hill states, and in many other parts of India. The successive governments of Bangladesh have denied it. There are also claims and counter claims by both India and Bangladesh of each hosting terrorist groups on their soil to conduct terrorist activities against each other.

Bangladesh claims that India has built an illegal fence without mutual agreement for a military rather than simply a civilian purpose. This claim is denied by India.[5] It may be mentioned that the 1974 Agreement envisaged that no defensive structure would be erected within 150 yards of the Bangladesh-India border. After 1982, barbed wire fencing was erected by India. Bangladesh viewed this as defensive structure which India rejected saying that the term "defensive structure" meant walls or bunkers which would impede the movement of military vehicles and since a tank can easily pass through it, the barbed wire was not a military barrier. Rather, India further contended, barbed wire fencing was needed to restrict movement of 'illegal immigrants', 'smugglers' and 'suspected militants'.

Then there is also the issue of the killing of over a thousand unarmed Bangladeshis by Indian BSF since 1990. This is seen as a "negation of the most elementary norms of inter-state behaviour unheard of in modern inter-state relations between two supposedly friendly countries having normal political, commercial and cultural relations."[6] According to a human rights body in Bangladesh *Odhikar*, on an average one unarmed Bangladeshi is killed every four days on the Indo-Bangladesh border by the BSF. In 2010 alone, 74 Bangladeshis were killed, 72 injured while 43 were kidnapped. The latest in the series is the killing of a 15-year-old Bangladeshi girl by BSF on Kurigram border. It merits repetition that the Bangladesh-India border is not like any other border, and for very compelling reasons requires sensitivity of management. Unfortunately, border killings have to some extent overshadowed the otherwise harmonious relationship between the two countries. It is also reported that there are regular violations of Bangladesh territory by intruders from across the border, who under protection of BSF take away crops grown by Bangladeshi farmers in their land. This usually happens in the Sylhet and north Bengal areas.

What can be done?

The Bangladesh-India relationship, after being in the doldrums for more than five years prior to 2009, began to witness a period of dynamism after the Grand Alliance government's assumption of office in January 2009. The relationship has been on a new trajectory. There is a change of mindset about India in Bangladesh, an attitude that has prompted proactive action on matters related to India, on the part of the Bangladesh leadership. In that positive frame of mind, Bangladesh has acted timely to address the security concerns of India. Its counter-extremist actions, which have a bearing on India's security too, are worth the mention. One would have liked Bangladesh's security concerns also to be addressed similarly -particularly border killings. If the border is a matter of concern for India, so are killings a highly sensitive matter for Bangladesh. For every mile of progress made in respect of bilateral relationship in other sectors, we regress two miles with the death of every Bangladeshi at the hands of the BSF. India has made a commitment to bring down the killings to zero. One hopes that this is not just another pledge among the many made by India in the last several years. Bangladesh would be reassured if the articulation of intent is translated into action on ground, in keeping with earlier assurance of 'gun freeze' on the border.

Bangladesh's undisputed resolve to combat terrorism contributed to India's comfort, in particular when the prime minister of Bangladesh sought to launch a South Asian anti terrorist task force. This has captured the attention of the vocal Indian media and even the columnists most critical of Bangladesh have taken note of it. Bangladesh has announced these unprecedented acts of friendship and taken tremendous risk from the revenge seeking insurgent organizations of North East India. Bangladesh has also handed over the Berubari enclave to India, lowered tariffs for Indian goods entering Bangladesh but these have not been duly reciprocated by India.[7]

It is high time that the roadblocks between the two friendly countries should be resolved on the basis of reciprocity, goodwill, cooperation and trust. In any case, it is India that should be taking the initiative to improve Bangladesh-India relations and play a dominant role, given its power position in South Asia. Bilaterally, both countries could take further steps in the following areas in order to maintain a balanced relationship:

- Fixing a final date and venue for Bangladesh-India Land Boundary Agreement of 1974 to solve the issues of the Tin Bigha Corridor, enclaves and border demarcation. Although the two countries have exchanged strip maps in 2011 regarding boundary demarcation, the Indian Parliament is yet to ratify it. Again, the text of the Bangladesh-India Land Border Agreement of 1974 has changed. Previously, there was mention of 'lease in perpetuity' about the Tin Bigha Corridor but now it is changed to '24 hours access'. The question thus arises whether the Agreement needs to be ratified by the Bangladesh Government again. The resolution of the issue calls for urgency. It will, no doubt, work as a major trust and confidence building measure between Dhaka and New Delhi, remove unnecessary suffering of the residents, and more importantly, it will de-escalate border conflicts.
- Hold frequent joint meetings between the border forces of the two countries and outlining a clear political indication from Indian part to put an end to the violent activities by the BSF in border areas;
- Terrorism is the most intractable threat which makes South Asia a volatile region. An inadequate legal mechanism, lack of

information sharing and lack of long term strategic planning are some of the major obstacles in the way of countering terrorism. Therefore, trans-border cooperation at the bilateral level is essential to combat terrorism. Thus, with the wholehearted cooperation and actions against militants from both countries, overall regional security conditions might improve :

- Addressing the issues of improving the land customs stations on both sides of Bangladesh-India border to prevent illegal trade/smuggling;
- Increasing people to people connection through exchange of visits to change the mindset and reduce distrust between the two countries. For this, relaxation of visa restrictions is necessary for the easy movement of people.
- It is important to highlight that the matters of security be treated as common, cooperative and indivisible based on pragmatism and realism.
- Both the countries' media need to act more responsibly. They must realise that parochial, partisan and speculative news coverage and misinterpretation of facts only create misunderstandings between the two countries thereby giving opportunity to different forces to exploit the situation in their favour.

Points to Ponder

Both Bangladesh and India must realise that they are tied to each other by common ideals and views and that their ties date back to the time of Bangladesh's independence movement. India must also realise that it can do very little to enhance its security on its own. It therefore must take its neighbours into confidence. The landslide victory of the Awami League demonstrated peoples' confidence in the party for taking the country towards development and prosperity. This should give India renewed confidence to deal with Bangladesh. Improvement of relations with India figured in the Awami League election manifesto. There is nothing in Bangladesh's foreign or domestic policy to antagonise India. In particular, when it comes to foreign policy, Bangladesh's opening up to the US and China goes in same spirit of friendship as it is with India.

Conclusion

Though the resolution of the issues are yet to take their final shape as they are still being negotiated, it would be important to take note that the negotiating process is continuing without any rupture which is a positive sign. Given the sensitive nature of the issues, both the governments should be responsive to the mood and sentiment of the people. To be frank, given the vast disparity between India and Bangladesh, relations between the two can never be equal, however, they can be based on equity, i,e.'justness'. At this critical juncture of India's rise to the status of a global power, it can, and probably has the capacity to make concessions to its smaller neighbours. This mind-set is believed to exist in today's India. What is needed is to translate this into reality. Perhaps there is no other greater occasion than the joint celebration of Tagore's 150th birth anniversary in 2011 by Bangladesh and India which will remain an invaluable example of Bangladesh-India cooperation - to be emulated in the future.

Notes

1. Abdus Salam Chowdhury, "Bangladesh-India Land Border Issues and Management", *NDC Journal*, June 2003.
2. Kulbir Krishnan, "Policing the Indo-Bangladesh Border", *Strategic Analysis*, New Delhi, XXV(5), 2001, pp. 664-665.
3. Sheikh Md. Monirul Islam *et. al,* "National Security of Bangladesh: Strategy and Cost Effectiveness", in Mustafa K. Mujeri and Shamsul Alam (eds.) *Sixth Five Year Plan of Bangladesh, 2011-2015, Background Papers,* Vol. I, Bangladesh Institute of Development Studies and General Economics Division, Planning Commission, Government of the People's Republic of Bangladesh, pp. 259-388.
4. M. Afsarul Qader, Management of Bangladesh-India Border, Paper Presented in a Roundtable on *Bangladesh-India Relations: Exploring New Horizons*, organized by Bangladesh Institute of International and Strategic Studies, Dhaka, 9 January 2010.
5. Robert Bradnock, "Introduction", in Farooq Sobhan (ed.) *Bangladesh-India Dialogue: Vision of Young Leaders*, Dhaka, Bangladesh Enterprise Institute and The University Press Limited, 2006.
6. M. Afsarul Qader, n. 4.
7. Ibid.

ANNEXURES

India Bangladesh Land Boundary Agreement, 1974

Agreement between the Government of the Republic of India and Government of the People's Republic of Bangladesh concerning the demarcation of the land boundary between India and Bangladesh and related matters, May 16, 1974

The Government of the Republic of India and the Government of the People's Republic of Bangladesh, BEARING IN MIND the friendly relations existing between the two countries, DESIRING TO define more accurately at certain points and to complete the demarcation of the land boundary between India and Bangladesh, HAVE AGREED as follows : Article1 The land boundary between India and Bangladesh in the areas mentioned below shall be demarcated in the following manner

MIZORAM-BANGLADESH SECTOR Demarcation should be completed on the basis of the latest perpetration notifications and records.

TRIPURA-SYLHET SECTOR Demarcation which is already in progress in this area on the agreed basis, should be completed as early as possible.

BHAGALPUR RAILWAY LINE The boundary should be demarcated at a distance of 75 feet parallel to the toe of the railway embankment towards the east.

SIBPUR-GAURANGALA SECTOR The boundary should be demarcated in continuation of the process started in 1951-52 on the basis of the District Settlement Maps of1915-1918.

MUHURI RIVER (BELONIA) SECTOR The boundary in this area should be demarcated along the mid-stream of the course of Muhuri River at the time of demarcation. This boundary will be a fixed boundary. The two Governments should raise embankments on their respective sides with a view to stabilizing the river in its present course.

REMAINING PORTION OF THE TRIPURA-NOAKHALI/ COMILLA SECTOR The demarcation in this sector should be completed on the basis ofChakia-Roshanabad Estate Maps of 1892-1894 and the District Settlement Maps of 1915-1918 for areas not covered by the CkaklaRoshanabad Maps.

FENNY RIVER The boundary should be demarcated along the mid-stream of the course at the time of demarcation of that branch of the Fenny River indicated as the Fenny River on Survey of India Map Sheet No. 79MI15, 1st Edition 1935, till it joins the stream shown as Asalong C on the said Map. From that point on, downstream, the boundary should be demarcated along the mid-stream of the course of the Fenny River at the time of demarcation of the boundary. The boundary in this sector will be a fixed boundary.

REST OF TRIPURA-CHI'ITAGONG HILL TRACT SECTOR The boundary will follow the mid-stream of that branch of the Fenny River, referred to in para 7 above, upto Grid reference 009779 (Map sheet as in para 7 above) from where the boundary will follow the mid-stream of the eastern-most tributary. From the source of this tributary, the boundary will run along the shortest distance to the mid-stream of the stream marked Bayan Asalong, on the map referred to above, and thence will run generally northwards along the mid-stream of this river till it reaches its source on the ridge (indicated by grid reference 046810 on the map referred to above). From there it will run along the crest of this ridge upto Boghoban Trig Station. From Boghoban Trig Station upto the tri-junction of the Bangladesh-Assam-Tripura boundary (Khan Talang Trig Station), the boundary will run along the watershed of the river systems of the two countries. In case of any difference between the map and the ground, the ground shall prevail. The boundary will be a fixed boundary in this sector.

BEANIBAZAR-KARIMGANJ SECTOR The undemarcated portion of the boundary west of Umapati village should be demarcated in accordance with the agreed basis of demarcation, leaving Umapati village in India.

HAKAR KHAL The boundary should be demarcated in accordance with the Nehru-Noon Agreement of September, 1958, treating Hakar Khal as a geographical feature distinct from the Ichhamati River. The boundary will be a fixed boundary.

BAIKARI KHAL In the Baikari Khal, the boundary should be demarcated on the agreed basis and principles, namely, that the ground shall prevail, i.e. as per the agreement reached between the Directors of Land Records and Surveys of West Bengal and erstwhile East Pakistan in 1949. The boundary will be a fixed boundary.

ENCLAVES The Indian enclaves in Bangladesh and the Bangladesh enclaves in India should be exchanged expeditiously, excepting the enclaves mentioned in paragraph 14 without claim to compensation for the additional area going to Bangladesh.

HILLI The area will be demarcated in accordance with Radcliffe Award and the line drawn by him on the map.

BERUBARI India will retain the southern half of South Berubari Union No.12 and the adjacent enclaves, measuring an area of 2.64 square miles approximately, and in exchange Bangladesh will retain the Dahagram and Angarpota enclaves. India will lease in perpetuity to Bangladesh an area of 178 metres x 85 metres ijear 'Tin Bigha' to connect Dahagram with Panbari Mouza (P.S. Patgram) of Bangladesh.

LATHITILLA-DUMABARI From point Y (the last demarcated boundary pillar position), the boundary shall run southwards along the Patharia Hills RF boundary upto the point where it meets the western boundary of Dumabari Mouza. Thence along the same Mouza boundary upto the tri-junction of Mouzas Dumabari, Lathitilla and Bara Putnigaon through the junction of the two Mouzas Dumabari and Lathitilla. From this point it shall run along the shortest distance to meet the mid-stream of Putni Chara. Thence it shall run generally southwards along the midstream of the course of Putni Chara at the time of demarcation, till it meets the boundary between Sylhet (Bangladesh) and Tripura (India). Article2 The Governments of India and Bangladesh agree that territories in adverse possession in areas already demarcated in respect of which boundary strip maps are already prepared, shall be exchanged within six months of the signing of the boundary strip maps by the plenipotentiaries. They 'may sign the relevant maps as early as possible and in any case not later than the

31st December, 1974. Early measures may be taken to print maps in respect of other areas where demarcation has already taken place. These should be printed by 31st May 1975 and signed by the plenipotentiaries thereafter in order that the exchange of adversely held possessions in these areas may take place by the 31st December 1975. In sectors still to be demarcated, transfer of territorial jurisdiction may take place within six months of the signature by plenipotentiaries on the concerned boundary strip maps. Article3 The Governments of India and Bangladesh agree that when areas are transferred, the people in these areas shall be given the right of staying on where they are, as nationals of the State to which the areas are transferred. Pending demarcation of the boundary and exchange of territory by mutual agreement, there should be no disturbance of the status quo and peaceful conditions shall be maintained in the border regions. Necessary instructions in this regard shall be issued to the local authorities on the border by the two countries. Article4 The Governments of India and Bangladesh agree that any dispute concerning the interpretation or implementation of this Agreement shall be settled peacefully through mutual consultations. Article5 This Agreement shall be subject to ratification by the Governments of India and Bangladesh and Instruments of Ratification shall be exchanged as early as possible. The Agreement shall take effect from the date of the exchange of the Instruments of Ratification. SIGNED in New Delhi on May 16, 1974, in two originals each of which is equally authentic.

For the Government of the Republic of India

Sd/-

INDIRAGANDHI
Prime Minister of India.

For the Government of the People's Republic of Bangladesh

Sd/-

SHEIKH MUJIBUR RAHMAN
Prime Minister of Bangladesh.

Terms of Lease in Perpetuity of Tin Bigha - Area, October 7, 1982

New Delhi

7 October 1982

Excellency,

I have the honour to refer to item 14 of Article 1 of the Agreement between the Government of Republic of India and the Government of the People's Republic of Bangladesh concerning the Demarcation of the Land Boundary between India and Bangladesh and Related Matters, signed in New Delhi on 16th of May 1974, and to state that in connection with the lease in perpetuity by India to Bangladesh of an area of approximately 178 metres x 85 metres near "Tin Bigha" to connect Dahagram with Panbari Mouza (P.S. Patgram) of Bangladesh, the follwoing understanding has been reached between our two Governments:

1 The lease in perpetuity of the aforementioned area shall be for the purpose of connecting Dahagram and Angarpota with Panbari Mouza (P.S. Patgram) of Bangladesh to enable the Bangladesh Government to exercise her sovreignty over Dahagram and Angorpota.

2 Sovereignty over the leased area shall continue to vest in India. The rent for the leased area shall be Bangladesh Tk. 1/- (Bangladesh Taka One) only per annum. Bangladesh shall not, however, be required to pay the said rent and the Government of India hereby waives its right to charge such rent in respect of the leased area.

3 For the purposes stated in para 1 above Bangladesh shall have undistributed possession and use of the area leased to her in perpetuity.

4. Bangladesh citizens including police, paramilitary and military personnel along with their arms, ammunition, equipment and supplies shall have the right of free and unfettered movement in the leased area and shall not be required to carry passports or travel documents of any kind. Movement of Bangladesh goods through the leased area shall also be free. There shall be no requirement of payment of customs duty, tax or levy of any kind whatsoever or any transit charges.

5. Indian citizens including police, paramilitary and military personnel along with their arms, ammunition, equipment and supplies shall continue to have the right of free and unfettered movement in the leased area in either direction. Movement of Indian goods across the leased area shall also be free. For the purposes of such passage the existing road running across it shall continue to be used. India may also build a road above and/or below the surface of the leased area in an elevated or subway form for her exclusive use in a manner which will not prejudice free and unfettered movement of Bangladesh citizens and goods as defined in paras 1 and 4 above.

6. The two governments shall cooperate in placing permanent makers along the perimeters of the leased area and put up fences where necessary.

7. Both India and Bangladesh shall have right to lay cables, electric lines, water and sewerage pipes etc. over or under the leased area without obstructing free movement of citizens or goods of either country as defined in paras 4 and 5 above.

8. The modalities for implementing the terms of the lease will be entrusted to the respective Deputy Commissioners of Rangpur (Bangladesh) and Cooch Behar (India). In case of differences, they will refer the matter to their respective Governments for resolution.

9. In the event of any Bangladesh/Indiaan national being involved in an incident in the leased area, constituting an offence in law, he shall be dealt with by the respective law enforcing agency of his own country in accordance with its national laws. In the event of an incident in the leased area involving nationals of both countries, the law enforcing agency on the scene of the

incident will take necessary steps to restore law and order. At the same time immediate steps will be taken to get in touch with the law enforcing agency of the other country. In such cases, any Indian national apprehended by a Bangladeshi law enforcing agency shall be handed over forthwith to the Indian side and any Bangladeshi national apprehended by an Indian law enforcing agency shall be handed over forthwith to the Bangladeshi side. India will retain residual jurisdiction in the leased area.

I shall be grateful if you kindly confirm that the above sets out correctly the understanding reached between our two Governments. I have also the honour to purpose that this letter and your reply confirming the understanding shall constitute an agreement between our two Governments in respect of the leased area, which shall be an integral part of the Agreement concerning the Demarcation of the Land Boundary between India and Bangladesh and Related Matters. Signed on the 16th of May 1974.

Accept, Excellency, the assurances of my highest esteem.

(P.V. Narshimha Rao)
Minister of External Affairs
Government of the Republic of India
H.E. Mr. A. R. Shams-Ud-Doha
Minister for Foreign Affairs
Government of the People's Republic of Bangladesh

Source: http://www.hcidhaka.org/terms_lease.php

Letter of Foreign Secretary of India Implementing Tin Bigha Lease, 26 March, 1992

New Delhi

26th March 1992

Excellency,

I have the honour to refer to item 14 of Article 1 of the Agreement of 16th May, 1974, signed by the Prime Ministers of India and Bangladesh concerning the demarcation of the land boundary between India and Bangladesh and related matters, and the Exchange of Letters dated 7 October, 1982, between the Minister of External Affairs of India and the Minister of Foreign Affairs of Bangladesh, regarding the terms of lease in perpetuity of the Tin Bigha Area. This is to confirm that in the subsequent discussions regarding the modalities for leasing out the above-mentioned area, the following understanding has been reached:

1 Indian flags will fly at the four corners of the Tin Bigha corridor as a manifestation of India's sovereignty over the area;

2 An East-West road to connect Dahagram (Bangladesh) with Patgram (Bangladesh) will be constructed by India before 26th June 1992 roughly at right angles to the existing North-South road. The new East-West road is to conform to the specifications and width of the existing North-South road;

3 Landscaping (horticulture) protected by fencing, on both sides, of the proposed road, is to be carried out and maintained by India, so as to prevent the possibility of encroachment and infiltration, keeping adequate provision for drains, laying of cables, water-supply etc., in future;

4 Two check points each are to be set up at both ends of the East-West road where it touches the Bangladesh boundary. They will be separately manned by Indian and Bangladesh authorities with a view to regulating the movement of traffic;

5 Traffic in the corridor will be regulated by the Indian authorities, and the opening and closing of the check points on the East-West road will be coordinated accordingly in such a manner that there is no intermixing of Indian and Bangladeshi streams of traffic;

6 At the intersection, i.e., the specific point where East-West road will cross the North-South road, there will be an Indian traffic Police control to direct the traffic movement;

7 Indian traffic movement on the North-South road will continue as heretofore. Bangladesh traffic will use the East-West road in the corridor at alternate hours during the daylight period. However, exceptions will be made at the local level to the above arrangements in cases of emergency, such as natural calamities, movement of civil administrators and medical emergencies;

8 Suitable lighting arrangements will be made for the entire corridor in order to facilitate monitoring by security agencies on both sides;

9 Differences, if any, regarding modalities for implementing the terms of lease will be resolved in the first instance through consultations between the Deputy Commissioner of Cooch Behar (India) and the Deputy Commissioner of Lalmonirhat (Bangladesh). Remaining differences, if any, will be referred to their respective Governments for resution;

10 India and Bangladesh will provide mutual judicial assistance to each other to the extent necessary, in all matters relating to the prosecution, trails, etc. concerning incidents constituting offences in the leased area;

11 Agreed arrangements will come into effect from 26th June, 1992.

I shall be grateful if Your Excellency could confirm that the above sets out correctly the understanding reached between out our two Governments.

Please accept, Excellency, the assurances of my highest consideration.

(J.N Dixit)
Foreign Secretary
H. E. Mr. A. H. Mahmood Ali,
Additional Foreign Secretary,
Ministry of Foreign Affairs,
Government of People's Republic of Bangladesh

http://www.hcidhaka.org/letter_sc.php

Ganges Water Treaty, 1996

TREATY BETWEEN THE GOVERNMENT OF THE PEOPLE'S REPUBLIC OF BANGLADESH AND THE GOVERNMENT OF THE REPUBLIC OF INDIA ON SHARING OF THE GANGA/GANGES WATERS AT FARAKKA

THE GOVERNMENT OF
THE PEOPLE'S REPUBLIC OF BANGLADESH

AND

THE GOVERNMENT OF THE REPUBLIC OF INDIA,

Determined to promote and strengthen their relations of friendship and good neighbourliness,

Inspired by the common desire of promoting the well-being of their peoples,

Being desirous of sharing by mutual agreement the waters of the international rivers flowing through the territories of the two countries and of making the optimum utilisation of the water resources of their region in the fields of flood management, irrigation, river basin development and generation of hydro-power for the mutual benefit of the peoples of the two countries,

Recognising that the need for making an arrangement for sharing of the Ganga/Ganges waters at Farakka in a spirit of mutual accommodation and the need for a solution to the long-term problem of augmenting the flows of the Ganga/Ganges are in the mutual interests of the peoples of the two countries,

Being desirous of finding a fair and just solution without affecting the rights and entitlements of either country other than those covered by this Treaty, or establishing any general principles of law or precedent,

Have agreed as follows:

ARTICLE - I

The quantum of waters agreed to be released by India to Bangladesh will be at Farakka.

ARTICLE - II

(i) The sharing between India and Bangladesh of the Ganga/Ganges waters at Farakka by ten day periods from the 1st January to the 31st May every year will be with reference to the formula at Annexure I and an indicative schedule giving the implications of the sharing arrangement under Annexure I is at Annexure II.

(ii) The indicative schedule at Annexure II, as referred to in sub para (i) above, is based on 40 years (1949-1988) 10-day period average availability of water at Farakka. Every effort would be made by the upper riparian to protect flows of water at Farakka as in the 40-years average availability as mentioned above.

(iii) In the event flow at Farakka falls below 50,000 cusecs in any 10-day period, the two Governments will enter into immediate consultations to make adjustments on an emergency basis, in accordance with the principles of equity, fair play and no harm to either party.

ARTICLE - III

The waters released to Bangladesh at Farakka under Article I shall not be reduced below Farakka except for reasonable uses of waters, not exceeding 200 cusecs, by India between Farakka and the point on the Ganga/Ganges where both its banks are in Bangladesh.

ARTICLE - IV

A Committee consisting of representatives nominated by the two Governments in equal numbers (hereinafter called the Joint Committee) shall be constituted following the signing of this Treaty. The Joint Committee shall set up suitable teams at Farakka and Hardinge Bridge to observe and record at Farakka the daily flows below Farakka Barrage, in the Feeder Canal, and at the Navigation Lock, as well as at the Hardinge Bridge.

ARTICLE - V

The Joint Committee shall decide its own procedure and method of functioning.

ARTICLE - VI

The Joint Committee shall submit to the two Governments all data collected by it and shall also submit a yearly report to both the Governments. Following submission of the reports the two Governments will meet at appropriate levels to decide upon such further actions as may be needed.

ARTICLE - VII

The Joint Committee shall be responsible for implementing the arrangements contained in this Treaty and examining any difficulty arising out of the implementation of the above arrangements and of the operation of Farakka Barrage. Any difference or dispute arising in this regard, if not resolved by the Joint Committee, shall be referred to the Indo-Bangladesh Joint Rivers Commission. If the difference or dispute still remains unresolved, it shall be referred to the two Governments which shall meet urgently at the appropriate level to resolve it by mutual discussion.

ARTICLE - VIII

The two Governments recognise the need to cooperate with each other in finding a solution to the long-term problem of augmenting the flows of the Ganga/Ganges during the dry season.

ARTICLE - IX

Guided by the principles of equity, fairness and no harm to either party, both the Governments agree to conclude water sharing Treaties/ Agreements with regard to other common rivers.

ARTICLE - X

The sharing arrangement under this Treaty shall be reviewed by the two Governments at five years interval or earlier, as required by either party and needed adjustments, based on principles of equity, fairness, and no harm to either party made thereto, if necessary. It would be open to either party to seek the first review after two years to assess the impact and working of the sharing arrangement as contained in this Treaty.

ARTICLE - XI

For the period of this Treaty, in the absence of mutual agreement on adjustments following reviews as mentioned in Article X, India shall release downstream of Farakka Barrage, water at a rate not less than 90% (ninety percent) of Bangladesh's share according to the formula referred to in Article II, until such time as mutually agreed flows are decided upon.

ARTICLE - XII

This Treaty shall enter into force upon signature and shall remain in force for a period of thirty years and it shall be renewable on the basis of mutual consent.

In witness whereof the undersigned, being duly authorised thereto by the respective Governments, have signed this Treaty.

Done at New Delhi on 12th December, 1996 in Hindi, Bangla and English languages. In the event of any conflict between the texts, the English text shall prevail.

Signed	Signed
(SHEIKH HASINA)	**(H.D. DEVE GOWDA)**
Prime Minister,	Prime Minister,
People's Republic of Bangladesh	Republic of India.

ANNEXURE-I

Availability at Farakka	*Share of India*	*Share of Bangladesh*
70,000 cusecs or less	50%	50%
70,000 cusecs -75,000 cusecs	Balance of flow	35,000 cusecs
75,000 cusecs or more	40,000 cusecs	Balance of flow

Subject to the condition that India and Bangladesh each shall receive guaranteed 35,000 cusecs of water in alternate three 10-day periods during the period March 11 to May 10.

ANNEXURE - II
Schedule

(Sharing of waters at Farakka between January 01 and May 31 every year.)

If actual availability corresponds to average flows of the period 1949 to 1988,the implication of the formula in Annex-I for the share of each side is:

Period		*Average of total flow 1949-88 (cusecs)*	*India's share (cusecs)*	*Bangladesh's share (cusecs)*
January	01-10	1,07,516	40,000	67,516
	11-20	97,673	40,000	57,673
	21-31	90,154	40,000	50,154
February	01-10	86,323	40,000	46,323
	11-20	82,859	40,000	42,859
	21-28/29	79,106	40,000	39,106
March	01-10	74,419	39,419	35,000
	11-20	68,931	33,931	35,000*
	21-31	64,688	35,000*	29,688
April	01-10	63,180	28,180	35,000*
	11-20	62,633	35,000*	27,633
	21-30	60,992	25,992	35,000*
May	01-10	67,351	35,000*	32,351
	11-20	73,590	38,590	35,000
	21-31	81,854	40,000	41,854

Joint Communiqué issued on the occasion of the visit to India of Her Excellency Sheikh Hasina, Prime Minister of Bangladesh January 12, 2010

1. Reaffirming the shared history, traditional links and the desire of the leaders of the two countries to launch a new phase in their bilateral relations, the Prime Minister of Bangladesh, Sheikh Hasina is paying a state visit to India from 10-13 January, 2010 at the invitation of Dr. Manmohan Singh, Prime Minister of India. Apart from attending the official programme in New Delhi, the Bangladesh Prime Minister will also visit Ajmer Sharif.
2. The Bangladesh Prime Minister was accorded a ceremonial reception at Rashtrapati Bhavan on 11 January 2010. She called on President of India Smt Pratibha Devisingh Patil.
3. Finance Minister Shri Pranab Mukherjee, External Affairs Minister Shri S.M. Krishna, Railway Minister Kumari Mamata Banerjee and Leader of the Opposition Smt. Sushma Swaraj called on Prime Minister Sheikh Hasina.
4. Reflecting the friendly relations existing between the two neighbouring countries, the Prime Minister of Bangladesh in her capacity as President of the Awami League and the Awami League-led Mohajote government also called on Smt Sonia Gandhi, Chairperson of the United Progressive Alliance. She also met with former Prime Minister Shri I.K. Gujral. The meetings and exchanges were marked by great warmth and cordiality on both sides.

5. The Prime Minister of Bangladesh paid tribute and respect to the memories of Mahatma Gandhi, Pandit Jawarlal Nehru, Smt Indira Gandhi and Shri Rajiv Gandhi at Rajghat, Shantivana, Shaktisthal and Virbhumi respectively.
6. During the visit, Prime Minister Sheikh Hasina was conferred the prestigious Indira Gandhi Prize for Peace, Disarmament and Development for 2009 at a ceremony at Rashtrapati Bhavan.
7. The Prime Minister of Bangladesh had a meeting with the Prime Minister of India on January 11, 2010, which was followed by delegation level talks. The talks were marked by great warmth, deep understanding and a spirit of close friendship between the two sides. Prime Minister Manmohan Singh hosted a banquet in honour of Prime Minister Sheikh Hasina and her accompanying delegation.
8. On the Bangladesh side, assisting the Prime Minister of Bangladesh in the talks were: Mr. Ramesh Chandra Sen, MP, Minister of Water Resources; Dr. Dipu Moni MP, Minister of Foreign Affairs, Advisers to the Prime Minister Mr. H.T. Imam, Mr. Mashiur Rahman and Mr. Gowher Rizvi; High Commissioner of Bangladesh to India Mr. Tariq A. Karim and other senior officials of the Bangladesh Government.
9. On the Indian side, assisting the Prime Minister of India were: Shri Pranab Mukherjee, Finance Minister; Shri P. Chidambaram, Home Minister; Shri S.M. Krishna, External Affairs Minister; Kumari Mamata Banerjee, Minister of Railways; Shri Anand Sharma, Minister of Commerce; Smt Preneet Kaur, Minister of State for External Affairs; Shri M.K. Narayanan, National Security Adviser; Shri T.K.A Nair, Principal Secretary to the Prime Minister and other senior officials of the Indian Government.
10. Prime Minister Dr. Manmohan Singh congratulated Prime Minister Sheikh Hasina on her party's impressive electoral victory in the general elections held in December 2008 and lauded the people of Bangladesh for their abiding faith in democracy, which eventually paved the way for return of multi-party democracy in Bangladesh. Both leaders agreed that the recent elections in both countries presented them with a historic opportunity to write a new chapter in their relationship.

11. The Bangladesh Prime Minister recalled the shared bonds of history, culture and aspirations that bind Bangladesh and India, and paid tribute to the sacred memory of the lives sacrificed for the freedom and independence of the two countries. She called for rededicating efforts to establish a society free from ignorance, fear and want.

12. Both the Prime Ministers agreed on a vision for the future in the pursuit of the common good - bilaterally, regionally and globally. In this context, they reiterated their commitment to work together to solve all issues through cooperation and mutual understanding. They also shared their outlook on the strengthening and reform of multilateral institutions in which developing countries have an effective voice and participation.

13. The Prime Minister of Bangladesh and the Prime Minister of India recognized that peace and stability in the region is necessary for development and well-being of the people of their respective countries. In this context, they emphasized the importance of close cooperation between India and Bangladesh and the need to effectively harness their respective resources for the good of the peoples of the two countries.

14. The two Prime Ministers agreed to put in place a comprehensive framework of cooperation for development between the two countries, encapsulating their mutually shared vision for the future, which would include cooperation in water resources, power, transportation and connectivity, tourism and education. They agreed on the need to operationalize the various areas of cooperation at the earliest.

15. Both Prime Ministers agreed to consider strengthening diplomatic and consular presence in each other's countries.

16. Both Prime Ministers reiterated their commitment to democracy, pluralism and rule of law. They expressed satisfaction that the people of both countries have rejected violence, extremism and terrorism and reaffirmed their faith in democracy and development. In this quest, the two leaders resolved to work together to strengthen the forces of democracy and moderation.

17. Both Prime Ministers condemned terrorism in all its forms and manifestations. They noted that security remained a priority for

both countries, as terrorists, insurgents and criminals respect no boundaries. They underscored the need for both countries to actively cooperate on security issues. Both leaders reiterated the assurance that the territory of either would not be allowed for activities inimical to the other and resolved not to allow their respective territory to be used for training, sanctuary and other operations by domestic or foreign terrorist/militant and insurgent organizations and their operatives.

18. Welcoming the Home Secretary level talks held in New Delhi in December 2009, the two Prime Ministers directed their respective Ministries and agencies to cooperate closely and implement all decisions taken during the talks. While recognizing the need to check cross border crimes, both Prime Ministers agreed that the respective border guarding forces exercise restraint and underscored the importance of regular meetings between the border guarding forces to curtail illegal cross border activities and prevent loss of lives.

19. The Prime Minister of Bangladesh thanked the Prime Minister of India for facilitating the provision of electricity in Dahagram-Angarpota and invited India to construct a flyover across Tin Bigha Corridor for exclusive Indian use, as agreed earlier.

20. Both Prime Ministers agreed to comprehensively address all outstanding land boundary issues keeping in view the spirit of the 1974 Land Boundary Agreement. In this context, they agreed to convene the Joint Boundary Working Group to take this process forward.

21. Both Prime Ministers agreed on the need to amicably demarcate the maritime boundary between India and Bangladesh. They noted the initiation of proceedings under Annex VII of the United Nations Convention on the Law of the Sea (UNCLOS) and, in this context, welcomed the visit of a delegation from Bangladesh to India.

22. It was agreed that Ashuganj in Bangladesh and Silghat in India shall be declared ports of call. The IWTT Protocol shall be amended through exchange of letters. A joint team will assess the improvement of infrastructure and the cost for one-time or longer term transportation of ODCs (Over Dimensional Cargo)

from Ashuganj. India will make the necessary investment. Both Governments agreed to expedite implementation. Contractors from both countries shall be eligible for the work.

23. It was agreed that Bangladesh will allow use of Mongla and Chittagong sea ports for movement of goods to and from India through road and rail. Bangladesh also conveyed their intention to give Nepal and Bhutan access to Mongla and Chittagong ports.

24. It was agreed that the construction of the proposed Akhaura – Agartala railway link be financed by grant from India. A joint team of the railway authorities of the two countries will identify the alignment for connectivity.

25. They welcomed the starting of "Maitree Express" between Kolkata and Dhaka and called for resumption of road and rail links between the two countries.

26. The Prime Ministers agreed that Rohanpur–Singabad broad gauge railway link would be available for transit to Nepal. Bangladesh informed of their intention to convert Radhikapur – Birol railway line into broad gauge and requested for railway transit link to Bhutan as well.

27. Recognizing the sufferings of the people of both sides in the face of scarcity of lean season flows of the Teesta River, the Prime Ministers expressed that the discussions on the sharing of the Teesta waters between India and Bangladesh should be concluded expeditiously. The two Prime Ministers directed their respective Water Resources Ministers to convene the Ministerial-level meeting of the Joint Rivers Commission in this quarter of 2010. The Joint Rivers Commission will also discuss issues relating to Feni, Manu, Muhuri, Khowai, Gumti, Dharla and Dudhkumar.

28. They also agreed that the following actions be taken:

    (a) Dredging of Ichhamati; and

    (b) River protection at Mahananda, Karatoa, Nagar, Kulik, Atrai, Dharla, and Feni

29. The Prime Minister of India agreed to support implementation of strategy of Government of Bangladesh to dredge rivers for

flood control, navigation and access to ports. In this context, India agreed to provide, inter alia, dredgers to Bangladesh on an urgent basis. Bangladesh indicated the need for 9 (nine) dredgers.

30. The Prime Minister of India reiterated the assurance that India would not take steps on the Tipaimukh project that would adversely impact Bangladesh.

31. The Prime Minister of India agreed to supply to Bangladesh 250 MW electricity from its grid. In this context, both Prime Ministers emphasized the need to expedite inter-grid connectivity. They also agreed that the two countries shall cooperate in development and exchange of electricity, including generation from renewable sources, and may set up joint projects or corporate entities for that purpose.

32. With a view to encouraging imports from Bangladesh, both countries agreed to address removal of tariff and non-tariff barriers and port restrictions and facilitate movement of containerized cargo by rail and water. In this context, Bangladesh welcomed India's initiative to provide duty-free access to SAARC LDCs to the Indian market. Bangladesh also welcomed the reduction of the number of items from India's negative list that were of direct interest to Bangladesh and requested for further reduction in the list.

33. The Prime Minister of India agreed to support the upgradation of the Bangladesh Standard Testing Institute with a view to building capacity on certification.

34. The Prime Ministers agreed that investments, including joint investment and joint ventures, shall be encouraged by both countries. They agreed that the participation of the private sector in both countries will give an added fillip to economic engagement between the two countries.

35. The Prime Ministers agreed to operationalize land customs stations at Sabroom-Ramgarh and Demagiri-Thegamukh, including putting in place necessary infrastructure and issue necessary notifications. Further, with respect to existing land custom stations, it was agreed to take measures for strengthening infrastructure.

36. It was agreed that border haats shall be established on a pilot basis at selected areas, including on the Meghalaya border, to allow trade in specified produces and products and in accordance with the regulations agreed and notified by both Governments.
37. It was agreed that trucks for movement from Bhutan and Nepal be allowed to enter about 200 meters into Zero Point at Banglabandh at Banglabandh-Phulbari land customs station. Necessary arrangements shall be mutually agreed and put in place by both countries.
38. The Prime Minister of India announced a line of credit of US$ 1 billion for a range of projects, including railway infrastructure, supply of BG locomotives and passenger coaches, rehabilitation of Saidpur workshop, procurement of buses including articulate buses and dredging projects.
39. Bangladesh requested for assistance to construct road infrastructure in Dhaka, including flyovers. India agreed to consider this request.
40. Recalling the shared legacy of the great poet laureate Rabindranath Tagore, the Prime Ministers agreed to oversee the joint celebrations of the 150th Birth Anniversary of Rabindranath Tagore in 2011 in a manner befitting his vision and spirit.
41. Government of India would offer Bangladesh 300 scholarships annually for a period of five years for study and training in Universities and training institutions in India, covering a wide range of disciplines as may be required by scholars and persons in government employment. The number may be increased through mutual consultation.
42. Both Prime Ministers underscored the role of SAARC in promoting regional cooperation. Both leaders agreed to work together in making SAARC a purposeful organization oriented towards implementation, which can revitalize the region through positive measures, concerted action and mutually reinforcing cooperation.
43. Both leaders welcomed the various steps taken to strengthen regional cooperation under BIMSTEC. In this context, Bangladesh requested India to support its aspiration to host the

BIMSTEC Secretariat in Dhaka. India agreed to give the request due consideration.

44. The two Prime Ministers welcomed the initiatives taken at the Climate Change Summit at Copenhagen in December 2009. They underlined that climate change was one of the most important global challenges. They reaffirmed the provisions and principles of the United Nations Framework Convention on Climate Change (UNFCCC), including that of common but differentiated responsibilities and respective capabilities, and underscored the importance of its full, effective and sustained implementation, giving due consideration to the needs of those which are most vulnerable, especially Least Developed Countries (LDCs), Small Island Developing States (SIDS) and Africa.

45. Both leaders recognized that the eradication of poverty and ensuring food security were great challenges of the century. They agreed that the international community should initiate a fully coordinated response and address these issues in a comprehensive manner, from short to medium and long term. They also recognized the need to give added focus on rural development policies, transfer and diffusion of technology and development, in particular to enhance agricultural productivity.

46. The Prime Ministers underscored the importance of an effective multilateral system, centered on a strong United Nations, as a key factor in tackling global challenges. In this context, they stressed the urgent need to pursue the reform of the United Nations, including the Security Council, to make it more representative, credible and effective, particularly with regard to its working method. They also advocated involvement of smaller countries in the reform process.

47. Responding to the Prime Minister of India, the Prime Minister of Bangladesh conveyed her country's support in principle for India's candidature for the permanent membership of the United Nations Security Council as and when the reform of the UN Security Council is achieved. Bangladesh conveyed its support to the Indian Candidature for a non-permanent seat in the UNSC for the term 2011-2012. India also conveyed its support to the Bangladesh's candidature for a non-permanent seat in UNSC for the term 2016-2017.

48. The two Prime Ministers witnessed the signing in their presence of the following accords:
    (a) Agreement on Mutual Legal Assistance on Criminal Matters
    (b) Agreement on the Transfer of Sentenced Persons
    (c) Agreement on Combating International Terrorism, Organized Crime and Illicit Drug Trafficking
    (d) Memorandum of Understanding on Cooperation in Power Sector
    (e) Cultural Exchange Programme

    The Prime Ministers also expressed the desire that Line of Credit and the comprehensive framework of cooperation for development be operationalized at the earliest.

49. The Prime Minister of Bangladesh thanked the Prime Minister of India and the Indian Government and people for the warm and gracious hospitality extended to her and the members of her delegation during their stay in India.

50. The Prime Minister of Bangladesh, on behalf of herself, her Government and the people of Bangladesh, extended her warm invitation to the Prime Minister of India and Mrs. Manmohan Singh to visit Bangladesh at a mutually convenient time. The Prime Minister of India thanked the Prime Minister of Bangladesh and accepted the invitation with great pleasure. The dates for the visit would be decided by mutual consultations through diplomatic channels.

New Delhi

January 12, 2010

http://www.mea.gov.in/mystart.php?id=530515482

Protocol on Demarcation of Land Boundary, 2011

PROTOCOL TO THE AGREEMENT BETWEEN THE GOVERNMENT OF THE REPUBLIC OF INDIA AND THE GOVERNMENT OF THE PEOPLE's REPUBLIC OF BANGLADESH CONCERNING THE DEMARCATION OF THE LAND BOUNDARY BETWEEN INDIA AND BANGLADESH AND RELATED MATTERS

The Government of the Republic of India and the Government of the People's Republic of Bangladesh,

Bearing in mind the friendly relations existing between the two countries,

Desiring to define more accurately at certain points and to complete the demarcation of the land boundary between India and Bangladesh,

Having regard to the Agreement between the Government of the Republic of India and the Government of the People's Republic of Bangladesh concerning the demarcation of the land boundary between India and Bangladesh and related matters, May 16, 1974 and Exchange of Letters dated December 26, 1974; December 30, 1974; October 7, 1982; and March 26, 1992 (hereinafter referred to as the 1974 Agreement),

Have agreed as follows:

ARTICLE 1

The provisions of this Protocol shall form an integral part of the 1974 Agreement.

ARTICLE 2

(I) Article 1 Clause 5 of the 1974 Agreement shall be implemented as follows:

Muhuri River (Belonia) sector

Boundary in this segment shall be drawn westwards from the existing Boundary Pillar No. 2159/48-S along the agreed line as depicted in the index map prepared jointly till it meets the southern limit of the Burning Ghat as shown in jointly surveyed map of Muhuri river area in 1977-78. Thereafter it shall follow the external limit of the Burning Ghat in South-West direction and then turn northwards along the external limit of the Burning Ghat till it meets the centre of the existing Muhuri River. Thereafter it shall run along the mid stream of the existing Muhuri River upto Boundary Pillar No. 2159/3-S. This boundary shall be the fixed boundary. The two Governments should raise embankments on their respective sides with a view to stabilising the river in its present course as stipulated in the 1974 Agreement. The Parties agree to fencing on 'zero line' in this area.

(II) Article 1 Clause 12 of the 1974 Agreement shall be implemented as follows:

Enclaves

111 Indian Enclaves in Bangladesh and 51 Bangladesh Enclaves in India as per the jointly verified cadastral enclave maps and signed at the level of DGLR&S, Bangladesh and DLR&S, West Bengal (India) in April 1997, shall be exchanged without claim to compensation for the additional areas going to Bangladesh.

(III) Article 1 Clause 15 of the 1974 Agreement shall be implemented as follows:

Lathitilla and Dumabari

Line drawn by Radcliffe from Boundary Pillar 1397(point Y) i.e. the last demarcated boundary pillar position, straight southward to the tri-junction of Mouzas Dumabari, Lathitilla and Bara Putnigaon i.e upto iron bridge, and thence it shall run generally southwards along the midstream of the course of Putni Chara as already demarcated on the ground, till it meets the boundary between Sylhet (Bangladesh) and Tripura (India) i.e. Boundary Pillar No. 1800.

(IV) The land boundary in the area mentioned below shall be demarcated in the following manner:

Daikhata 56 (West Bengal-Jalpaiguri) / Panchagarh

Boundary in this segment shall be drawn as fixed boundary from existing Boundary Pillar 774/32-S in the strip sheet 444/6 along the mouza boundary of Daikhata-56 as surveyed in 1997-98 and thereafter will follow the southern boundary of Daikhata-56 (from east to west) upto Point No 18 and therefrom it will follow the western boundaiy of Daikhata-56 (from south to north) till it meets the center of River Sui at Point No 15 and thereafter, will run along the center of the River Sui upto Point No 1, the points as depicted in the sketch map jointly prepared and mutually agreed on August 3, 2011. Thereafter the International Boundary shall follow the already delineated boundary through Main Pillar (MP) 775.

ARTICLE 3

(I) Article 2 of the 1974 Agreement shall be implemented as follows:

The Government of India and the Government of Bangladesh agree that the boundary shall be drawn as a fixed boundary for territories held in Adverse Possession as determined through joint survey and fully depicted in the respective adversely possessed land area index map (APL map) finalized by the Land Records and Survey Departments of both the countries between December 2010 and August 2011, which are fully described in clause (a) to (d) below.

The relevant strip maps shall be printed and signed by the Plenipotentiaries and transfer of territorial jurisdiction shall be completed simultaneously with the exchange of the enclaves. The demarcation of the boundary, as depicted in the above-mentioned Index Maps, shall be as under:-

(a) West Bengal Sector

(i) **Bousmari – Madhugari (Kushtia-Nadia) area :** The boundary shall be drawn from the existing Boundary Pillar Nos. 154/5-S to 157/1-S to follow the centre of old course of river Mathabanga, as depicted in consolidation map of 1962, as surveyed jointly and agreed in June 2011.

(ii) **Andharkota (Kushtia-Nadia) area :** The boundary shall be drawn from existing Boundary Pillar No 152/5-S to Boundary Pillar No 153/1-S to follow the edge of existing River Mathabanga as jointly surveyed and agreed in June 2011.

(iii) **Pakuria (Kushtia-Nadia) area :** The boundary shall be drawn from existing Boundary Pillar No 151/1-S to Boundary Pillar No 152/2-S to follow the edge of River Mathabanga as jointly surveyed and agreed in June 2011.

(iv) **Char Mahishkundi (Kushtia-Nadia) area :** The boundary shall be drawn from existing Boundary Pillar No 153/1-S to Boundary Pillar No 153/9-S to follow the edge of River Mathabanga as jointly surveyed and agreed in June 2011.

(v) **Haripal/ Khutadah/ Battoli/ Sapameri/ LNpur (Patari) (Naogaon- Malda) area :** The boundary shall be drawn as line joining from existing Boundary Pillar No 242/S/13, to Boundary Pillar No 243/7-S/5 and as jointly surveyed and agreed in June 2011.

(vi) **Berubari (Panchagarh-Jalpaiguri area) :** The boundary in the area Berubari (Panchagarh-Jalpaiguri) adversely held by Bangladesh, and Berubari and Singhapara Page Khudipara (Panchagarh-Jalpaiguri), adversely held by India shall be drawn as jointly demarcated during 1996-1998.

(b) Meghalaya Sector

(i) **Lobachera-Nuncherra :** The boundary from existing Boundary Pillar No 1315/4-S to Boundary Pillar No 1315/15-S in Lailong - Balichera, Boundary Pillar No 1316/1-S to Boundary Pillar No 1316/11-S in Lailong- Noonchera, Boundary Pillar No 1317 to Boundary Pillar No 1317/13-S in Lailong- Lahiling and Boundary Pillar No 1318/1-S to Boundary Pillar No 1318/2-S in Lailong- Lubhachera shall be drawn to follow the edge of tea gardens as jointly surveyed and agreed in Dec 2010.

(ii) **Pyrdiwah/ Padua Area** : The boundary shall be drawn from existing Boundary Pillar No 1270/1-S as per jointly surveyed and mutually agreed line till Boundary Pillar No 1271/1-T. The Parties agree that the Indian Nationals from Pyrdiwah village shall be allowed to draw water from Piyang River near point No 6 of the agreed Map.

(iii) **Lyngkhat Area :**

(aa) Lyngkhat-I / Kulumcherra & Lyngkhat-II/ Kulumcherra : The boundary shall be drawn from existing Boundary Pillar No. 1264/4-S to Boundary Pillar No 1265 and BP No 1265/6-S to 1265/9-S as per jointly surveyed and mutually agreed line.

(ab) Lyngkhat-III/ Sonarhat : The boundary shall be drawn from existing Boundary Pillar No 1266/13-S along the nallah southwards till it meets another nallah in the east-west direction, thereafter it shall run along the northern edge of the nallah in east till it meets the existing International Boundary north of Reference Pillar Nos.1267/4-R-B and 1267/3-RI.

(iv) **Dawki/ Tamabil area :** The boundary shall be drawn by a straight line joining existing Boundary Pillar Nos 1275/1-S to Boundary Pillar Nos 1275/7-S. The Parties agree to fencing on 'zero line' in this area.

(v) **Naljuri/ Sreepur Area**

(aa) Naljuri I : The boundary shall be a line from the existing Boundary Pillar No 1277/2-S in southern direction upto three plots as depicted in the strip Map No 166 till it meets the nallah flowing from Boundary Pillar No 1277/5-T, thereafter it will run along the western edge of the nallah in the southern direction upto 2 plots on the Bangladesh side, thereafter it shall run eastwards till it meets a line drawn in southern direction from Boundary Pillar No 1277/4-S.

(ab) Naljuri III: The boundary shall be drawn by a straight line from existing Boundary Pillar No 1278/2-S to Boundary Pillar No 1279/ 3-S.

(vi) **Muktapur/ Dibir Hawor Area :** The Parties agree that the Indian Nationals shall be allowed to visit Kali Mandir and shall also be allowed to draw water and exercise fishing rights in the water body in the Muktapur / Dibir Hawor area from the bank of Muktapur side.

(c) Tripura Sector

(i) **Chandannagar-Champarai Tea Garden area in Tripura/ Moulvi Bazar sector** : The boundary shall be drawn along Sonaraichhera river from existing Boundary Pillar No 1904 to

Boundary Pillar No 1905 as surveyed jointly and agreed in July 2011.

(d) Assam Sector

(i) **Kalabari (Boroibari) area in Assam sector :** The boundary shall be drawn from existing Boundary Pillar No 1066/24-T to Boundary Pillar No 1067/16-T as surveyed jointly and agreed in August 2011.

(ii) **Pallathal area in Assam sector :** The boundary shall be drawn from existing Boundary Pillar No. 1370/3-S to 1371/6-S to follow the outer edge of the tea garden and from Boundary Pillar No. 1372 to 1373/2-S along outer edge of the pan plantation.

ARTICLE 4

This Protocol shall be subject to ratification by the Government of the Republic of India and the Government of the People's Republic of Bangladesh and shall enter into force on the date of exchange of Instruments of Ratification.

Signed at Dhaka on the Sixth day of September, 2011, in two originals in the English language.

For the Government of the Republic of India	**For the Government of the People's Republic of Bangladesh**

Framework Agreement on Cooperation for Development

FRAMEWORK AGREEMENT ON COOPERATION FOR DEVELOPMENT BETWEEN GOVERNMENT OF THE REPUBLIC OF INDIA AND GOVERNMENT OF THE PEOPLE'S REPUBLIC OF BANGLADESH

The Government of the Republic of India (hereinafter Government of India) and the Government of the People's Republic of Bangladesh (hereinafter Government of Bangladesh)

Recalling the two countries' shared bonds of history, culture and common values;

Desirious of living in peace and harmony with each other and fostering good neighbourly relations based on sovereign equality, noninterference in each other's internal affairs, and mutual respect and mutual benefit;

Inspired by an abiding faith in and total commitment to democracy, development, pluralism and peaceful co-existence;

Reiterating their common objective of eradicating poverty, hunger, illiteracy and disease and promoting social justice and inclusive growth with a view to enabling their peoples to realize their potential to the full;

Desirous of promoting trans-border cooperation in the management of shared water resources, hydropower potentials and eco-systems and in the areas of connectivity and trade and economic cooperation;

Convinced that cooperation at the bilateral, sub-regional and regional levels will accelerate development and enable the two countries to realise their developmental aspirations, shared destiny and common vision of a peaceful and prosperous South Asia;

Have Agreed as under:

ARTICLE 1

To promote trade, investment and economic cooperation, which is balanced, sustainable and builds prosperity in both countries. Both Parties shall take steps to narrow trade imbalances, remove progressively tariff and non-tariff barriers and facilitate trade, by road, rail, inland waterways, air and shipping. Both Parties will encourage the development of appropriate infrastructure, use of sea ports, multimodal transportation and standardization of means of transport for bilateral as well as sub-regional use.

ARTICLE 2

To enhance cooperation in sharing of the waters of common rivers, both Parties will explore the possibilities of common basin management of common rivers for mutual benefit. The Parties will cooperate in flood forecasting and control. They will cooperate and provide necessary assistance to each other to enhance navigability and accessibility of river routes and ports.

ARTICLE 3

To develop mechanisms for technical cooperation and exchange of advance information with respect to natural disasters. The Parties shall also promote training and capacity building initiatives and cooperation between respective disaster management authorities, with a view to upgrading response mechanism.

ARTICLE 4

To establish arrangements for cooperation in generation, transmission, and distribution of electricity, including electricity from renewable or other sources. The Parties also agree to use power grid connectivity to promote power exchanges to mutual economic advantage.

ARTICLE 5

To promote scientific, educational, cultural and people to people exchanges and cooperation between the two countries. These shall be implemented through programmes and joint initiatives in areas such as agriculture, education and culture, health, tourism, sports, science & technology and any other area that the Parties may agree. The Parties shall cooperate by means of exchange of data, scientific knowledge, collaborative research, training, common programmes and in any other manner as may be agreed between the two Parties.

ARTICLE 6

To develop and implement programmes for environmental protection and responding to the challenges of climate change through adaptation. The Parties shall collaborate on projects of mutual interest to preserve common eco-systems and, as far as practicable, coordinate their response in international fora.

ARTICLE 7

To harness the advantages of sub-regional cooperation in the power sector, water resources management, physical connectivity, environment and sustainable development for mutual advantage, including jointly developing and financing projects.

ARTICLE 8

To cooperate closely on issues relating to their national interests. Both parties shall work together to create a peaceful environment conducive for inclusive economic growth and development.

ARTICLE 9

To cooperate on security issues of concern to each other while fully respecting each other's sovereignty. Neither party shall allow the use of its territory for activities harmful to the other.

ARTICLE 10

To establish a Joint Consultative Commission for effective and smooth implementation of this Agreement that shall meet once a year.

ARTICLE 11

The Agreement may be amended by mutual consent in order to enhance, deepen and widen the scope of cooperation, including regional / sub-regional expansion.

ARTICLE 12

This Agreement shall come into force on the date of its signing by the two Parties and shall remain in force until terminated by mutual consent in accordance with Para 2 of this Article. Either Party may seek termination of this Agreement by giving a written notice to the other Party providing the reasons for seeking such termination. Before this Agreement is terminated, the Parties shall consider the relevant circumstances and hold consultations to address the reasons cited by the Party seeking termination in the Joint Consultative Commission. Actions taken or agreements reached pursuant to this Agreement shall not be affected by its expiry or termination.

Done in Dhaka on the Sixth day of September, 2011, in two originals in English Language.

Dr. Manmohan Singh
Prime Minister
Government of the
Republic of India

Sheikh Hasina
Prime Minister
Government of the People's
Republic of Bangladesh

Cooperation on Renewable Energy 2011

Memorandum of Understanding
On
Renewable Energy Cooperation
Between
Government of the People's Republic of Bangladesh
AND
Government of the Republic of India

The Power Division, Ministry of Power, Energy and Mineral Resources, Government of the People's Republic of Bangladesh AND the Ministry of New and Renewable Energy, Government of the Republic of India, hereinafter referred to as 'The Parties';

Desiring to enhance traditional ties of friendship between the two countries through development of economic cooperation;

Having identified New and Renewable Energy as a common area of interest; and

Desiring to establish New and Renewable Cooperation in this area with the aim of developing new and renewable energy technologies;

Have reached the following understanding:

Article I

OBJECTIVE

The objective of this Memorandum of Understanding is to establish the basis for a cooperative institutional relationship to encourage and promote technical bilateral cooperation on new and renewable energy issues on the basis of mutuai benefit equality and reciprocity.

Article II

MODALITIES OF COOPERATION

Cooperation under this Memorandum of Understanding may take the following modalities.

(a) exchange and training of scientific and technical personnel;

(b) exchange of scientific and technological available information and data;

(c) organization of workshops seminars and working groups;

(d) transfer of equipment know-how and technology and technical standards on non-commercial basis;

(e) development of joint research or technical projects on subjects of mutual interest;

(f) exchange visit of Government officials and technical experts for sharing of experiences on renewable energy practices, policies, framework, incentive and technologies with financing mechanism;

(g) other modalities as may be agreed upon by the Parties.

Article III

WORKING GROUP

In order to coordinate the above-mentioned activities and decide upon project proposals related to design and development of various new and renewable energy technologies such as but not restricted to Solar Energy, Wind Energy and Bio-Energy the Parties intend to establish a "Joint Working Group" with the objectives of:

- Identifying areas of mutual interest and cooperation for development of new and renewable energy technologies, systems, sub-systems, devices, components, etc.
- Monitoring and evaluating cooperation activities.
- Financing mechanism and cost sharing of activities under this MOU.

The Parties shall designate one main representative not below the rank of Joint Secretary from each representative ministries to the Joint Working Group. For the aforesaid activities, the Joint Working Group shall to the extent possible conduct its work through electronic communication, but meet alternately in India and Bangladesh, when this is deemed necessary.

The Joint Working Group can co-opt other members from Government agencies, scientific institutions, research centers, universities or any other entity, as and when considered essential.

Article IV

AMENDMENT

This Memorandum of Understanding can be amended by the Parties through mutual consultation. The amendments shall be enclosed with this Memorandum of Understanding and shall form an integral part of it thereof.

Article V

ENTRY INTO FORCE, DURATION AND TERMINATION

This Memorandum of Understanding will enter into force on the date of signing and shall remain in force unless revoked by the consent of the Parties.

Either of the Parties may terminate this Memorandum of Understanding by giving the other party a written notice of 90 (ninety) days in advance of its decision to terminate this Memorandum of Understanding. Termination will not affect activities covered by a collaborative contract between the executive agencies and already underway at the time of termination.

In witness thereof, the undersigned representatives of the contracting parties being duly authorized thereto have signed this Memorandum of Understanding.

Signed at Dhaka on the Sixth day of September 2011 in two originals, in English language.

For and on behalf of the
Government of the
Republic of India

For and on behalf of the
Government of the
People's Republic of
Bangladesh

Joint Statement on the occassion of the visit of the PM of India to Bangladesh September 07, 2011

1. At the invitation of the Prime Minister of the People's Republic of Bangladesh, Sheikh Hasina, the Prime Minister of the Republic of India, Dr. Manmohan Singh, paid a State visit to Bangladesh from 6-7 September 2011. He was accompanied by Smt. Gursharan Kaur.
2. During the visit, the Prime Minister of India called on H.E. Md. Zillur Rahman, Hon'ble President of Bangladesh. Foreign Minister Dr. Dipu Moni called on the Prime Minister of India. The Leader of the Opposition Begum Khaleda Zia, and President of Jatiya Party Mr. H.M. Ershad also called on the Prime Minister of India. The meetings and exchanges were marked by warmth and cordiality on both sides.
3. The Prime Minister of India paid tribute and respect to the memory of Bangabandhu Sheikh Mujibur Rahman at Bangabandhu Museum in Dhaka. He laid a wreath at the National Martyr's Mausoleum at Savar as a mark of respect to the memory and contribution of the great freedom fighters of Bangladesh.
4. The official talks between Bangladesh and India were held on 6 September 2011 in an extremely warm, cordial and friendly atmosphere reflecting the excellent bilateral relations and friendship that exist between the two countries. The two Prime Ministers led their respective sides. Prime Minister Sheikh Hasina hosted a banquet in the honour of Prime Minister Dr. Manmohan Singh and the accompanying delegation.
5. During the official talks, the Prime Minister of India was assisted

by External Affairs Minister Shri S M Krishna, Chief Minister of Assam Shri Tarun Gogoi, Chief Minister of Meghalaya Dr. Mukul Sangma, Chief Minister of Mizoram Shri Lal Thanhawla, Chief Minister of Tripura Shri Manik Sarkar, National Security Advisor Shri Shivshankar Menon, Foreign Secretary Shri Ranjan Mathai, High Commissioner of India to Bangladesh Shri Rajeet Mitter, Secretary Ministry of Water Resources Shri Dhruv Vijai Singh and other senior officials.

6. The Prime Minister of Bangladesh was assisted by Foreign Minister Dr. Dipu Moni, Finance Minister Mr. A.M.A. Muhith, Home Minister Advocate Sahara Khatun, Minister for Land Mr. Rezaul Karim Hira, Water Resources Minister Mr. Ramesh Chandra Sen, Commerce Minister Mr. Faruk Khan, Advisor for Economic Affairs Dr. Moshiur Rahman, Advisor for Energy Dr. Tawfique-e-Illahi Chowdhury, Advisor for International Affairs Dr. Gowher Rizvi, High Commissioner of Bangladesh to India Mr. Tariq A. Karim, Ambassador-at-Large M. Ziauddin, Principal Secretary Mr. Abdul Karim, Foreign Secretary Mr. Mijarul Quayes and other senior officials.

7. During the talks, the two Prime Ministers reiterated the shared faith in and commitment to the values of secularism, democracy and social justice. They recognised that the destinies of the peoples of the two countries were interlinked in their search for peace, prosperity and stability.

8. Prime Minister Dr. Manmohan Singh lauded the steps taken by Prime Minister Sheikh Hasina towards strengthening democracy and promoting peace, security and stability in the region. He added that Bangladesh is a high growth economy with promising prospects.

9. The Prime Minister of India, on behalf of the Government and people of India, conveyed appreciation to the Government of Bangladesh for conferring the Bangladesh Swadhinata Sammanona (Bangladesh Freedom Honour), the highest Award of Bangladesh for foreign nationals, on former Prime Minister of India, Smt. Indira Gandhi, for her extraordinary contribution to the historic Liberation War of Bangladesh.

10. The two Prime Ministers noted that India and Bangladesh have

entered a new phase in bilateral relations with a pragmatic and practical approach based on sovereignty, equality, friendship, trust and understanding for the mutual benefit of their peoples and collective prosperity of the region.

11. They recalled the landmark visit of H.E. Sheikh Hasina to India in January 2010 and noted that, during the visit, the two sides had reached agreement on a set of initiatives that had elevated the bilateral relations to new heights. The two Prime Ministers noted with satisfaction the recent exchange of high level visits and agreed that these exchanges had helped reach understanding on many of the issues under discussion. They agreed to encourage more such high level interactions between the two sides.

12. They also welcomed the regular holding of institutional mechanisms for promoting bilateral relations, such as Foreign Office Consultations, Commerce Secretary level talks, Joint River Commission meetings, Home Secretary level talks, BGB-BSF DG level border conferences as well as meetings of the Joint Working Groups on various issues.

13. In their desire for the common good, they recognized the need to exploit the synergies between the two countries for further deepening of cooperation and widening of the relationship into newer areas and towards that end, agreed on a number of measures.

14. The two sides signed the following historic accords:
    (i) Framework Agreement on Cooperation for Development
    (ii) Protocol to the Agreement Concerning the Demarcation of the Land Boundary between India and Bangladesh and Related Matters

15. The following bilateral documents were also signed during the visit:
    (i) Addendum to the MoU between India and Bangladesh to Facilitate Overland Transit Traffic between Bangladesh and Nepal
    (ii) Memorandum of Understanding on Renewable EnergyCooperation

(iii) Memorandum of Understanding on Conservation of the Sundarban

(iv) Protocol on Conservation of the Royal Bengal Tiger of the Sunderban

(v) Memorandum of Understanding on Cooperation in the field of Fisheries

(vi) Memorandum of Understanding on Mutual Broadcast of Television Programmes

(vii) Memorandum of Understanding between Jawaharlal Nehru University and Dhaka University

(viii) Memorandum of Understanding on Academic Cooperation between National Institute of Fashion Technology (NIFT), India and BGMEA Institute of Fashion and Technology (BIFT), Bangladesh.

16. Both sides welcomed the conclusion of the comprehensive "Framework Agreement on Cooperation for Development" that outlines the shared vision for durable and long-term cooperation to achieve mutual peace, prosperity and stability.

17. Both sides decided to establish a Joint Commission led by the Ministers of Foreign/External Affairs to jointly coordinate and oversee implementation of initiatives as well as to explore newer avenues for cooperation, including progress of activities under the Framework Agreement.

18. The two Prime Ministers welcomed that there has been progress on the principles and modalities of interim agreements on sharing of waters of Teesta and Feni Rivers on fair and equitable basis. They directed the concerned officials to work towards concluding the agreements at the earliest.

19. The Prime Ministers noted that the Joint Rivers Commission (JRC), Secretary and technical level meetings were discussing various aspects relating to sharing of waters of the Manu, Muhuri, Khowai, Gumti, Dharla and Dudhkumar rivers.

20. The two Prime Ministers noted with satisfaction that the following decisions flowing from the Joint Communiqué of January 2010 had been implemented:

(a) Dredging of the river Ichhamati along the common reach between Angrail and Kalanchi bridges has been completed;

(b) The river bank protection works along Mahananda, Karatoa, Nagar, Kulik, Atrai, Dharla, Punarbhaba, Feni, Khowai, Surma etc. are being carried out in phases.

21. The Prime Minister of India reiterated the assurance that India would not take steps on the Tipaimukh project that would adversely impact Bangladesh.

22. The Prime Ministers expressed satisfaction at the level of cooperation between the two countries on security related issues and reaffirmed their unequivocal and uncompromising position against terrorism in all its forms and manifestations, including insurgency. They reiterated the assurance that their respective territories would not be allowed for any activity inimical to the other and by any quarter.

23. They noted with satisfaction the signing of the Coordinated Border Management Plan during the visit of the Home Minister of India to Bangladesh in July 2011. They expressed confidence that it would enhance cooperation between the border guarding forces of the two countries, and enable them to manage the identified vulnerable areas with a view to preventing criminal activities, illegal movement, acts of violence and loss of lives along the border areas. The Prime Ministers directed the concerned agencies to implement the Plan immediately. They welcomed the decision to henceforth hold annual consultations at the level of Home Ministers.

24. The two Prime Ministers underscored the need to conclude an Extradition Treaty between the two countries expeditiously to complete the legal framework for bilateral security cooperation while expressing satisfaction that the Agreement on Mutual Legal Assistance on Criminal Matters, Agreement on the Transfer of Sentenced Persons and Agreement on Combating International Terrorism, Organised Crime and Illicit Drug Trafficking, signed in January 2010, were now in force following their ratification.

25. The Prime Ministers expressed deep satisfaction at the conclusion of the Protocol to the 1974 Land Boundary Agreement which paves the way for settlement of the long pending land

boundary issues including the undemarcated areas, territories under adverse possession and exchange of enclaves. The historic agreement, which is based on ground realities, would further contribute to amity and harmony in border areas and create a conducive environment for enhanced bilateral cooperation. The two Prime Ministers also expressed satisfaction at the signing of strip maps by the Plenipotentiaries. They resolved to complete the ratification process and implement the Agreement expeditiously.

26. Prime Minister Sheikh Hasina expressed deep appreciation of the Government of Bangladesh for facilitating 24-hour unfettered access to Bangladesh nationals through the Tin Bigha Corridor. She noted that the fulfillment of the long pending promise would have a significantly positive impact on the lives of the people of Angarpota-Dahagram.

27. The Prime Ministers agreed to promote trade, investment and economic cooperation in a sustainable manner and facilitate trade by road, rail, inland waterways, shipping and air. Both sides underscored the need to increase trade volumes and address trade imbalance. Prime Minister Dr. Manmohan Singh announced the decision of the Government of India to remove all forty six textile lines which are of interest to Bangladesh from India's Negative List for LDCs under the provisions of SAFTA, thereby reducing the applicable duty rate to zero with immediate effect. Prime Minister Sheikh Hasina conveyed appreciation for this major step on improved market access extended to Bangladesh aimed at reducing the existing trade imbalance.

28. The Prime Ministers underscored the importance of harmonization of standards and mutual recognition of certificates for promoting bilateral trade and expressed appreciation for efforts being taken towards this end. The Prime Minister of Bangladesh thanked the Indian side for undertaking the upgradation of laboratories of the BSTI and for training of the Bangladesh Standards Testing Institute (BSTI) personnel in India. It was agreed that a bilateral cooperation agreement between the Bureau of Indian Standards (BIS) and the Bangladesh Standards Testing Institute (BSTI) would be concluded at an early date.

29. Recognizing the need to address factors including non tariff and para tariff barriers and port restrictions that hamper the natural growth of bilateral trade, the Prime Ministers directed concerned officials to identify and remove all barriers to unfettered bilateral trade.

30. The two Prime Ministers welcomed the opening of Banglabandha-Fulbari Land Port for bilateral trade between Bangladesh and India. They also expressed satisfaction at the Indian initiative to develop seven Integrated Check Posts (ICPs), and noted that this would facilitate trade between the two countries. They directed the concerned officials to hold the meetings of the Sub-Group on Infrastructure so that necessary infrastructure could be developed at the identified Land Ports / Land Custom Stations (LCS) on both sides expeditiously.

31. The two Prime Ministers welcomed the inauguration of the border haat in Baliamari (Kurigram)-Kalaichar (West Garo Hills) and the proposed inauguration in Balat (East Khasi Hills)-Dalora (Sunamganj) as a fulfillment of the long standing demand of the local people of the area. They noted that the resulting economic activity would contribute to the economic upliftment of the people of the area surrounding the border haats. Both sides agreed to open new border haats at mutually agreed locations.

32. Welcoming the exchange of Instruments of Ratification of the Bilateral Investment Promotion and Protection Agreement, the two Prime Ministers reiterated their call for increasing investments including joint ventures in each other's country. They underscored the role of the private sector as very important in bringing qualitative and quantitative change in the development process. The Indian Prime Minister appreciated the announcement of the Bangladesh Prime Minister regarding the establishment of a Special Economic Zone for Indian investments.

33. Both sides agreed to examine the establishment of new land ports / LCS / immigration points to facilitate trade and movement of people.

34. The two Prime Ministers noted that both sides had already signed the Standard Operating Procedures allowing movement of trucks carrying goods from Nepal and Bhutan to Land Customs Stations

in Bangladesh. It was agreed to work towards concluding Motor Vehicles Agreement for regulation of Passenger and Cargo traffic.

35. Prime Minister Dr. Manmohan Singh thanked the government of Bangladesh for allowing passage of ODC cargo for the Palatana power project in Tripura.

36. The Prime Ministers noted with satisfaction the operationalisation of Ashuganj and Silghat as additional Ports of Call under the bilateral Inland Water Transit and Trade Protocol. He also expressed his appreciation for the successful commencement of trial run of the bulk cargo for Tripura using multi-modal facilities through Ashuganj port. It was agreed that the construction of an Inland Container Terminal at Ashuganj would be expedited and pending that, the port could be used for movement of bulk cargo immediately as far as practicable.

37. Both sides agreed to expedite works for enabling night navigation facilities on the Protocol routes. They agreed to allow movement of containerized cargo by rail and water and to work towards its early operationlisation.

38. Both the Prime Ministers directed that necessary steps be taken to expedite construction of a bridge over river Feni as per the alignment already agreed between the two sides.

39. The Prime Ministers directed the concerned officials that the MoU regarding development of railway infrastructure at the border point between Agartala and Akhaura should be concluded and the execution of rail line commenced at the earliest.

40. Bangladesh Prime Minister expressed her appreciation to the Indian Prime Minister for amendment of the MoU between the Bangladesh and Indian Railways allowing Rohanpur-Singabad as an additional route for both bulk and container cargo for Nepalese rail transit traffic. Bangladesh side also appreciated the assistance from India for the movement of fertilizers from Bangladesh to Nepal by rail route. They also agreed to re-establish rail connections between Chilahati-Haldibari and Kulaura-Mahishashan in the spirit of encouraging revival of old linkages and transport routes between the two countries.

41. The Prime Ministers directed that necessary formalities for the use of Chittagong and Mongla seaports for movement of goods

to and from India through water, rail and road should be completed urgently.

42. Both the Prime Ministers noted that road, rail and waterways were building blocks to an inter-dependent and mutually beneficial relationship among the countries of the region. The establishment of physical infrastructure would promote exchange of goods and traffic, and lead to the connectivity of services, information, ideas, culture and people.

43. The two sides welcomed the signing of the MoU for cooperation in the Renewable Energy sector between the two countries, noting that cooperation in this sector was essential to meet the growing energy demands of the two countries and to supplement the conventional sources.

44. The two Prime Ministers urged expeditious conclusion of Power Purchase Agreement between BPDB and NTPC for purchase of 250MW power from India by Bangladesh. It was agreed that Bangladesh would procure the additional 250MW of power from the open market in India utilizing the full capacity of the power transmission line being established through inter-grid connectivity at Bheramara and Behrampur.

45. The two Prime Ministers noted that BPDB and NTPC were working towards concluding a Joint Venture Agreement for setting up of 1320MW coal based power plant in Bagerhat. They directed the concerned officials to complete all formalities for operationalising the project expeditiously. They also directed the concerned officials to undertake necessary steps for conducting feasibility reports for the setting up of a similar 1320MW coal based power plant at a suitable location in Chittagong.

46. Both the Prime Ministers agreed to promote and support joint research projects and exchange of scientific personnel. In this context, the Prime Minister of India conveyed that India would invite from Bangladesh eminent scientists and researchers to participate in the Indian National Science Congress, and school children to participate in the Annual National Children Science Congress.

47. The two Prime Ministers expressed satisfaction at the

programmes orgainsed for the joint celebration to commemorate the 150th birth anniversary of Rabindranath Tagore. They directed officials of both sides to remain engaged in the joint effort and take it to a successful conclusion in May 2012. They noted that the joint celebration had enthused the people on both sides to explore the common cultural heritage and linkages and had promoted exchanges not only among Tagore experts, but also a whole range of artists, singers, dancers, dramatists, poets, writers, actors, etc. which had led to greater understanding among the two sides. It was agreed that the 90th Anniversary of the publication of Bidrohi by Poet Nazrul Islam would be jointly celebrated. Bangladesh Prime Minister conveyed her intention to set up a Bangladesh Bhaban in Shantiniketan as a resource centre for use of the visiting academicians and researchers from Bangladesh.

48. Recognizing the urgent need of trained doctors and specialists in the field of healthcare in Bangladesh, the two Prime Ministers agreed to set up a programme for training of Bangladesh doctors in premier Indian medical institutes.

49. Bangladesh Prime Minister appreciated the concurrence of the Government of India to the opening of a Deputy High Commission of Bangladesh in Mumbai. In addition, both sides agreed to consider further strengthening diplomatic and consular presence in each other's countries.

50. Recognizing the value of television channels as a means to promote cultural exchange and dissemination of information, the two Prime Ministers welcomed the signing of MoU on Mutual Broadcast of Television Programmes between Doordarshan and Bangladesh Television. Noting that there are no restrictions, they encourgaed private channels to explore opportunities to expand the viewership in each other's countries.

51. The two Prime Ministers underscored the need to preserve the memory of freedom fighters by undertaking various initiatives, including observance of anniversaries of their martyrdom. The Indian side informed that it would enhance scholarships to the heirs of Muktijoddhas from Bangladesh to pursue higher secondary and graduate studies. Bangladesh side requested

facilitation for setting up of memorial plaques and visits of family members to the identified graves of freedom fighters buried along the border in the Indian States of Tripura, Meghalaya, Assam and West Bengal.

52. The Prime Minister of Bangladesh expressed appreciation for the assistance provided by the Indian side in the construction of 2800 core shelters for families affected by the Sidr cyclone and the construction of Theatre and Music Departments of Kalabhaban in the University of Dhaka.

53. The Prime Ministers expressed satisfaction at the utilisation of the US$ 1 billion Line of Credit extended by India and noted that it would significantly enhance infrastructure and capacities in Bangladesh. The credit would finance a number of projects identified by Bangladesh, including for supply of BG locomotives, tank wagons, passenger coaches and infrastructure projects such as Khulna-Mongla rail line and rail bridges over Titas and Bhairab rivers for strengthening Bangladesh Railways, purchase of buses for Dhaka city public transportation and dredgers for capital and maintenance dredging of Bangladesh rivers. They directed the concerned officials of both India and Bangladesh to complete all necessary measures for the speedy implementation of the projects so that the benefits would accrue to the people at an early date.

54. The Prime Minister of India Dr. Manmohan Singh announced grant to Bangladesh for several cooperation and developmental projects and other initiatives, including :

    (a) Construction of state-of-the-art India-Bangladesh Culture Centre in Dhaka;

    (b) Undertaking feasibility study for upgradation of Dhaka-Chittagong railway line;

    (c) Construction of railway line between Akhaura and Agartala;

    (d) New Indian Scholarship to 100 students at graduate, post graduate and Doctoral/ research level;

    (e) Setting up of an IT Lab in a model school in each of the 64 districts in Bangladesh;

    (f) Setting up of IT centres in Bangladesh Public

Administration Training Centre, Military Institute of Science and Technology and Bangladesh Police Academy;

(g) Provision of solar lanterns to 2800 families affected by the Sidr Cyclone.

55. Recognizing the urgency of protecting and conserving the fragile ecosystem of Sundarban, the world's largest mangrove forest, the two Prime Ministers expressed satisfaction at the signing of the MoU on Conservation of the Sundarban and a Protocol on the Conservation of the Royal Bengal Tiger of the Sundarban. They expressed confidence that the combined efforts of the two sides would lead to the sustenance and preservation of this common heritage.

56. Reiterating the role of SAARC in promoting regional cooperation, they agreed to work together in further strengthening SAARC, including by expanding areas of cooperation, and as partners in achieving the full implementation of all existing SAARC projects and Agreements.

57. Both sides reviewed various steps taken to strengthen sub-regional and regional cooperation, including under BIMSTEC and other regional initiatives.

58. Both Prime Ministers agreed that the two sides would harness advantages of regional and sub-regional cooperation in power, water resources, transport and other forms of connectivity, food security, education, environment and sustainable development to mutual advantage. They directed relevant authorities of both sides to study and formulate, in consultation with experts of the countries of the region, necessary terms for undertaking joint projects in the field of water resources management and hydro-power.

59. The two leaders agreed to promote trade in services under the SAARC Agreement on Trade in Services and directed early completion of work for harmonization of education curricula and mutual recognition of degrees between the two countries.

60. Both Prime Ministers reiterated the importance of an effective multilateral system, centred on a strong United Nations, as a key factor in tackling global challenges. In this context, they

also recognized the need to pursue the reform of the main UN bodies, including the Security Council. The Prime Minister of Bangladesh reiterated her country's support for India's candidature for permanent membership of an expanded and reformed UN Security Council. Both sides noted with satisfaction contributions of both countries to UN peacekeeping operations.

61. The two Prime Ministers underscored the need for strengthening and reform of multilateral financial institutions and enhancing the voice and participation of developing countries in international economic decision-making.

62. Both sides agreed that climate change was one of the most important global challenges. They reaffirmed the provisions and principles of the United Nations Framework Convention on Climate Change (UNFCCC), including that of common but differentiated responsibilities. It was agreed that adaptation programmes for environment protection were essential to combat climate change. They agreed to collaborate on matters of mutual interest to preserve common eco-systems and coordinate their response in international fora. They also stressed the need to meet the over-riding priority of poverty eradication and sustainable development and agreed to enhance cooperation on issues related to bio-diversity.

63. The two sides expressed their conviction that Prime Minister Dr Manmohan Singh's visit to Bangladesh and signing of historic documents between the two countries marks a watershed in the bilateral relationship between two close and friendly neighbours.

64. The Prime Minister of India thanked the Prime Minister of Bangladesh for the warmth, cordiality and gracious hospitality extended to him and members of his delegation during their stay in Bangladesh.

65. Prime Minister Dr Manmohan Singh extended an invitation to Prime Minister Sheikh Hasina to pay a visit to India. The invitation was accepted and it was agreed that the dates of the visit would be finalised through diplomatic channels.

Dhaka

September 7, 2011

Index